THE

ARABIC MANUAL

THE ARABIC MANUAL

COMPRISING A

CONDENSED GRAMMAR

OF BOTH THE

CLASSICAL AND MODERN ARABIC

BY

PROF. E. H. PALMER, M.A.

GYAN

Published by

Gyan Publishing House
5, Ansari Road
Daryaganj, New Delhi-110002
Phone: 011-47034999, 9811692060
E-mail: books@gyanbooks.com

Distribution Network
gyanbooks.com
India, USA, Canada, UK, Australia

ISBN: 978-81-212-7063-2 (PB)
First Published, 1881

2nd Impression 2024

Printed at: Gyan Press, Delhi.

THE ARABIC MANUAL
Author: E. H. PALMER

THE

ARABIC MANUAL.

COMPRISING A

CONDENSED GRAMMAR

OF BOTH THE

CLASSICAL AND MODERN ARABIC;

Reading Lessons and Exercises, with Analyses;

AND A

VOCABULARY OF USEFUL WORDS.

BY

PROF. E. H. PALMER, M.A.,

FELLOW OF ST. JOHN'S COLLEGE, AND LORD ALMONER'S READER AND PROFESSOR OF ARABIC IN THE UNIVERSITY OF CAMBRIDGE;
AUTHOR OF A GRAMMAR OF THE ARABIC LANGUAGE, ETC., ETC.

SECOND EDITION.

LONDON:
W. H. ALLEN & CO., 13 WATERLOO PLACE,
PALL MALL. S.W.
Publishers to the India Office.

1885.

PREFACE.

THIS little work is intended to form a complete introduction to the Arabic language as written and spoken at the present day. Without a knowledge of the grammatical construction of the ancient tongue it is impossible fully to understand that of the modern dialect, which, however, becomes quite easy with such aid. The student, after mastering the grammatical portion of the book, is recommended to study carefully the Reading Lessons, pp. 100–115; he should then do all the Exercises for Translation, pp. 146–160; after which he should carefully peruse the translations from English into Arabic, pp. 160–177, referring where necessary to the Transliteration and Notes, pp. 193–216. He will then have acquired a sufficient vocabulary and insight into the language to enable him to read any ordinary work in literary Arabic, or to commence, with the help of the second part of the Manual, the study of the spoken dialect.

As a subsequent course of reading, he should take the Ḳor'án (Ed. Flügel, Lipsiæ, MDCCCLVIII.), with my translation (Max Müller's Sacred Text Series, vols. vi. and ix. Clarendon Press, Oxford, 1881), and my edition and translation of "The Poetical Works of Behá-ed-dín Zoheir of Egypt" (Cambridge, University Press, 1876). The Ḳor'án, being the standard of elegant style, and being constantly quoted and imitated by Arabic authors, an acquaintance with it is absolutely necessary to the student of the language. The poems of Behá-ed-dín Zoheir are written in a very elegant post-classical style, and the vocabulary employed in them is as useful at the present day as it was when they were composed. Both books have the advantage of being pointed with all the vowels throughout, and of being accompanied with translations, which are as literal and idiomatic as I could make them.

I would strongly advise the student to learn pieces of Arabic poetry by heart, acquiring the correct pronunciation and rythm orally and, when possible, from a native. This is one of the best methods for learning to speak a language, since the rhyme and rhythm assist the memory, and ensure a correct accent.

For mere colloquial purposes, however, the Manual itself will, I hope, be found sufficient for all the learner's ordinary wants.

E. H. PALMER.

London, June 1881.

CONTENTS.

The Numerals.

Particles.

Section II.—Syntax.

ARABIC MANUAL.

PART I.—CLASSICAL ARABIC.

SECTION I.—THE GRAMMAR.

The Alphabet.

The Arabs write from right to left.

Their alphabet consists of twenty-eight letters, *all consonants.*

Arabic Letters.	Names.	English equivalents.	Pronunciation.
ا	Alif	A	This at the commencement of a word is a mere prop for the letter *hemzeh*, or soft breathing, and has no sound of itself; after a consonant it serves merely to prolong the vowel *fetḥah.*
ب	Bá	B	as in English, but more forcibly.
ت	Tá	T	a soft dental, like the Italian *t.*
ث	Thá	Th	as in *thing* (sometimes *s*).
ج	Jím	J	as in *John.*
ح	Ḥá	H	a strong pectoral aspirate.
خ	Khá	Kh	guttural, something like the Scotch *ch* in *loch*, or Welsh *ch* in *chwi.*
د	Dál	D	soft dental, like the Italian *d.*

Arabic Letters.	Names.	English equivalents.	Pronunciation.
ذ	Dhál	Dh	like *th* in *that.*
ر	Rá	R	as in English, but more forcibly.
ز	Zá	Z	
س	Sín	S	
ش	Shín	Sh	
ص	Ṣád	Ṣ	a lisping *s.*
ض	Ḍhád	Ḍh	a hard palatal *ḍ.*
ط	Ṭ(h)á	Ṭ	a hard palatal *ṭ.*
ظ	D̲h̲á	D̲h̲	*th* in *this* (sometimes *ź*).
ع	‘Ain	‘	a guttural vowel.
غ	G̲h̲ain	G̲h̲	a guttural sound, something between *g̲h̲* and *r.*
ف	Fá	F	as in English, but more forcibly.
ق	Ḳáf	Ḳ	like *ck* in *stuck,* pronounced very gutturally.
ك	Káf	K	as in English, but more forcibly.
ل	Lám	L	
م	Mím	M	
ن	Nún	N	
ه	Há	H.	
و	Waw	W.	
ی	Yá	Y.	

To which is added لا Lám-alif, LÁ.

These are joined to the preceding letter by prefixing a small curve or stroke, and to the following letter by removing the curve with which they all, except *alif,* end.

In ذ د ز ر و the removal of the curve would leave the letter unrecognizable; these, therefore, as well as the *alif,* are not joined to the left.

The following table shows the initial, medial, and final forms of the several groups of letters:

Detached.	Initial.	Medial.	Final.
ا	ا	ـا	ـا
ث ت ب	ثـ تـ بـ	ـثـ ـتـ ـبـ	ـث ـت ـب
ى ن	يـ نـ	ـيـ ـنـ	ـى ـن
خ ح ج	خـ حـ جـ	ـخـ ـحـ ـجـ	ـخ ـح ـج
ذ د	ذ د	ـذ ـد	ـذ ـد
و ز ر	و ز ر	ـو ـز ـر	ـو ـز ـر
ض ص	ضـ صـ	ـضـ ـصـ	ـض ـص
ظ ط	ظ ط	ـظ ـط	ـظ ـط
غ ع	غـ عـ	ـغـ ـعـ	ـغ ـع
ق ف	قـ فـ	ـقـ ـفـ	ـق ـف
ك	كـ	ـكـ	ـك
ل	لـ	ـلـ	ـل
م	مـ	ـمـ	ـم
ه	هـ	ـهـ ـهـ	ـه

ه is sometimes written ة: it is then called *há-tá, and when followed by a vowel* is pronounced like ت *t.*

Vowels.

The vowels and other orthographical signs are written above and below the letters. The vowels are ـَ *fetḥah*, ـُ *ḍhammah*, and ـِ *kesrah*, pronounced respectively ـَ *a*, as in *fat;* ـُ *u*, as in *full;* and ـِ *i*, as in *fit.*

Tenwín.

When the vowels are doubled, thus ـً ـٌ ـٍ, they are pronounced respectively *an, un* and *in*. This is called تَنوِين *tenwín*, i.e. "giving the *n* sound."

The *tenwín* shows that a noun is indefinite; if it be defined by the article or otherwise the *tenwín* is lost.

Thus: اَلْكِتَابُ *al-kitábu*, "THE book," كِتَابٌ *kitábUN*, "A book," مَلِكٍ *malikIN*, "OF A king," but كِتَابُ مَلِكٍ KITA'BU *malikin*, "the BOOK of A king."

The short vowels ـَـِـُ correspond to the weak consonants و ا ى and the long vowels are formed by a combination of the two; thns, بَا *bá*, بُو *bú*, بِى *bí*. و and ى preceded by *fetḥah* form diphthongs بَوْ *bau* (pronounced as *ow* in *now*) and بَىْ *bai* (pronounced as *y* in *by*).

Hemzeh.

In endeavouring to pronounce a vowel without a consonant, we make a distinct, though slight, effort with the muscles of the throat: this the Arabs represent by *hemzeh* أ, and the long vowels accordingly become at the beginning of a word أَا *aa*, أُو *uu*, إِي *ii*, = *á*, *ú*, *í*.

Meddah.

In the case of أَا *aa* the second *alif* is written over the first thus آ *á*, or ~ without the *hemzeh*, and is called *meddah*, "prolongation."

Jezmeh or Sukún.

There are only two kinds of syllables in Arabic. 1. A consonant with a short vowel, as بَ *ba*. 2. Two consonants with a short vowel between, as بِتْ *bit*. In this case the mark ـْـ is placed over the last, and is called *sukún*, "rest," or *jezmeh*, "cutting off." A letter without a vowel is called "quiescent."

Teshdíd.

When the article أَلْ *al* precedes any *dental, liquid,* or *sibilant* letter, it is assimilated with it, and the letter itself is doubled to compensate for the elision; thus we say أَلشَّمْسُ *ash-shemsu,* not *al-shemsu.* Like all other permutations of letters in Arabic, this is obviously merely a euphonic change.

Letters of this class are called أَلْحُرُوفُ ٱلشَّمْسِيَّةُ *al-ḥurúf ash-shamsíyeh,* "solar letters," because the word شَمْسٌ "sun" begins with one of them. The remainder are called أَلْحُرُوفُ ٱلْقَمَرِيَّةُ *al-ḥurúf al-ḳamaríyeh,* "lunar letters," for a similar reason.

The mark of reduplication is called *teshdíd,* "strengthening," and is written thus ـّـ.

Hemzet el-waṣl.

The Arabs cannot utter two consonants together at the beginning of a word without a vowel; but to facilitate the utterance of the first they employ a *hemzet el-waṣl,* or "point of conjunction": thus, the English word "smith" in an Arab's mouth would become اِسْمِث *ismith.*

The *hemzet el-waṣl,* when following a vowel, is elided in pronunciation, and the mark *waṣlah* ـٱـ is placed over the *alif* to denote this fact; thus, إِبْنُ ٱلْمَلِكِ *ibnu 'l-meliki,* not *ibnu al-meliki.*

If the *hemzet el-waṣl* come at the beginning of a sentence, or after a *tenwín* or a word that has no final vowel, it is pronounced with *kesrah*; except after كُمْ *kum,* "you," "your," هُمْ *hum,* "them," "their," أَنْتُمْ *antum,* "you," and مُذْ *mudh*, "since," when it is pronounced with *ḍhammah*; and after ي *í*, نى *ní*, "me," "my," مِن *min*, "from," and مَعَ *ma'*, "with," where it is pronounced with *fetḥah*.

Hemzet el-kaṭa'.

Hemzet el-kaṭa', "the point of disjunction, or hiatus" (because a hiatus is felt before the vowel introduced by it is pronounced), is either a radical letter or a sign of inflection prefixed to verbs; as in أَفْعَلُ "I act," where it denotes the first person singular of the aorist. In such cases it is, of course, not elided.

Hemzet el-waṣl, when following a vowel or *tenwín*, is written ٱ; but when it stands at the beginning of a sentence, it is written أَ *a*, أُ *u*, إِ *i*.

Hemzet el-kaṭa' is always written in full أ. When the latter occurs in the middle of a word, and introduces ـُ *ḍhammah* or ـِ *kesrah*, the *alif*, which serves as its prop, is changed into the semi-vowel analogous to the short vowel; as مُؤْمِنٌ *mu'-minun* (not مُأْمِنٌ), "a believer," جِئْتُ (not جِأْتُ), "I came." When ى is so used, the dots are omitted, to distinguish it from the letter of prolongation.

The Pause.

The final short vowels are dropped in pronunciation at the end of a sentence; thus:

بِسْمِ ٱللّٰهِ ٱلرَّحْمٰنِ ٱلرَّحِيمْ

Bismi'lláhi 'rraḥmáni 'rraḥím, not . . . . . *'rraḥími*.

ةُ, with or without *tenwín*, becomes هْ in the pause; as جَاءَتْ رَحْمَةٌ pronounced *já-at raḥmah.* *Tenwín kesrah* and *ḍhammah* ـٍ ـٌ are dropped; as جَاءَ زَيْدٌ and مَرَرْتُ بِزَيْدٍ, pronounced *já'a Zeid* and *marartu bi-Zeid;* but *tenwín fetḥah* اً becomes اَ, as رَأَيْتُ زَيْدًا, pronounced *ra'aitu Zeidá.*

The single emphatic ن *nún*, which is sometimes added to the imperative and aorist of verbs, also becomes اَ; as اِضْرِبَنْ, pronounced at the end of a sentence اِضْرِبَا *idhribá.*

Words of one letter add ه in the pause; as رَهْ *rah* and قِهْ *ḳih* for رَ *ra* and قِ *ḳi.*

Words like قَاضٍ, in which the *tenwín kesrah* stands for a ى which has dropped out, reject the *tenwín* in the pause; as مَرَرْتُ بِقَاضٍ pronounced *marartu bi-ḳádh.*

Examples for Practice in Reading.

شِ	سَ	زُ	رِ	ذَ	دُ	خِ	حَ	جُ	ثِ	تَ	بُ	إِ	أُ	أَ
shi	*sa*	*zu*	*ri*	*dha*	*du*	*k̲h̲i*	*ḥa*	*ju*	*thi*	*ta*	*bu*	*i*	*u*	*a*

يَ	هُ	وَ	نِ	مَ	لُ	كَ	قِ	فُ	غِ	عَ	ظُ	طِ	ضَ	صُ
ya	*hu*	*wa*	*ni*	*ma*	*lu*	*ka*	*ḳi*	*fu*	*g̲h̲i*	*'a*	*d̲h̲u*	*ṭi*	*ḍha*	*ṣu*

رِي	ذَا	دُو	خِي	حَا	جُو	ثِي	تَا	بُو	أَيْ	إِي	أَوْ	أُو	آ
rí	*dhá*	*dú*	*k̲h̲í*	*ḥá*	*jú*	*thí*	*tá*	*bú*	*ai*	*í*	*au*	*ú*	*á*

مَا	لُو	كَا	قِي	فُو	غِي	عَا	ظُو	طِي	ضَا	صُو	شِي	سَا	زُو
má	*lú*	*ká*	*ḳí*	*fú*	*g̲h̲í*	*'á*	*d̲h̲ú*	*ṭí*	*ḍhá*	*ṣú*	*shí*	*sá*	*zú*

يَا	يُو	هُو	وِي	وَيْ	وَا	نِي
yá	*yú*	*hú*	*wí*	*wai*	*wá*	*ní*

تَبْ فُتْ بِتْ مِتْ قَدْ هَجْ رُحْ قَطْ خُذْ قَعْ صَرْ مُذْ

mudh ṣar ḳ'a khudh ḳaṭ ruḥ haj ḳad mit bit fut tab

دُرْ دَسْ زُرْ بَلْ كَمْ صَفْ

ṣaf kam bal zur das dur

---

* لِلنَّاسِ * فِى ٱلزَّمَانِ * فِى ٱلْحَرْبِ * عَلَيْهِ * فِى ٱلْحَيٰوةِ * وَٱللّٰهِ *

wa'lláhi fi'l-ḥayáti 'alaihi fi'l-ḥarbi fi'z-zamáni linnási

لِلّٰهِ * لَبِثْتُ إِلَى ٱلْيَوْمِ * لِلْحَيَاةِ ٱلدُّنْيَا *

lil-ḥayáti 'd-dunyá labittu ila 'l-yaumi li'lláhi

The learner is recommended to study these examples carefully at first in order to acquire facility in reading the Arabic character, as the language cannot be studied in the Roman character.

The Measures of Words.

Every word in Arabic may be referred to a significant root, consisting of either three or four letters, the triliterals being by far the more common.

In English we add the termination *er* to express the active participle or agent of a verb, and *ing* to express the infinitive or gerund; as make, mak*er*, mak*ing*. In Arabic, however, such modifications are obtained not only by prefixing or affixing, but by inserting letters in the root. فعل *fa'l*, signifying mere *action*, is taken as the typical root for exhibiting these modifications, and the *formulæ* thus obtained are called the "measures of words." For instance, the insertion of an *alif* between the first and second radical, and pointing the latter with a vowel *kesrah*, gives the sense of the agent or active participle; thus فَعْلٌ becomes فَاعِلٌ "one who does," and this word is the *measure* upon which all other agents of this kind are formed.

It is, in fact, a mere formula, like the letters used in Algebra; for as $(a+b)$ may represent $(2+3)$, $(4+5)$, or any other numbers, so for the triliteral root فعل in فَاعِلٌ we may substitute any other triliteral root and obtain the same modification of meaning by *a word of the same shape;* as

ضَرْبٌ *ḍharbun*, "striking," ضَارِبٌ "a striker."

قَتْلٌ *ḳatlun*, "killing," قَاتِلٌ "a murderer."

where ضَارِبٌ and قَاتِلٌ are said to be the فَاعِلٌ of the respective triliteral roots to which they belong.

The triliteral root may contain one or more of the weak consonants or semivowels أ ى و, in which case certain euphonic and other changes will take place. These changes are called the Permutations of weak consonants, and depend upon the principle stated above, that the three weak consonants أ و ى are respectively homogeneous to the three vowels ـَـُـِ. When the vowel and the weak consonant in any derived form do not correspond, *the vowel changes the weak consonant into another weak consonant analogous to itself.*

If, instead of the three radical letters of a significant root ف ع ل, we substitute the signs (1) (2) (3), and then proceed to form "measures" of nouns and verbs in the ordinary manner, we shall obtain such results as the following:

1. فِعْلٌ "doing" = (3)ٌ (2)ْ (1)ِ
2. فَاعِلاً "doer"* = (3)ً (2)ِ ا(1)َ
3. فَعَلَ "he does" = (3)َ (2)َ (1)َ
4. فُعِلَ "it is done" = (3)َ (2)ِ (1)ُ

The vowels are the real or characteristic part of the measure, as they give the general sense of the form, while the radicals only define the particular case to which it is to be applied; they must therefore of necessity be preserved at any sacrifice to the consonant.

Now, in the four forms given above, let us substitute for the numerical signs of the letters و ز غ, an existing Arabic triliteral root, and we have:

1. (3)ٌ (2)ْ (1)َ = غَزْوٌ "A raid or foray."
2. (3)ً (2)ِ ا(1)َ = غَازِواً Here the *kesrah* and the *wáw* do not correspond, but the former, being the more important, changes the latter into ى; that is, into the weak letter analogous to itself, and the word becomes غَازِياً "a raider."

---

* I have adopted the objective case with *tenwín fetḥah* in this illustration, because *tenwín ḍhammah* or *tenwín kesrah* would involve the question of a further permutation, the discussion of which is left for the paragraph on the declension of nouns, *q.v.*

3. (3) (2) (1)= غَزَوَ Here the two *fethahs* absorb the و, changing it into ا, and the word becomes غَزَا "he made a foray."

4. (3) (2) (1) (from قَوْل "saying") قَوِلَ=قِيلَ.

In the 3rd person preterite active of the same verb قَالَ the two *fethahs* conquer the و. In the 1st person قُلْتُ the long و being quiescent conquers, and the accent falling on it, it becomes قُولْتُ; but this is naturally shortened in pronunciation, and the following rule holds. *that two quiescent letters cannot come together*.

This, then, is the general principle of permutation:—*When a vowel and a weak letter which is not analogous to it come together in a form*, the ordinary laws of euphony require that one should yield, and in Arabic the *vowel conquers: e.g.*

The measure مِفْعَالٌ, from وزن, would be مِوْزَانٌ and the measure مُفْعِلٌ, from يقن, would be مُيْقِنٌ; but مِوْزَانٌ *miwzánun* and مُيْقِنٌ *muykinun* are repugnant to the ear, and therefore become مِيزَانٌ *mízánun* and مُوقِنٌ *múkinun.*

A permutation of other than weak letters occasionally takes place; as, for instance, when two letters which it is impossible to pronounce together occur in the same form; then the softer of the two is changed into the corresponding hard one. This can only take place in *dental* or *palatal* letters, for they are the only ones in which such a difficulty is likely to arise: *e.g.*

Forming the measure اِفْتَعَلَ *ifta'ala* from the root ضرب we should have اِضْتَرَبَ *i<u>dh</u>taraba;* this, however, would be unpronounceable, and as the soft *t* ت will actually sound like the hard *ṭ* ط, the latter is written instead, and the form becomes اِضْطَرَبَ.

Another euphonic change of which letters are susceptible is

Assimilation.

One letter is often assimilated by another, which is then doubled. This naturally occurs when the same letter is repeated without the intervention of a vowel, as مَدٌّ for مَدْدٌ *maddun;* or when two letters of the same kind come together, as مَكَتَّ *makatta* for مَكَثْتَ *makathta.*

Parts of Speech.

The parts of speech in Arabic are three :—1. The Verb. 2. The Noun (including the pronoun and adjective, and what we are accustomed to call the participle). 3. The Particle (including the preposition, adverb, conjunction, and interjection).

The Verb.

Arabic Verbs are of two kinds, *sound* and *weak.*

These are further subdivided into *transitive* and *neuter, active* and *passive.*

They are either *simple* or *augmented,* y the addition of other letters to modify the meaning.

The simple verb cannot contain less than three letters or more than five.

It may happen that in conjugating, all the letters but one may disappear, so that a simple form may seem to have been one letter, as in تِ *ti*, the shortened form of اِيتِ *íti*, from أَتَى *atá*, "he came."

The letters thus employed to augment or conjugate verbs and inflect nouns are called *servile.* It may also happen that some of these letters occur as radicals in a verb, but in such a case nothing save a knowledge of the grammatical measures will enable the student to discriminate.

We are accustomed to speak of the first, second, and third radical letter of a triliteral verb as the ف *fá*, ع *'ain*, or ل *lám* respectively.

Parts of the Verb.

The Arabic Verb has two voices,—active and passive; three tenses,—preterite, aorist, and imperative; fifteen conjugations. These last, however, are nothing more than *augmented* or derived verbs formed from the simple root by the addition of certain letters which modify or extend the sense.

The noun which expresses the simple action is considered as the source, مَصْدَر, from which all derived forms, whether nouns or verbs, are taken, as ضَرْب *ḍharbun*, "striking"; and this occasionally supplies the place of the infinitive or gerund, which parts of the verb are wanting in Arabic.

Note.—As this noun of action is variable in form, it has been found convenient in practice to treat the third person singular masculine as the form from which all others are derived. *This is, therefore, the form under which all words are ranged in grammars and dictionaries.*

Tenses of Verbs.

The Preterite.—There are three classes of simple verbs distinguished by the middle vowel of the preterite active, viz. فَعَلَ , فَعِلَ , or فَعُلَ .

The preterite passive is invariably of the form فُعِلَ .

The Persons are formed as follows:

Plural.		Dual.		Singular.		
Fem.	Masc.	Fem.	Masc.	Fem.	Masc.	
فَعَلْنَ	فَعَلُوا	فَعَلَتَا	فَعَلَا	فَعَلَتْ	فَعَلَ	* 3rd person.
فَعَلْتُنَّ	فَعَلْتُمْ	فَعَلْتُمَا		فَعَلْتِ	فَعَلْتَ	2nd ,,
فَعَلْنَا				فَعَلْتُ		1st ,,

---

* This paradigm applies equally to the forms فَعِلَ فَعُلَ , and to the passive فُعِلَ , which are declined in the same way—

فَعِلَ فَعِلَتْ فَعِلْتَ . . . .

فَعُلَ فَعُلَتْ فَعُلْتَ . . . .

فُعِلَ فُعِلَتْ فُعِلْتَ . . . .

The Aorist.—The aorist active of the simple verb is formed as follows:

Plural. Fem.	Plural. Masc.	Dual. Fem.	Dual. Masc.	Singular. Fem.	Singular. Masc.	
يَفْعَلْنَ	يَفْعَلُونَ	تَفْعَلَانِ	يَفْعَلَانِ	تَفْعَلُ	يَفْعَلُ	* 3rd person.
تَفْعَلْنَ	تَفْعَلُونَ	تَفْعَلَانِ		تَفْعَلِينَ	تَفْعَلُ	2nd "
نَفْعَلُ				أَفْعَلُ		1st "

The aorist passive is declined in precisely the same manner, merely substituting the vowel ـُ for ـَ in the *prefixes* and pointing the second radical with ـَ, thus:

Plural. Fem.	Plural. Masc.	Dual. Fem.	Dual. Masc.	Singular. Fem.	Singular. Masc.	
يُفْعَلْنَ	يُفْعَلُونَ	تُفْعَلَانِ	يُفْعَلَانِ	تُفْعَلُ	يُفْعَلُ	3rd person.
تُفْعَلْنَ	تُفْعَلُونَ	تُفْعَلَانِ		تُفْعَلِينَ	تُفْعَلُ	2nd "
نُفْعَلُ				أُفْعَلُ		1st "

Moods of the Verb.

The aorist is declinable like the noun; that is to say, the final vowel is susceptible of certain changes to express modifications of the meaning.

1. It changes from ـُ to ـَ to express the conditional or subjunctive mood, and when preceded by certain particles: in this case the ن is also dropped from all the

---

* So, too, يَفْعِلُ and يَفْعُلُ are declined throughout.

persons which end in that letter preceded by a long vowel, thus:

Plural.		Dual.		Singular.		
Fem.	Masc.	Fem.	Masc.	Fem.	Masc.	
يَفْعَلْنَ	يَفْعَلُوا	تَفْعَلَا	يَفْعَلَا	تَفْعَلُ	يَفْعَلُ	3rd person.
تَفْعَلْنَ	تَفْعَلُوا	تَفْعَلَا		تَفْعَلِي	تَفْعَلُ	2nd ,,
نَفْعَلُ				أَفْعَلُ		1st ,,

2. It may lose its last vowel altogether when preceded by certain particles, or used as an imperative, or in a conditional or alternative sentence. It will then be declined:

Plural.		Dual.		Singular.		
Fem.	Masc.	Fem.	Masc.	Fem.	Masc.	
يَفْعَلْنَ	يَفْعَلُوا	تَفْعَلَا	يَفْعَلَا	تَفْعَلْ	يَفْعَلْ	3rd person.
تَفْعَلْنَ	تَفْعَلُوا	تَفْعَلَا		تَفْعَلِي	تَفْعَلْ	2nd ,,
نَفْعَلْ				أَفْعَلْ		1st ,,

To the conditional form of the aorist a *nún* نْ, either single or doubled نَّ, and preceded by *fetḥah*, is sometimes added to impart emphasis: it is chiefly used when this tense is employed as an imperative. It is then declined as follows:

1. With the doubled *nún* نَّ.

Plural.		Dual.		Singular.		
Fem.	Masc.	Fem.	Masc.	Fem.	Masc.	
يَفْعَلْنَانِّ	يَفْعَلُنَّ	تَفْعَلَانِّ	يَفْعَلَانِّ	تَفْعَلَنَّ	يَفْعَلَنَّ	3rd person.
تَفْعَلْنَانِّ	تَفْعَلُنَّ	تَفْعَلَانِّ		تَفْعَلِنَّ	تَفْعَلَنَّ	2nd ,,
نَفْعَلَنَّ				أَفْعَلَنَّ		1st ,,

2. With the single *nún* نْ.

Plural.		Dual.		Singular.		
Fem.	Masc.	Fem.	Masc.	Fem.	Masc.	
Wanting	يَفْعَلُنْ	Wanting	Wanting	تَفْعَلَنْ	يَفْعَلَنْ	3rd person.
Wanting	تَفْعَلُنْ	Wanting		تَفْعَلِنْ	تَفْعَلَنْ	2nd ,,
نَفْعَلَنْ					أَفْعَلَنْ	1st ,,

The long vowels و and ى are elided before the نَ or نَّ.

The Imperative.—The imperative is formed from the second person of the apocopated form of the aorist by removing the prefix تَ *ta.* But from تَفْعَلْ, by removing the تَ, we should have فْعَلْ; that is to say, a word beginning with a quiescent letter, and therefore inadmissible. To remedy this defect we add a *hemzet el waṣl* pointed with ـُ if the vowel of the aorist be ـُ, as أُفْعُلْ; but with ـِ if the vowel is either ـَ or ـِ, as إِفْعَلْ or إِفْعِلْ.

Plural.		Dual.	Singular.	
Fem.	Masc.	Common.	Fem.	Masc.
أُفْعُلْنَ	أُفْعُلُوا	أُفْعُلَا	أُفْعُلِي	أُفْعُلْ

The remaining persons of the imperative are formed by prefixing لِ to the apocopated aorist, as لِيَضْرِبْ "let him strike."

The Noun of Action.

The noun of action corresponds in many respects to our infinitive. In simple verbs it is irregular in its formation, but the following are the most usual measures: transitive verbs having the form فَعْلٌ and neuter verbs فَعَلٌ or فُعُولٌ.

1*st*, 2*nd*, *and* 3*rd Classes.*

Transitive فَعْلٌ; Neuter فُعُولٌ.

	Measures.			Examples.			
	Pret.	Aor.	Noun.	Pret.	Aor.	Noun.	
Transitive	فَعَلَ	يَفْعُلُ	فَعْلٌ	نَصَرَ	يَنْصُرُ	نَصْرٌ	To assist
Neuter			فُعُولٌ	قَعَدَ	يَقْعُدُ	قُعُودٌ	To sit
Transitive	فَعَلَ	يَفْعِلُ	فَعْلٌ	ضَرَبَ	يَضْرِبُ	ضَرْبٌ	To strike
Neuter			فُعُولٌ	جَلَسَ	يَجْلِسُ	جُلُوسٌ	To sit
Transitive	فَعَلَ	يَفْعَلُ	فَعْلٌ	قَطَعَ	يَقْطَعُ	قَطْعٌ	To cut
Neuter			فُعُولٌ	خَضَعَ	يَخْضَعُ	خُضُوعٌ	To be humble

4*th Class.*

Transitive فَعْلٌ; Neuter فَعَلٌ.

	Pret.	Aor.	Noun.	Pret.	Aor.	Noun.	
Transitive	فَعِلَ	يَفْعَلُ	فَعْلٌ	فَهِمَ	يَفْهَمُ	فَهْمٌ	To understand
Neuter			فَعَلٌ	طَرِبَ	يَطْرَبُ	طَرَبٌ	To rejoice

5*th Class.*

Verbs implying an innate quality make their noun of action in فَعَالَةٌ فُعُولَةٌ or فِعَلٌ.

	Pret.	Aor.	Noun.	Pret.	Aor.	Noun.	
Neuter	فَعُلَ	يَفْعُلُ	فَعَالَةٌ	ظَرُفَ	يَظْرُفُ	ظَرَافَةٌ	To be charming
Neuter			فُعُولَةٌ	سَهُلَ	يَسْهُلُ	سُهُولَةٌ	To be easy.
Neuter			فِعَلٌ	عَظُمَ	يَعْظُمُ	عِظَمٌ	To be grand.

Augmented or Derived Conjugations.

The meaning of the simple verb may be extended or modified in various ways by the addition of one or more letters to the root.

There are in all fourteen of these derived conjugations, which may be divided into four groups, namely:

1. Adding one letter to the root, which in transitive verbs strengthens or intensifies the action, and in neuter verbs imparts a transitive sense.
2. Prefixing تَ to imply "consequence" or "effect."
3. Adding two or more letters to the root to modify the original meaning.
4. Distorting the original form of the root as well as adding letters to it. This implies a corresponding distortion of the meaning, and indicates either colour, defect, or intensity.

The simple triliteral verb is considered as the first conjugation, and the fourteen derived forms are numbered 2, 3, and so on, up to 15. In the following account of the signification of the derived forms these numbers are placed against the measures, but they are described in a somewhat different order.

Signification of the Derived Forms.

First Group (adding One Letter to the Root).

4th Conjugation, أَفْعَلَ.

The prefix of *hemzet el kaṭa'* to the root gives a transitive sense to neuter verbs, and a doubly transitive or causal sense to those which are already transitive.

The following are the most usual significations :

Transitive or causal ; as أَنْزَلَ "he caused to descend," from نَزَلَ "to descend."

Going to, or making for, a place : أَعْرَقَ "he went to 'Iráḳ."

Being or becoming at a certain time ; as أَصْبَحَ "he was in the morning."

2nd Conjugation.

Doubling the middle consonant intensifies the meaning of the root, and makes it, if neuter, transitive. Its most usual significations are :

Transitive ; as قَدَّمَ "he sent forward," from قَدَمَ "to be in front."

Intensive or frequentative ; as كَسَّرَ "he broke to pieces," from كَسَرَ "he broke."

Attributing to, regarding as, or making out to be ; as صَدَّقَ "he looked upon him as, or proved him, truthful."

This form is used in deriving a verb from a noun ; as خَيَّمَ "he pitched his tents," from خَيْمَةٌ "a tent."

This use is almost identical with that of the English verb formed from a noun ; as *to water, to skin, to peel,* etc.

3rd Conjugation, فَاعَلَ

The insertion of *alif* between the first and second radicals gives an idea of reciprocity to the action ; as قَاتَلَ "he fought," from قَتَلَ "he killed." The notion of a second party who reciprocates the action is always implied.

Second Group (adding Two Letters).

5th Conjugation, تَفَعَّلَ.

This, by the prefix of ت, expresses the consequence of the 2nd conjugation فَعَّلَ; as قَدَّمَ "he brought forward;" تَقَدَّمَ "he was (so) brought forward."

When the original root is a concrete noun, this form will imply simply adopting or employing; as تَوَسَّدَ "he reclined his head on a pillow," from وَسَّدَ 2nd conjugation (from وِسَادَةٌ) "a pillow."

6th Conjugation, تَفَاعَلَ.

This is formed by prefixing to the 3rd conjugation فَاعَلَ ت, implying *consequence,* with the same results as in the 5th conjugation; thus, تَقَاتَلَ "he was one of the parties engaged in a fight between two," from قَاتَلَ 3rd conjuga-tion of قَتَلَ.

The sense of feigning is sometimes contained in this form; as تَمَارَضَ "to feign illness." It appears to come somewhat in the following manner:

A hypothetical form مَارَضَ must have existed, which in such a word as this, from مَرِضَ "to be ill," can only mean that his illness was merely for the sake of affecting a second party, and this, again, could only mean that he displayed it to deceive another, and the prefix ت limiting the consequence of such action to himself, تَمَارَضَ will mean that he was one who was afflicted with illness in order to produce an effect upon another, *i.e.* he assumed illness.

7th Conjugation, إِنْفَعَلَ.

This conjugation expresses the state or condition resulting from the action of the simple triliteral verb فَعَلَ ; as قَطَعْتُهُ "I cut it"; إِنْقَطَعَ "it was cut."

8th Conjugation, إِفْتَعَلَ.

This does not differ materially from the 7th conjugation, the only difference being that while the last indicates the state or condition resulting from, or exhibits the *effects* of the action of the simple triliteral verb, the 8th conjugation conveys the notion of being *affected* by the action; as جَمَعْتُهُ "I collected it"; إِجْتَمَعَ "it was gathered together, or was in a collected state."

9th Conjugation, إِفْعَلَّ.

The form of noun used to express a colour or quality is, as we shall presently see, أَفْعَلُ; the 9th conjugation appears to be formed from this by doubling the last consonant to imply action, and thus making it into a verb.

This form is used to express any quality which is very conspicuous, especially colour or distortion; as إِحْمَرَّ "to be red," from أَحْمَرُ "red;" إِحْدَبَّ "to be hump-backed," from أَحْدَبُ "a hunchback."

Third Group (adding Three Letters).

10th Conjugation, إِسْتَفْعَلَ.

This conjugation implies asking or seeking, as إِسْتَغْفَرَ "he asked pardon."

Finding or considering a thing to be possessed of the attribute implied in the original verb, as إِسْتَعْظَمَ "to consider grand or mighty."

From the sense of "desiring" comes that of "desiring to be," إِسْتَكْبَرَ "he was proud," "desired to be thought great," and hence becoming or turning into, as إِسْتَحْجَرَ ٱلطِّينُ "The clay began to turn into stone," or "petrify," *i.e.* to become stone-hard.

11*th Conjugation*, إِفْعَالَّ.

This is of very rare occurrence, and is merely an extension of the 9th conjugation إِفْعَلَّ both in form and signification: *e.g.* إِصْفَارَّ "to be very yellow."

12*th Conjugation*, إِفْعَوْعَلَ. 13*th Conjugation*, إِفْعَوَّلَ.

These imply great intensity, as إِخْشَوْشَنَ "to be very rough and rugged," from خَشُنَ "to be rough."

The grammars give two other forms—14th Conjugation إِفْعَنْلَلَ, and 15th إِفْعَنْلَى; but these are very rare, and may be regarded as varieties of the quadriliteral verb. See p. 26.

No verb is susceptible of *all* these forms; those in use will depend upon the nature of the original verb, and it must be left to practice and the common sense of the student to distinguish which may or may not be employed.

The Tenses of Derived Forms.

(1) *The Preterite.*

The numbers and persons of the preterite of the derived conjugations are formed as in the simple triliteral verb; as فَعَلَ, فَعَلَتْ, فَعَلْتَ, etc.

(2) *The Aorist.*

The forms of the aorist and the nouns of action of derived verbs will be seen from the following table :

Tables of the Derived Conjugations.

Active.

	Preterite.	Aorist.	Imperative.	Noun of Action.
First Group. One letter added to the root.				
2. Doubled radical, expressing action or intensity	فَعَّلَ	يُفَعِّلُ	فَعِّلْ	تَفْعِيلٌ or تَفْعِلَةٌ
4. Prefixed *alif*, expressing action	أَفْعَلَ	يُفْعِلُ	أَفْعِلْ	إِفْعَالٌ
3. Inserted *alif*, expressing reciprocity or emulation	فَاعَلَ	يُفَاعِلُ	فَاعِلْ	فِعَالٌ or مُفَاعَلَةٌ
Aor. act. عِلُ . . . يُفَ ; pass. عَلُ . . . يُفَ				
Second Group. ت prefixed to root, implying consequence.				
5. Consequence of 2	تَفَعَّلَ	يَتَفَعَّلُ	تَفَعَّلْ	تَفَعُّلٌ
6. Consequence of 3	تَفَاعَلَ	يَتَفَاعَلُ	تَفَاعَلْ	تَفَاعُلٌ
Aor. act. عَلُ . . . يَتَفَ ; pass. عَلُ . . . يُتَفَ				

Tables of the Derived Conjugations—*cont.*

Active—cont.

	Preterite.	Aorist.	Imperative.	Noun of Action.
Third Group. Two or more letters added, modifying the sense of the root.				
7. Exhibiting the effect of the action of the root	اِنفَعَلَ	يَنفَعِلُ	اِنفَعِلْ	اِنفِعَالْ
8. Being affected by the action of the root	اِفتَعَلَ	يَفتَعِلُ	اِفتَعِلْ	اِفتِعَالْ
10. Asking for or regarding as the original idea expressed by the root	اِستَفعَلَ	يَستَفعِلُ	اِستَفعِلْ	اِستِفعَالْ
Aor. act. يُ . . . عِلُ ; pass. يُ . . . عَلُ				
Fourth Group.				
9. Colour or defect	اِفعَلَّ	يَفعَلُّ	اِفعَلِلْ	اِفعِلَالْ
11. Colour or defect	اِفعَالَّ	يَفعَالُّ	اِفعَالِلْ	اِفعِيلَالْ
Aor. act. يَفْ . . . عَلُّ.				
12. Great intensity	اِفعَوعَلَ	يَفعَوعِلُ	اِفعَوعِلْ	اِفعِيعَالْ
13. Great intensity	اِفعَوَّلَ	يَفعَوِّلُ	اِفعَوِّلْ	اِفعِوَّالْ
Aor. act. يَفْ . . . ِلُ.				

Passive.

	Preterite.	Aorist.		Preterite.	Aorist.
2	فُعِّلَ	يُفَعَّلُ	7	اُنْفُعِلَ	يُنْفَعَلُ
4	أُفْعِلَ	يُفْعَلُ	8	اُفْتُعِلَ	يُفْتَعَلُ
3	فُوعِلَ	يُفَاعَلُ	10	اُسْتُفْعِلَ	يُسْتَفْعَلُ
5	تُفُعِّلَ	يُتَفَعَّلُ	9	Wanting	Wanting
6	تُفُوعِلَ	يُتَفَاعَلُ	11	Wanting	Wanting
			12	اُفْعُوعِلَ	يُفْعَوْعَلُ
			13	اُفْعُوِّلَ	يُفْعَوَّلُ

Quadriliteral and quinquiliteral verbs are rare, and are conjugated like augmented verbs.

Nouns derived from Verbs.

Certain nouns derived from verbs may be considered as particular forms of the latter; they therefore range themselves naturally under the same head. The principal forms will be found in the accompanying table (pp. 28, 29).

Examples of the use of the table:—

Take the root ضَرَبَ of which the aorist (to be found only by the dictionaries) is يَضْرِبُ. In the table we find that the imperative of this class is اِفْعِلْ, and by substituting (1) ض for ف (2) ر for ع and (3) ب for ل we get اِضْرِبْ, which is the imperative of the verb in question.

Coming next to the noun of action, we find that for transitive verbs the form is فَعْلٌ and ضَرَبَ belonging to this class, its noun of action should be ضَرْبٌ, which is the proper form. Similarly we get

Noun of Unity.	Agent.	Patient.	Noun of Action in *mím*.
ضَرْبَةٌ	ضَارِبٌ	مَضْرُوبٌ	مَضْرِبٌ

Again, amongst the derived conjugations, suppose we wish to form the third; we have then

Preterite.	Aorist.
ضَارَبَ=فَاعَلَ	يُفَ . . . عِلُ = يُضَ . . . رِبُ

i.e. (the dots implying that any letters coming between the first and second radicals are unchanged) يُضَارِبُ.

Passive (Preterite).	Passive (Aorist).
ضُورِبَ=فُوعِلَ	يُ . . . عَلُ = يُ . . . رَبُ

i.e. (all intermediate letters remaining unchanged) يُضَارَبُ.

Noun of Action.	Agent.
مُضَارَبَةٌ=مُفَاعَلَةٌ	مُ . . . عِلٌ

i.e. (the letters represented by the dots being unchanged as before) مُضَارِبٌ.

Patient.
Noun of Action in *mím*. } مُ . . . عَلٌ = as before مُضَارَبٌ.
Noun of Time and Place.

And so on with all the other forms.

As it is in this method of deriving its forms that Arabic differs from all non-Semitic languages, the importance of early acquiring practice in it cannot be over-estimated.

When the learner has once mastered the table, every fresh root that he learns adds some six or seven score of fresh words to his vocabulary together with the different shades of meaning of each.

SIMPLE TRILITERAL VERB.		Active.		Passive.		Impera-tive.	Noun of Action.	
		Preterite.	Aorist.	Preterite.	Aorist.		Transitive.	Neuter.
1. (See p.19.)	Class 1	فَعَلَ	يَفْعُلُ	فُعِلَ	يُفْعَلُ	اُفْعُلْ	فَعْلٌ	فُعُولٌ
	,, 2	,,	يَفْعِلُ	,,	,,	اِفْعِلْ	,,	,,
	,, 3	,,	يَفْعَلُ	,,	,,	اِفْعَلْ	,,	,,
	,, 4	فَعِلَ	يَفْعَلُ	,,	,,	اِفْعَلْ	,,	فَعَلٌ
	,, 5	,,	يَفْعِلُ	,,	,,	اِفْعِلْ	,,	,,
	,, 6	فَعُلَ	يَفْعُلُ	,,	,,	اُفْعُلْ	,,	فَعَالَةٌ / فُعُولَةٌ / فَعْلٌ
DERIVED CONJUGATIONS. 1st Group. (One letter added.)	2	فَعَّلَ	يُفَـ...عِلُ	فُـ...عِلَ	يُـ...عَلُ	فَـ...عِّلْ	تَفْعِيلٌ / تَفْعِلَةٌ	
	3	فَاعَلَ	,,	فُوعِلَ	,,	,,	فِعَالٌ / مُفَاعَلَةٌ	
	4	أَفْعَلَ	,,	أُفْعِلَ	,,	أَفْعِلْ	إِفْعَالٌ	
2nd Group. (ت prefixed.)	5	تَفَعَّلَ	يَتَفَـ...عَلُ	تُـ...عِلَ	,,	تَفَـ...لْ	تَـ...عُلٌ	
	6	تَفَاعَلَ	,,	,,	,,	,,	,,	
3rd Group. (Two or more letters added.)	7	اِنْفَعَلَ	يَـ...عِلُ	,,	,,	اِ...عِلْ	اِ...عَالٌ	
	8	اِفْتَعَلَ	,,	,,	,,	,,	,,	
	10	اِسْتَفْعَلَ	,,	,,	,,	,,	,,	
4th Group. (Colour or Defect.)	9	اِفْعَلَّ	يَفْـ...عَلُّ	,,	,,	اِ...لِلْ	......لَالٌ	
	11	اِفْعَالَّ	يَفْعَالُّ	,,	,,	,,	,,	
	12	اِفْعَوْعَلَ	يَفْـ...عِلُ	,,	,,	اِ...لِلْ	......الٌ	
	13	اِفْعَوَّلَ	,,	,,	,,	,,	,,	

Noun of Unity.	Noun of Species.	Agent.	Patient.	Noun of Action in *mím.*	Noun of Time or Place.	Noun of Instrument, or Intransitive Agent.	Noun of Quality.	Noun of Superiority (Comparative and Superlative.)	Intensive Agent.
فعلة	فعلة	فَاعِلٌ	مفعول	مفعل	مفعل	مفعل مفعال مفعلة	فَاعِلٌ	أفعل	فَعُولٌ
,,	,,	,,	,,	,,	,,	مفعل مفعلة	,,	,,	,,
,,	,,	,,	,,	,,	مفعل	,,	,,	,,	,,
,,	,,	,,	,,	,,	مفعل	,,	فعلان	,,	,,
,,	,,	,,	,,	,,	مفعل	,,	,,	,,	,,
,,	,,	,,	,,	,,	مفعل	,,	فَاعِلٌ فَعِلٌ	,,	فَعِيلٌ
adding ة to the Noun of Action. ,,		مُ...عِلٌ	مُ...عَلٌ	مُ...عَلٌ	مُ...عَلٌ	Wanting	مُ...عِلٌ	Wanting	فَعُّولٌ فِعِّيلٌ فَعَّالٌ
,,		,,	,,	,,	,,	,,	,,	,,	فَاعُولٌ
,,		,,	,,	,,	,,	,,	,,	,,	,,
,,		,,	,,	,,	,,	,,	,,	,,	
,,		,,	,,	,,	,,	,,	,,	,,	
,,		,,	,,	,,	,,	,,	,,	,,	
,,		,,	,,	,,	,,	,,	,,	,,	
,,		,,	,,	,,	,,	,,	,,	,,	
,,		,,	,,	,,	,,	,,	أفعل	,,	
,,		,,	,,	,,	,,	,,	,,	,,	
,,		,,	,,	,,	,,	,,	,,	,,	
,,		,,	,,	,,	,,	,,	,,	,,	

Irregular Verbs.

Irregular verbs are those of which the second and third radicals are alike, or which contain one or more of the weak letters أ, و or ى. They are of five kinds:

I. *Doubled*, in which the second and third radical are alike.

II. *Hemzated*, in which one of the three radicals is a *hemzeh*.

III. *Assimilated*, in which the first radical is either و or ى.

IV. *Hollow*, which have one of the weak letters و or ى for the medial letter.

V. *Defective*, of which the final radical is a weak letter; as غَزَا (for غَزَوَ) "he made a raid," رَمَى (for رَمَيَ) "he threw," رَضِيَ (for رَضِوَ).

Combinations of these may of course occur, and a verb may have all the three radicals weak; as أَوَى "he repaired to," "he had recourse to."

It will be noticed that the weak consonants or semi-vowels are أ *hemzeh* (not *alif*), و *wáw*, and ى *yá*: *alif* is not regarded as a consonant at all, but only as a prop for *hemzeh* or as a letter of prolongation.

I. *Doubled Verbs.*

The Doubled verb differs from the simple triliteral only in the assimilation of the two similar consonants in the preterite and aorist, as مَدَّ for مَدَدَ, and يَمُدُّ for يَمْدُدُ; as this throws back the vowel of the second radical in the aorist, the *hemzet el-waṣl* is no longer required in the imperative, which then becomes مُدَّ.

The derived conjugations of the doubled verb are regularly formed from the first, as from مَدَّ we get 4th أَمَدَّ, 2nd مَدَّدَ, and so on. In the 3rd and 6th the ا (which is the characteristic letter of the conjugation), is in the passive changed by the ـُ (which is the characteristic vowel of the voice), into the corresponding semi-vowel, namely و. The forms مَادَّ, تَمَادَّ, etc., as well as مادّ for مادِد), in the agent, are exceptions to the rule which prohibits a quiescent letter from following a long vowel. There are two reasons which make this exception admissible: first, that if a long vowel were shortened it would be impossible to distinguish between such forms as the 3rd conj. active and the passive of the first; and, second, because when the assimilation is resolved, the first letter is found to be only *apparently* quiescent, *e.g.* مادّ = مادِد, and not مادْدْ.

The tenses, preterite and aorist, are regularly formed, but two other forms of the 2nd person preterite are admissible, namely: مَدْتُ, etc., as ظَلْتُ or مَدَيْتُ, etc. as ظَلَيْتُ. The last is constantly used in modern Arabic.

It will be observed that the assimilated letters are resolved whenever the second of the two letters would be quiescent, because otherwise it would violate the rule which prohibits two quiescent letters from occurring together, as مَدَدْنَا (not مَدّْنا) يَمْدُدْنَ (not يَمُدّْنَ).

II. *Hemzated Verbs.*

1. Verbs having *hemzeh* for the first radical are conjugated exactly like the sound verbs. The only change is that when the *alif* ا which supports the *hemzeh* is preceded by a vowel, َ or ُ, characteristic of the form, it is changed into the corresponding semi-vowel, as يُوثِرُ for يُأْثِرُ, see p. 6.

In the derived forms also of verbs with initial *hemzeh*, the only changes are those undergone by the *alif* ا, which serves as the prop to *hemzeh*, as آثَرَ for أَأْثَرَ, يُوثِرُ for يُأْثِرُ as before. In the 4th and 8th, إِيثَارٌ and إِيتَثَرَ are for إِئْثَارٌ and إِئْتَثَرَ, where the second of two *hemzehs* which come together yields and is changed into the ى, corresponding to the preceding vowel *kesrah*. So, too, in the passive of the 4th, أُوثِرَ is for أُأْثِرَ. In the verbal noun of the 7th and 10th the *hemzeh* with *kesrah* beginning a syllable but not a word, has for its prop a ى without dots. See p. 6. In the 8th إِيتَثَرَ is sometimes further contracted into إِتَّثَرَ, as إِتَّخَذَ from أَخَذَ.

2. Verbs having *hemzeh* for the medial radical.—All the changes in this and the derived forms, depend upon the rule that a *hemzeh* beginning a syllable, but not a word, takes as its prop the semi-vowel homogeneous to the vowel by which it is surmounted, and if this be ى the dots are omitted, as يَسْئَلُ and أَسْآلٌ.

The ء is sometimes dropped in the imperative, in

which case the *hemzet el-waṣl* is no longer needed. Thus اسأل becomes سَل .

3. Verbs with the *hemzeh* for the final radical.—All the changes in these and their derived forms, depend upon the rule that the prop for *hemzeh* may be a weak consonant homogeneous to the preceding vowel, as يبرِى , أبرأ ; تبرأ , تبرو .

The tenses of the *hemzated* verbs do not differ from those of the sound verb.

III. *Assimilated Verbs.*

The changes that take place in these verbs are: (1) when either *kesrah* or *ḍhammah* precedes the weak letter, they change it into the homogeneous weak consonant; N.B. when *fetḥah* precedes it, a diphthong is formed; as وعد , pret. 4th أوعد , aor. 4th يوعد , verbal noun 4th ايعاد . Note, when the verb begins with و and is of the measure يفعِل in the aorist, the و of verbs beginning with that letter is dropped in that tense, as وعد , يعِد , to promise.

The tenses are declined exactly like the sound verb, *e.g.*:

Preterite	وعد	وعدْت	وعدَت , etc.
Aorist	يعد	تعد , etc.	
Ditto	يوسم	توسم , etc.	

The و in most of these verbs is also rejected in forming the verbal noun, but a ة is added by way of compensation, as

Preterite.	Aorist.	Noun.
وعد	يعِد	عِدَة

The initial ى does not make any change in the form, unless it be preceded by ـُ , in which case it becomes و , as مُوقِن for مُيْقِن .

IV. *The Hollow Verb.*

A verb of which the middle radical is و or ى , is called "hollow." Thus قَالَ , aorist يَقُولُ , is in the dictionaries and grammars said to be a verb with a medial و of the measure فَعَلَ , aorist يَفْعُلُ , *i.e.* it belongs to class 1 ; (see p. 18). In this case the قَالَ stands for قَوَلَ and يَقُولُ for يَقْوُلُ ; the second is an obviously euphonic change, but the first is not so evidently required, since قَوَلَ *ḳawala* would be as easy to pronounce as قَبَلَ *ḳabala*.

If, however, we regard it as a *really* hollow verb, *i.e.* without a middle radical at all, the measure will be فَ*لَ ; then instead of saying that its medial radical is *w* و (in which case, having a medial radical, it could not be hollow), let us refer it to the class of sound verbs to which it belongs, namely يَفْعُلُ , فَعَلَ , and we get قَ*لَ , يَقْ*ُلُ . Here the two *fetḥahs* in قَ*لَ coalesce into ا ; and the ـُ *dhammah* in يَقْ*ُلُ , from its position in the penultimate, where it naturally receives an accent, has a long sound. The form is then written يَقُولُ , and *the* و *thus obtained is treated as the radical letter of the root.* Similarly بَاعَ , aorist يَبِيعُ . with a medial *ya* ى , may be written بَ*عَ and referred to class 2, فَعَلَ , يَفْعِلُ becoming بَ*عَ , يَبْ*ِعُ , that is بَاعَ , يَبِيعُ .

In the noun of action of verbs with a weak medial this

radical is elided and ة added at the end to make up for it, as from قَامَ the nouns of action of the 4th and 10th conjugations are—

إِقَامَةٌ for إِقْوَامٌ
إِسْتِقَامَةٌ „ إِسْتِقْوَامٌ

The preterite and aorist are regularly formed except that whenever a long vowel is followed by a *sukún* it is changed into a short one, as قُلْتُ, not قُولْتُ, which would violate the rule that two sukúns cannot come together.

V. *The Defective Verb.*

The defective verb is that which occasions most trouble to learners; the rules however which govern its permutations are very simple, and are all contained in the following table:—

Changes in the Termination of the Preterite.

a.	وَ	becomes	ا	In the Preterite of the 1st conj. only; in all the derived forms وَ becomes ى like *c.*
b.	وِ	„	ىِ	
c.	ىَ	„	ى	Here the final vowel is dropped and the ى is then silent, the *fethah* alone being pronounced. This letter is called *short alif.*

Changes in the Termination of the Aorist.

d′. ـُوُ becomes ـُو	i. ـُوُّ / ـُيُو become ـُو
e. (ـُو remains unchanged ـُو)	
f. ـَوُ / ـَى become ـَى	j. ـِوِي / ـِيِي become ـِي
g. ـِوُ / ـِى become ـِى	k. ـُوُّ / ـُيُو become ـُوْ
h. (ـِى remains unchanged ـِى)	l. ـِيِي becomes ـِىْ

Similarly in nouns.

f′. ـَوٌ / ـَى become ـًى.

g′. ـِوٌ / ـِى „ ـٍ, the و and ى not being required to support *tenwín kesrah.*

ـُوٌّ becomes ـُوْ (but in verbs of the form رَضِوَ(=رَضِىَ) ـِىْ is more commonly used).

ـِوْىٌ „ ـِىْ.

From this it follows that the subjunctive mood of the aorist, which is formed by changing the final ـُ into ـَ, can only be formed from verbs of the form يَفْعِلُ or يَفْعُلُ, as يَرْمِى (by *h*) يَغْزُو (by *e*).

m. The final vowel is, as we have seen, dropped in all cases except *e* and *h*. In order therefore to represent the apocopated forms of the aorist we must drop the *weak radical*; thus from يَرْمِى the form يَفْعِلْ becomes يَرْمِ.

The defective verb in the 2nd conjugation always makes its noun of action تَفْعِلَةٌ instead of تَفْعِيل which is the most common form in the sound verb, as تَصْفِيَة from صَفَا

The feminine of the third person singular and of the dual active, being formed directly from the masculine, drops the ا because اْتْ would bring two *sukúns* together. Thus غَزَا fem. غَزَتْ, not غَزَاْتْ.

Doubly Imperfect Verbs.

1. Initial و and Final و or ى.

These are mere combinations of the defective with the initial و, and follow the rules given for each. Thus—وَقَى is of the form فَعَلَ يَفْعِلُ; like وَعَدَ it rejects its *wáw* in the aorist, and like رَمَى it changes ىَ into ى, and ىُ into ىِ by *f* and *g* becoming in the aorist يَقِى.

2. Medial و and Final و or ى.

In these no change takes place in the second radical, which retains its power as a consonant. The final ى follows the rule of ى and ى in رَمَى and رَضِىَ.

Note.—The Verb حَيِىَ, although in all other cases conforming to the foregoing rules, in the tenth conjugation loses its second radical; as—

Preterite	اِسْتَحْيَى	or	اِسْتَحَى	
Aorist	يَسْتَحْيِى	„	يَسْتَحِى	
Imperative	اِسْتَحْيِ	„	اِسْتَحِ	and so on.

Combinations with أ *hemzeh* and the other weak letters also occur; in these cases it is only necessary to apply to each letter the required rule according to the foregoing explanations. Thus أَوَى, which is of the form فَعَلَ يَفْعِلُ, becomes أَوَى يَأْوِى by *c* and *g* for اَوَىَ يَأْوِىُ. Similarly to form the imperative اِفْعِلْ we have ايوِ by the rule on p. 32 and by *m* for اأْوِىْ.

Again, رَأَى of the measure فَعَلَ يَفْعَلُ becomes رَأَى يَرْأَى by *c* and *f* for رَأَىَ يَرْأَىُ; the *hemzeh* is then rejected, and the form becomes رَأَى يَرَى. Similarly the apocopated form of aorist is يَرَ by *m*, and the imperative رَ or رَهْ by the pause (7).

Hollow Verbs declined as Strong Verbs.

A few verbs with a weak medial radical pointed with *kesrah* are declined like strong verbs.

Preterite.	Aorist.	Agent.	
عَوِرَ	يَعْوَرُ	عَاوِرٌ	to be one-eyed.
عَوِزَ	يَعْوَزُ	عَاوِزٌ	to be wanting.
حَوِلَ	يَحْوَلُ	حَاوِلٌ	to squint.
صَيِدَ	يَصْيَدُ	صَايِدٌ	afflicted with glanders (a camel).
غَيِدَ	يَغْيَدُ	غَايِدٌ	to be delicate in body.

In the form أَفْعَلُ, from verbs with a medial weak radical, the strong form is used, as أَسْوَدُ (not أَسَادُ), black.

To conjugate a weak or irregular verb.—First find the form required amongst the derived conjugations of the strong verb (p. 24); next apply the rules for euphonic change (pp. 9 and 35). Then if it be a tense, refer to the paradigms of the preterite, aorist, or imperative. If any further change be then required, again apply the rules of permutation, p. 35.

Thus to find the first person aorist of the 3rd conjugation from غَزَا "to make a raid or foray." We look in the table (p. 24 or 28) for the third conjugation, which we find to be فَاعَلَ; the corresponding form of غَزَا will obviously be غَازَا. Again, the aorist of the third is of the measure يُفَـ.....عِلُ, which in this case will be يُغَازِوُ; but وِ by 9 becomes ى, and the whole word becomes يُغَازِى.

A further reference to the table of persons in the aorist, p. 15, teaches us to substitute the prefix of the first person أُ for the يُ of the third person, and we get أُغَازِى *ughází*, the form required.

The final short vowel ـُ of the aorist is variable, depending upon the action of particles, etc., but the remaining vowels of the forms are constant, and therefore exert a stronger influence upon a weak letter.

By applying these principles, all difficulties as to the conjugation of verbs containing weak radicals will disappear; and we shall find that such a thing as a really irregular verb does not exist in the Arabic language.

The student is recommended to practise this process

until he is completely familiar with all the permutations which can occur in conjugating a weak verb.

Indeclinable Verbs.

Indeclinable verbs are those which have only one tense. They are—(1) لَيْسَ "he is not," عَسَى "perhaps," which have only a preterite.

(2) The following, which are only found in the imperative: هَاتِ "give," تَعَالَ "come."

These are declined like a regular imperative, thus—

Plural.		Dual.	Singular.	
Fem.	Masc.	Common.	Fem.	Masc.
هَاتِينَ	هَاتُوا	هَاتِيَا	هَاتِي	هَاتِ

Some grammarians include هَلُمَّ, which is, however, not properly a verb; it is most frequently found in the expression هَلُمَّ جَرًّا, literally, "take and drag along"="and so on."

THE NOUN.

In the category of nouns the Arabs include also pronouns and certain prepositions, adverbs, and interjections. Nouns are either primitive or derived.

Primitive Nouns.

Primitive nouns are those which cannot be referred to any verbal root such as فَرَسٌ horse, قَلْبٌ heart, جَعْفَرٌ small stream.

Nouns derived from Verbs.

Besides the nouns immediately derived from verbs, included in the table on pp. 28–29, and corresponding more or less to our participles, there are a great many other forms expressive of specific ideas which may be studied with advantage; the principal of these are the following:

1. Trades and offices are of the measure فِعَالَةٌ; as تِجَارَةٌ trading, خِيَاطَةٌ tailoring, خِلَافَةٌ office of Caliph.

2. Pains of the body are of the measure فُعَالٌ; as صُدَاعٌ headache, سُعَالٌ cough.

3. Sounds are of the measure فُعَالٌ or فَعِيلٌ; as صُرَاخٌ cry, صَفِيرٌ whistling.

4. Motion, commotion, or emotion are expressed by the form فَعَلَانٌ, and sometimes فَعِيلٌ; as خَفَقَانٌ palpitating, fluttering, رَحِيلٌ departure.

5. Flight or avoidance by فِعَالٌ; as فِرَارٌ flight.

6. A small portion is expressed by فِعْلَةٌ; as كِسْرَةٌ a broken crust, قِطْعَةٌ a fragment.

7. A small quantity, by فُعْلَةٌ; as قُبْضَةٌ a handful.

8. Colour in the abstract, by فُعْلَةٌ; as حُمْرَةٌ redness, صُفْرَةٌ yellowness.

9. Small pieces, refuse, by فُعَالَةٌ; as قُرَاضَةٌ clippings, filings.

The Genders of Nouns.

There are only two genders in Arabic, masculine and feminine; some words, however, have only one form for both, and may therefore be called of the common gender.

The neuter does not exist, but its place is most commonly supplied by the feminine.

The following are feminine :

Proper names of women, and nouns applicable only to females, as أُمّ "a mother," أُخْتٌ "a sister," حَامِلٌ "pregnant."

Nouns ending in ة, as ضَارِبَةٌ "a striker," unless the sense be opposed to it ; خَلِيفَةٌ "Caliph."

Nouns ending in ى, as حُسْنَى "most beautiful" (female), دُنْيَا (for دُنْيَى) "the world."

[If this ى is not a grammatical termination, but belong to the *root*, it may be masculine.]

Nouns ending in آء, as صَحْرَآء "desert."

Proper names of towns and countries.

Names of wind, fire, or wine, as رِيحٌ "wind," شَمَالٌ "the north wind," نَارٌ "fire," خَمْرٌ "wine."

The double parts of the body, as يَدٌ "hand," عَيْنٌ "eye," كَتِفٌ "shoulder," رِجْلٌ "foot." (Some others which are not double are also feminine, as سِنٌّ "tooth," كَبِدٌ "liver.")

Collective nouns, especially when they add ة to express an individual of the species, as حَمَامٌ "dove" (the *genus* dove), حَمَامَةٌ "a dove."

All "broken" plurals, which will be described afterwards.

The following nouns are also considered as feminine, although they do not all come under the heads given above :—

أَرْضٌ "earth," شَمْسٌ "sun," أَرْنَبٌ "hare," ضَبُعٌ "hyena,"

أَفْعَى "viper," ضِلَعٌ "rib," بِئْرٌ "well," عَرُوضٌ "prosody," ثَعْلَبٌ "fox," عَصًا "staff," جَهَنَّمُ , جَحِيمٌ , سَعِيرٌ , سَقَرُ , or لَظَى , "hell," عَقْرَبٌ "scorpion," فَهْدٌ "cheetah" (hunting leopard), فَأْسٌ "axe," فِرْدَوْسٌ "Paradise," قَوْسٌ "bow," حَرْبٌ "war," كَأْسٌ "cup," خَمْرٌ "wine," مُوسَى "razor," دَارٌ "house," نَارٌ "fire," دِرْعٌ "coat of mail," نَعْلٌ "sandal," دَلْوٌ "bucket," نَفْسٌ "soul," رَحًى "hand-mill," يَمِينٌ "oath," سُوقٌ "market."

Formation of the Feminine from the Masculine.

The feminines of masculine nouns are formed as follows :—

1. The ordinary method is by adding ة; as ضَارِبٌ fem. ضَارِبَةٌ "a striker"; مَضْرُوبٌ fem. مَضْرُوبَةٌ "struck."

ى and ـا before ة become ا; as فَتًى "a youth," fem. فَتَاةٌ "a young girl."

2. Nouns of the form فَعْلَانُ make their feminines in فَعْلَى; as سَكْرَانُ "drunk," fem. سَكْرَى.

But فَعْلَانٌ and فُعْلَانٌ make their feminines in the usual manner, فَعْلَانَةٌ and فُعْلَانَةٌ; as نَدْمَانٌ "repentant," fem. نَدْمَانَةٌ; عُرْيَانٌ "naked," fem. عُرْيَانَةٌ.

3. أَفْعَلُ when it expresses the comparative or superlative makes its feminine فُعْلَى; as أَكْبَرُ "greatest," fem. كُبْرَى; أَوَّلُ "first" (for أَأْوَلُ), fem. أُولَى; آخَرُ (for أَأْخَرُ), fem. أُخْرَى.

4. أَفْعَلُ when it is descriptive of colour or deformity has for its feminine فَعْلَاءُ; as أَحْمَرُ "red," fem. حَمْرَاءُ; أَحْدَبُ "hump-backed," fem. حَدْبَاءُ.

5. فَعُولٌ when it has an active signification has no different form for the feminine, as رَجُلٌ صَبُورٌ "a patient man," إِمْرَأَةٌ صَبُورٌ "a patient woman," except عَدُوٌّ "an enemy," fem عَدُوَّةٌ.

But فَعُولٌ with a passive signification makes فَعُولَةٌ in the feminine, as مَرْكُوبٌ "a riding horse or camel," fem مَرْكُوبَةٌ ; رَسُولٌ "one sent," fem. رَسُولَةٌ.

6. *Vice versâ* فَعِيلٌ in the passive sense has only one form for the masculine and feminine, as رَجُلٌ قَتِيلٌ "a murdered man," إِمْرَأَةٌ قَتِيلٌ "a murdered woman," while فَعِيلٌ with an active meaning makes فَعِيلَةٌ in the feminine : شَفِيعٌ "an intercessor," fem. شَفِيعَةٌ.

The other forms of the intensive nouns مِفْعَلٌ , مِفْعَالٌ , and مِفْعِيلٌ , being also nouns of instrument, do not take the feminine termination, with the exception of مِسْكِينٌ "a poor person," fem. مِسْكِينَةٌ ; مِيقَانٌ "speaking the truth," fem. مِيقَانَةٌ.

Common Gender.

The following nouns are used either as masculine or feminine :—

إِزَارٌ "veil," صَاعٌ "a dry measure," إِصْبَعٌ "finger," ضُحًى "forenoon," ثَدْيٌ "breast," ضَرَبٌ "honey," ثَرًى "earth," طَرِيقٌ "road," جَنَاحٌ "wing," عَجُزٌ "buttocks," حَالٌ "state, condition," عُرْسٌ "wedding," حَانُوتٌ "store, shop," عَسَلٌ "honey (wild)," رَحِمٌ "womb," عُقَابٌ "eagle," رُمْحٌ "lance," عُنُقٌ "neck," سَبِيلٌ "road," عَنْكَبُوتٌ "spider," سُرًى "night ourney," فَرَسٌ "horse or mare," سِكِّينٌ "knife," فُلْكٌ "ship," سِلاحٌ "arms," قِدْرٌ "pot, kettle," سُلْطَانٌ "dominion," قَفًا "nape of the neck," سِلْمٌ "peace," قَوْسٌ "bow," سُلَّمٌ "staircase, adder," كُرَاعٌ "shin-bone," سَمَاءٌ "heaven," لِسَانٌ "tongue," شَعِير "barley," لَيْلٌ "night," صِرَاطٌ "way," مِسْكٌ "musk," صُلْحٌ "peace," مِعًى "intestines," صَلِيفٌ "side of the neck," مِلْحٌ "salt."

All nouns not included in the foregoing categories are masculine.

Declension of Nouns.

The Cases.—Arabic nouns have three cases, the nominative or subjective, accusative or objective, and genitive or dependent. [I shall use the terms subjective, dependent, and objective as more in accordance with the principles of Arabic grammar.] The nasal vowels (*tenwín*) are employed for the indefinite noun, and the short vowels for the definite noun, thus:

Indefinite.	Definite. With the Article.	Definite. With Pronouns.	
Subjective كِتَابٌ a book.	اَلْكِتَابُ	كِتَابُهُ	كِتَابِي
Dependent كِتَابٍ of a book.	اَلْكِتَابِ	كِتَابِهِ	كِتَابِي
Objective كِتَابًا a book.	اَلْكِتَابَ	كِتَابَهُ	كِتَابِي

The following nouns, أَبٌ "father," أَخٌ "brother," حَمٌ "father-in-law," هَنٌ "thing," ذُو "possessor," فَمٌ "mouth," are declined with long vowels when in construction with a noun, or when they have an affixed pronoun.

	Indefinite.	With the Article.	With Pronouns.	In Construction.
Subjective	أَبٌ a father	اَلْأَبُ	أَبِى أَبُوهُ	أَبُو زَيْدٍ
Dependent	أَبٍ	اَلْأَبِ	أَبِى أَبِيهِ	أَبِى زَيْدٍ
Objective	أَبًا	اَلْأَبَ	أَبِى أَبَاهُ	أَبَا زَيْدٍ

The Cases of Nouns with a weak Final Radical.

The existence of a weak radical at the end of a noun must obviously affect the case endings; the following results (already treated of, see p. 36) must be remembered:

Nouns of the measure فَعَلٌ from verbs with a final و in the root, change the وٌ into ا by *f′*, as رِضًا for رِضَوٌ.

Nouns of the measure فَعَلٌ from verbs with a final ى, change the يٌ into ىً, as فَتًى.

Nouns of more than three letters of the form عَلٌ * * *, whether from a final radical وٍ or يٍ, make their termination in ىً: as مُرْتَمًى, from رَمَى : مَلْهًى, from لَهَا (لَهَوَ).

Nouns ending in وٍ or يٍ change that termination into ٍ by *g′*.

Examples: رِضًا "satisfaction," فَتًى "a youth," قَاضٍ "a Cadi."

Measure.		Indefinite.	Definite. With Article.	With Pronoun.
فِعَلٌ	Subjective	رِضًا for رِضَوٌ	اَلرِّضَا	رِضَاهُ
	Dependent	رِضًا „ رِضَوٍ	اَلرِّضَا	رِضَاهُ
	Objective	رِضًا „ رِضَوًا	اَلرِّضَا	رِضَاهُ

Measure.		Indefinite.	Definite. With Article.	Definite. With Pronoun.
فَعَلٌ	Subjective	فَتًى for فتىً	أَلْفَتَى	فَتَاهُ (or فَتَيُهُ)
	Dependent	فَتًى „ فَتًى	أَلْفَتَى	فَتَاهُ (or فَتَيْهُ)
	Objective	فَتًى „ فَتًى	أَلْفَتَى	فَتَاهُ (or فَتَيْةُ)
فَاعِلٌ	Subj.	قَاضٍ for قَاضِيٌ	أَلْقَاضِي	قَاضِيهِ
	Depend.	قَاضٍ „ قَاضِيٍ	أَلْقَاضِي	قَاضِيهِ
	Obj.	قَاضِيًا „ قَاضِيًا (regular)	أَلْقَاضِيَ (regular)	قَاضِيَهُ

Imperfectly declined Nouns.

Certain words are not susceptible of *tenwín*, and employ *fetḥah* both in the dependent (instead of *kesrah*) as well as in the objective case. These will be seen in the examples of the declensions of nouns.

Note.—All imperfectly declined nouns when in construction or preceded by the article take *kesrah* in the oblique case, as مَرَرْتُ بِأَفْضَلِكُمْ "I passed by the most accomplished of you."

The Numbers of Nouns.

There are three numbers in Arabic nouns, singular, dual, and plural.

The Dual.—The dual has only one form to express the dependent and objective cases; the terminations are—

	Masculine.	Feminine.
Subjective	ـــانِ	ـــتَانِ
Dependent, Objective,	ـــيْنِ	ـــتَيْنِ

In construction, or when followed by an affixed pronoun, the نِ is dropped, كِتَابَا زَيْدٍ "Zeid's two books," فى كِتَابِيْهِ "in his two books."

The rules of permutation which hold in verbs apply equally to nouns.

The Plural.—The plural in Arabic is formed either by affixes or by a modification of the original form of the singular, as in English we say "ship," pl. "ships"; "man," pl. "men."

The first kind is called technically a regular plural; the second a "broken" plural.

Regular Masculine Plural.—The regular plural has only one form for the dependent and objective cases.

Masc.	ـُونَ	nom.	This is an expansion of the singular termination ـٌ ـٍ, for as ـٌ *un* = ُو *ú*, so ُونَ *úna*= ُوُو *úú*.
,,	ـِينَ	oblique	
Fem.	ـَاتٌ		This is an expansion of the regular feminine affix ة.
,,	ـَاتٍ		

The regular masculine affixed form is only used for—

1. Nouns of a participial form derived from verbs making their feminine in ة and signifying rational beings.

2. Proper names of men, provided they consist of a single word, and do not end in ة.

3. Diminutives of proper names of the description just mentioned, and diminutives of ordinary nouns, provided

they denote rational beings, and are of the masculine gender, as

رُجَيْلٌ a little man, plural, رُجَيْلُونَ

4. Relative adjectives ending in يٌّ.

5. Nouns of the measure أَفْعَلُ provided they have the comparative or superlative meaning.

It cannot be used in nouns which are common to both genders, as

جَرِيحٌ wounded. صَبُورٌ patient.

There are a few words which form exceptions to the rules above given; they are

اِبْنٌ	son,	plural,	بَنُونَ
أَهْلٌ	family,	,,	أَهْلُونَ
ذُو	possessor,	,,	ذَوُو and أُولُو
عَالَمٌ	world, universe,	,,	عَالَمُونَ
أَرْضٌ	earth,	,,	أَرَضُونَ
عَشْرٌ	ten,	,,	عِشْرُونَ twenty.

(And the other cardinal numbers, thirty, forty, etc., between twenty and ninety.)

سَنَةٌ year, plural سِنُونَ

Together with all nouns similar to the last, *i.e.* nouns of which the last radical is cut off and a ة added by way of compensation, as مِائَةٌ "a hundred," مِئُونَ; عِضَةٌ "a thorny tree," عِضُونَ.

A peculiarity of the class of plurals last mentioned is

that in the dependent case they may be treated as broken plurals, and declined throughout; *e.g.*

Sub. سِنِينٌ Dep. سِنِينٍ Obj. سِنِينًا

When the last letter of a noun is weak و, ى or *tenwín* ـٍ the rules given on p. 36 for the change in the termination of the aorist of verbs and of nouns must be applied.

قَاضٍ a judge, plural { قَاضُونَ by *i.*
قَاضِينَ „ *j.*

مُصْطَفًى Mustafá, „ مُصْطَفَوْنَ „ *k.*

Before a *hemzet el-waṣl* these lose their نَ and take ـَ and ـِ respectively, as مُصْطَفَى ٱللّٰهِ, "chosen of God," pl. مُصْطَفَو ٱللّٰهِ.

In construction with a following noun the regular plural loses its final نَ, as

ضَارِبُو زَيْدٍ the strikers of Zeid.

N.B.—ة whether singular or plural becomes ت when followed by another letter, as إِخْوَةٌ "brothers," إِخْوَتُهُ "his brothers."

The regular feminine plural in اَتٌ is frequently used in nouns which have a neuter sense, as

حَمَّامٌ bath, pl. حَمَّامَاتٌ.

Broken Plurals.

There are two kinds of broken plurals recognized by the Arabic grammarians; namely, the plural of paucity, and the plural of multitude.

The plural of paucity expresses any number between three and ten.

The plural of multitude denotes any number from ten to infinity.

Plural of Paucity.—There are four measures of the plural of paucity:

أَفْعُلٌ as أَرْجُلٌ from رِجْلٌ foot.
فِعْلَةٌ „ غِلْمَةٌ „ غُلَامٌ slave.
أَفْعِلَةٌ „ أَكْسِيَةٌ „ كِسَاءٌ dress. (This only occurs in words which have the penultimate a long vowel.)
أَفْعَالٌ „ أَحْمَالٌ „ حِمْلٌ load. This is common to plurals of multitude also.

Broken plurals are invariably treated as feminine.

These broken plurals are one of the greatest difficulties the beginner has to encounter in learning Arabic; a reference to the accompanying table, however, will show that they are not so arbitrary or unsystematic as might at first appear. The left-hand column contains the measures of the singular, the horizontal line at the top of the page gives the measures of the plural. Some forms, such as فُعْلَى, it will be seen, have only one plural فُعَلٌ, while others have several. The first four forms are those which have the greatest variety of plurals, thus the measure فَعَلٌ may have for its plural either فِعْلَةٌ, فُعْلٌ, فُعُلٌ, فُعُولٌ, فِعَالٌ,

4 *

أَفْعَال , أَفْعُل , أَفْعِلَة , فِعْلَان , فِعَال , or مَفَاعِل . Practice and the dictionaries alone can teach the student which of these various forms of plural a particular noun of the measure فَعَل takes, but he may approximately arrive at it by observing the nature of various plural forms. For example, the first فِعْلَة is generally used with words that have a weak consonant for the first or last radical, as أَخ (for أَخَو) "a brother," إِخْوَة the forms فُعْل , فُعُل , and فُعُول are chiefly used with substantives implying concrete ideas, and the same noun may make its plural in any one of the three, as أَسَد "a lion," أُسْد , أُسُد , or أُسُود ; if a number between three and ten is to be expressed, the plural of paucity is used, as جَبَل pl. of paucity أَجْبُل ; if the substantive make its feminine in ة and has not a weak radical, the form فِعَال is often used as جَمَل "a camel," pl. جِمَال, and so on. Sometimes a word if used in different meanings, will take one plural in one sense and one in another, as بَيْت "a house," pl. بُيُوت , but بَيْت "a verse of poetry," makes its pl. أَبْيَات . Words of four or more syllables need occasion no difficulty, as their plurals may be represented by the formula (4) (3) ا (2) (1), as is shown below.

The tables of broken plurals with examples which are given in my larger grammar may be consulted with advantage by the student.

Plural of Quadriliterals.—The measure for the plurals of words of four letters may be regularly represented by the signs (4) (3) ا (2) (1), which will be found to embrace all the forms فَوَاعِل , فَعَاعِل , مَفَاعِل , etc., as the position of any of the three radicals in the form is immaterial. Thus from مِفْتَاح "key," we get (4) ح (3) تا (2) فـ (1) مـ (= مَفَاتِيح the ـِ changing the ا into ى), where the first radical ف of the root occurs in the second place of the measure (2); and from جَوْهَر "jewel," we have (4) ر (3) هـ (2) و (1) جـ = جَوَاهِر, where the first radical ج occurs in the first place (1).

In words of five or more letters all above four are cut off in forming the plural, as

عَنْدَلِيب nightingale, plural عَنَادِل (يب) (4) ل (3) د (2) ن (1) ع

سَفَرْجَل quince „ سَفَارِج (ل) (4) ج (3) ر (2) ف (1) س

In the measures of the broken plurals, as in the mea sures of the verbs, the vowels are the characteristic and really important part of the form.

They will therefore exert their usual influence upon a weak letter; thus مِفْتَاح = (4) ا(3) ْ(2) (1), and should by the rule for the formation of broken plurals from quadri-literal nouns make (4) (3) ا(2) (1), that is مَفَاتَاح; but the ـِ is the most important form to preserve, and the ا therefore yields and is changed to ى, the word becoming مَفَاتِيح.

Plurals of Plurals.

In the measure of quadriliterals and quinqueliterals are formed plurals of plurals; thus,

يَدٌ (يَدِى) pl. أَيْدٍ (أَيْدِى), hands, pl. of pl. أَيَادٍ (أَيَادِى) gifts.

Or a regular plural may be formed from the broken plural, but it must be a feminine plural; see

طَرِيقٌ road, pl. طُرُقٌ, pl. of pl. طُرُقَاتٌ.

Irregular Plurals.

Plurals formed from singulars obsolete and other than those to which they are referred are

أُمٌّ mother, pl. أُمَّهَاتٌ as if from أُمَّهَةٌ

فَمٌ mouth, „ أَفْوَاهٌ „ فُوهٌ

مَاءٌ water, „ أَمْوَاهٌ „ مَاهٌ

The two following are also irregular.

نِسَاءٌ women, pl. نِسْوَةٌ and نِسْوَانٌ

إِنْسَانٌ man, „ أَنَاسٌ (rare and poetic) and نَاسٌ.

From relative adjectives a collective plural may be formed by simply adding the feminine termination ة; as,

شَافِعِيٌّ Shafiite, coll. pl. شَافِعِيَّةٌ the Shafiite sect.

Examples of the Declensions of Nouns.

Regularly declined Nouns.—1. Nouns derived from a verb (except أَفْعَلُ) and denoting rational beings; as مُذْنِبٌ, fem. مُذْنِبَةٌ "a sinner."

Plural.		Dual.		Singular.		
Fem.	Masc.	Fem.	Masc.	Fem.	Masc.	
مُذْنِبَاتٌ	مُذْنِبُونَ	مُذْنِبَتَانِ	مُذْنِبَانِ	مُذْنِبَةٌ	مُذْنِبٌ	Subjective.
مُذْنِبَاتٍ	مُذْنِبِينَ	مُذْنِبَتَيْنِ	مُذْنِبَيْنِ	مُذْنِبَةٍ	مُذْنِبٍ	Dependent.
do.	do.	do.	do.	مُذْنِبَةً	مُذْنِبًا	Objective.

2. Proper names consisting of three letters the middle of which is quiescent; as زَيْدٌ *Zeid*, a man's name; هِنْدٌ *Hind*,* a woman's name.

Plural. Fem.	Plural. Masc.	Dual. Fem.	Dual. Masc.	Singular. Fem.	Singular. Masc.	
هِنْدَاتٌ	زَيْدُونَ	هِنْدَانِ	زَيْدَانِ	هِنْدٌ	زَيْدٌ	Subjective.
هِنْدَاتٍ	زَيْدِينَ	هِنْدَيْنِ	زَيْدَيْنِ	هِنْدٍ	زَيْدٍ	Dependent.
do.	do.	do.	do.	هِنْدًا	زَيْدًا	Objective.

3. Proper names of men having an intelligible signification in Arabic; مُحَمَّدٌ Mohammed (Praised).

Plural. Masc.	Dual. Masc.	Singular. Masc.	
مُحَمَّدُونَ	مُحَمَّدَانِ	مُحَمَّدٌ	Subjective.
مُحَمَّدِينَ	مُحَمَّدَيْنِ	مُحَمَّدٍ	Dependent.
do.	do.	مُحَمَّدًا	Objective.

4. Broken plurals, except those of the form (4) (3) ا 2) (1), (4) ءِ (3) ا (2) (1), and those ending in ى or آءِ; as أُسُدٌ "lions," قِرَدَةٌ "apes."

Plural.		
قِرَدَةٌ	أُسُدٌ	Subjective.
قِرَدَةٍ	أُسُدٍ	Dependent.
قِرَدَةً	أُسُدًا	Objective.

---

* Words of this class, *i.e.* triliteral names of females, may be also imperfectly declined, *i.e.* without *tenwín* in singular, and with only one form from the dependent and objective cases.

Imperfectly declined Nouns.—1. Proper names of men or women not included in classes 2 and 3 of the previous section: عُثْمَانُ "Othman," زَيْنَبُ "Zeinab."

Plural. Fem.	Plural. Masc.	Dual. Fem.	Dual. Masc.	Singular. Fem.	Singular. Masc.	
زَيْنَبَاتٌ	عُثْمَانُونَ	زَيْنَبَانِ	عُثْمَانَانِ	زَيْنَبُ	عُثْمَانُ	Subjective.
زَيْنَبَاتٍ	عُثْمَانِينَ	زَيْنَبَيْنِ	عُثْمَانَيْنِ	زَيْنَبَ	عُثْمَانَ	Dependent and Objective.

2. Nouns of the form أَفْعَلُ, whether comparative or descriptive of colour and deformity; as أَفْضَلُ "more accomplished."

Plural. Masc.	Dual. Masc.	Singular. Masc.	
أَفْضَلُونَ	أَفْضَلَانِ	أَفْضَلُ	Subjective.
أَفْضَلِينَ	أَفْضَلَيْنِ	أَفْضَلَ	Dependent and Objective.

Those expressing deformity do not take the regular plural. See p. 49.

3. Nouns of the form فَعْلَانُ, adjectival and descriptive, and which do not make their feminine by the addition of ة.

These are declined like عُثْمَانُ in the last paradigm but one.

4. Broken plurals of the form (4)(3)ا(2)(1),(4)يـ(3)ا(2)(1); as دَرَاهِمُ "dirhems" (drachmæ); مَفَاتِيحُ "keys."

مَفَاتِيحُ	دَرَاهِمُ	Subjective.
مَفَاتِيحَ	دَرَاهِمَ	Dependent. and Objective.

Declension of Nouns ending in a weak letter.—**1.** Nouns ending in ٓاءٌ, the *hemzeh* being radical.

These are declined quite regularly; as قُرَّآءٌ "a reader."

Plural.	Dual.	Singular.	
قُرَّآؤُونَ	قُرَّآءَانِ	قُرَّآءٌ	Subjective.
قُرَّآئِينَ	قُرَّآءَيْنِ	قُرَّآءٍ	Dependent.
		قُرَّآءً	Objective.

2. Nouns ending in ٓاءٌ, this termination being derived from a final radical و or ى; as كِسَآءٌ for كِسَاوٌ "a suit of clothes."

Plural.	Dual.	Singular.	
A regular plural cannot be formed from such a noun as this.	كِسَآءَانِ } كِسَاوَانِ }	كِسَآءٌ	Subjective.
	كِسَآءَيْنِ	كِسَآءٍ	Dependent.
	كِسَاوَيْنِ	كِسَآءً	Objective.

رِدَآءٌ for رِدَایٌ "a mantle," is similarly declined.

When the termination ٓاءٌ is added to the root but is not a sign of the feminine, as عِلْبَآءٌ "a sinew," it is declined in the same manner, but the form عِلْبَاوَانِ is preferable in the dual.

3. Nouns ending in ٓاءُ.

Plural.	Dual.	Singular.	
The regular plural is wanting.	عَذْرَاوَانِ	عَذْرَآءُ	Subjective.
	عَذْرَاوَيْنِ	عَذْرَآءَ	Dependent and Objective.

Broken plurals in آء are declined like the singular of this last form.

4. Proper names of men ending in آء; as زَكَرِيَّآء "Zachariah."

Plural.	Dual.	Singular.	
زَكَرِيَّآؤُونَ	زَكَرِيَّآءَانِ or زَكَرِيَّاوَانِ	زَكَرِيَّآءُ	Subjective.
زَكَرِيَّآئِينَ	زَكَرِيَّآءَيْنِ / زَكَرِيَّاوَيْنِ	زَكَرِيَّآءَ	Dependent and Objective.

5. Triliterals ending in اً for وٌ.

Plural.	Dual.	Singular.	
Regular plural wanting.	عَصَوَانِ	عَصاً	Subjective.
	عَصَوَيْنِ	عَصاً	Dependent.
	do.	عَصاً	Objective.

Similarly أَبٌ, أَخٌ, etc., for أَبَوٌ, أَخَوٌ, make أَبَوَانِ, أَخَوَانِ, etc. in the dual, the last radical weak letter being restored in the other forms.

6. Nouns ending in ىً for يٌ.

Plural.	Dual.	Singular.	
Regular plural wanting.	فَتَيَان	فَتىً	Subjective.
	فَتَيَيْنِ	فَتىً	Dependent.
	do.	فَتىً	Objective.

Nouns ending in یَ (without the *tenwín*) are similarly declined in the dual.

7. Quadriliterals ending in ٍ for وٍ or یٍ.

Plural.	Dual.	Singular.	
قَاضُونَ	قَاضِيَانِ	قَاضٍ	Subjective.
قَاضِينَ	قَاضِيَيْنِ	قَاضٍ	Dependent.
		قَاضِيًا	Objective.

The Noun of Relation.—The noun of relation is formed by affixing the syllable یّ and rejecting all such inflections as the ة of the feminine, or the signs of the dual and plural, as مَكَّةُ, relative مَكِّیّ "Meccan"; زَيْدَانِ "two Zeids," rel. زَيْدِیّ; زَيْدُونَ; rel. زَيْدِیّ.

In nouns which themselves end in the termination یّ, the relative is formed by rejecting this, if preceded by more than two letters, and adding the termination یّ, as as كُرْسِیّ, rel. كُرْسِیّ, so that the two are identical in form; but if preceded by only one letter, the first of the two *yás* ی is pointed with *fetḥah* and the second is changed into و, as حَیّ "an Arab village," rel. حَيَوِیّ. If the first of the two *yás* ی stand in place of a و, it is also changed into that letter, as طَیّ "a fold," rel. طَوَوِیّ.

In forming the noun of relation from nouns ending in a weak letter, the same rules apply as for the declensions.

Another form of the relative termination is انِیّ. This is principally used in technical or scientific terms; as

جِسْمَانِىٌّ "corporeal," رُوحَانِىٌّ "spiritual," بَرَّانِىٌّ "external," جَوَّانِىٌّ "internal."

Very irregular forms are شَآمٍ "Syrian," يَمَانٍ "of Yemen." (These are declined like قَاضٍ.)

Abstract Noun.

From the Noun of Relation an Abstract Substantive is formed by the addition of the feminine termination ةٌ, as اِلٰهٌ "a god," اِلٰهِىٌّ "divine," اِلٰهِيَّةٌ "divinity." In theological works (especially Christian) the termination وتٌ is used instead, as لَاهُوتٌ "divinity," "deity," مَلَكُوتٌ "kingdom (of heaven)."

The Diminutive.

The diminutive is formed by inserting يْ (quiescent *yá*) after the second letter of the noun, and pointing the initial letter with *ḍhammah* and the second letter with *fetḥah*, as رَجُلٌ "a man," dim. رُجَيْلٌ.

If the noun has more than three letters, all which follow the inserted يْ are pointed with *kesrah*, as دِرْهَمٌ "a drachma," dim. دُرَيْهِمٌ.

Declinable nouns only are susceptible of a diminutive.

THE PRONOUN.

The Pronouns are of two kinds, separate and affixed.

Personal Pronouns.

1. The separate pronouns are:

	Singular. Masc.	Singular. Common.	Singular. Fem.	Dual. Common.	Plural. Masc.	Plural. Common.	Plural. Fem.
1st person		أَنَا I.				نَحْنُ we.	
2nd „	أَنْتَ thou.		أَنْتِ thou.	أَنْتُمَا ye two.	أَنْتُمْ ye.		أَنْتُنَّ ye.
3rd „	هُوَ he.		هِيَ she.	هُمَا they two.	هُمْ they.		هُنَّ they.

These only express the nominative case.

2. The affixed pronouns are:

	Singular. Masc.	Singular. Common.	Singular. Fem.	Dual. Common.	Plural. Masc.	Plural. Common.	Plural. Fem.
1st person		ى my, me.				نَا we.	
2nd „	كَ thy, thee.		كِ thy, thee.	كُمَا your, you two.	كُمْ your, you.		كُنَّ your, you.
3rd „	هُ his, him.		هَا her.	هُمَا their, them two.	هُمْ their, them.		هُنَّ their, them.

These only express the oblique or objective cases.

With verbs, and certain particles which resemble verbs, the ى of the first person becomes نِى; as ضَرَبَنِى "he struck me," اِنَّنِي "verily I."

After a long vowel ى becomes يَ, as خَطَايَا "sins," خَطَايَايَ "my sins."

The pronouns of the third person, when preceded by *kesrah* ـِ or ى, change their *ḍhammah* to *kesrah*, as كِتَابِهِ, "(of) his book"; عَلَيْهِمْ "upon them."

N.B.—If a *hemzet el-waṣl* follows the plural masculine pronoun, the *mím* must be pointed with ـُ , as عَلَيْهِمُ ٱلسَّلَامُ "peace be upon them!"

The feminine termination ةَ becomes ـَتـ before the affixed pronoun, as كِتَابَةٌ "writing," كِتَابَتُهَا "her writing."

As the addition of the affixed pronoun serves to make the noun definite, the *tenwín* necessarily disappears before the affixed pronoun (see p. 4).

The نَ of the regular plural and the نِ of the dual are omitted before the affixed pronouns, as كِتَابَاهُ "his two books;" ضَارِبُوهُ "his strikers."

The mute ا is dropped in the third person masc. plural of the preterite, as كَتَبُوهُ "they wrote it."

A Verb governing two Accusative Pronouns.—When a verb governs two accusatives, and both of these happen to be affixed pronouns, as أَعْطَيْتُكَهُ "I gave thee it," the second may be either joined or written separately, the word إِيَّا being used as a peg on which to hang it; thus أَعْطَيْتُكَ إِيَّاهُ "I gave thee it."

If the two pronouns are joined, the natural order of the persons must be followed, the first preceding the 2nd, and the second coming before the 3rd.

When pronouns of the second person plural are followed by another affixed pronoun, a long و is introduced between the two, as أَعْطَيْتُكُمْ "I gave you," أَعْطَيْتُكُمُوهُ "I gave you it," أَعْطَيْتُمْ "you gave," أَعْطَيْتُمُوهُ "you gave it"; (مُو appears to have been the original full form of the termination of these pronouns).

Demonstrative Pronouns.

The Demonstrative pronoun is ذا "that," and is thus declined:

Plural.	Dual. Fem.	Dual. Masc.	Singular. Fem.	Singular. Masc.	
أُولَى or أُولَاءِ	تَانِ	ذَانِ	ذِى	ذَا	Subjective.
”	تَيْنِ	ذَيْنِ	”		Dependent and Objective.

ذَا is seldom used by itself, and when it forms a compound the feminine singular assumes the form تِى or ذِهِ at the end of a word is formed, and تَا or تِ at the beginning.

When ذُو signifies "possessor" (see p. 45), it is fully declined as follows:

Plural. Fem.	Plural. Masc.	Dual. Fem.	Dual. Masc.	Singular. Fem.	Singular. Masc.	
ذَوَاتُ (أُولَاتُ)	ذَوُو (أُولُو)	ذَوَاتَا	ذَوَا	ذَاتُ	ذُو	Subjective.
ذَوَاتِ (أُولَاتِ)	ذَوِي (أُولِي)	ذَوَتَيْ	ذَوَيْ	ذَاتِ	ذِي	Dependent.
				ذَاتَ	ذَا	Objective.

For the ordinary demonstrative denoting distant objects ذٰلِكَ is used:

Plural.	Dual. Fem.	Dual. Masc.	Singular. Fem.	Singular. Masc.	
أُولَٰئِكَ (أُولَالِكَ)	تَانِّكَ	ذَانِّكَ	تِلْكَ	ذٰلِكَ	Subjective.
”	تَيْنِّكَ	ذَيْنِّكَ	”		Dependent and Objective.

The ordinary demonstrative for near objects is formed by prefixing هَا "lo!" "here," to ذَا, the ا being generally defectively written, thus هٰذَا "this," which is declined as follows:

	Plural.	Dual. Fem.	Dual. Masc.	Singular. Fem.	Singular. Masc.
Subjective.	هَاؤُلَاءِ	هَتَانِ	هٰذَانِ	هٰذِهِ	هٰذَا
Dependent and Objective.	"	هَتَيْنِ	هٰذَيْنِ	"	

For additional emphasis كَ may be added to the above, as هٰذَاكَ "this here," which is then declined:

	Plural. Common.	Dual. Fem.	Dual. Masc.	Singular. Fem.	Singular. Masc.
Subjective.	هَاؤُلَائِكَ	هَتَانِكَ	هٰذَانِكَ	هَاتِيكَ	هٰذَاكَ
Dependent and Objective.	"	هَتَيْنِكَ	هٰذَيْنِكَ	"	

The Relative and Interrogative Pronouns.

The Relative pronoun أَلَّذِى=(أَلْ+لَ+ذِى) is thus declined:

	Plural. Fem.	Plural. Masc.	Dual. Fem.	Dual. Masc.	Singular. Fem.	Singular. Masc.
Subjective.	أَللَّاتِى or أَللَّوَاتِى	أَلَّذِينَ [or أَلْأُولَاءِ]	أَللَّتَانِ	أَللَّذَانِ	أَلَّتِى	أَلَّذِى
Dependent and Objective.			أَللَّتَيْنِ	أَللَّذَيْنِ		

Other relatives are—مَنْ "who," مَا "what." مَنْ and مَا are also used as Interrogatives.

مَا is indeclinable. مَنْ only very rarely declined.

The Article.

The article أَلْ "the" is indeclinable.

For the use of the Relative pronouns and of the Article see the Syntax.

The Numerals.

The Cardinal Numbers.

		Masculine.	Feminine.	
1	١	أَحَدٌ وَاحِدٌ	إِحْدَى وَاحِدَةٌ	
2	٢	إِثْنَانِ	اِثْنَتَانِ ثِنْتَانِ	This is declined as an ordinary dual noun.
3	٣	ثَلٰثَةٌ ثَلَاثَةٌ	ثَلٰثٌ ثَلَاثٌ	From 3 to 10 the numerals assume the feminine form for the masculine, and *vice versâ*. *From three to ten the numerals govern a broken plural of the noun numbered, which is put in the oblique case.* If the noun have a plural of paucity, this is to be preferred, as غِلْمَةٍ ثَلَاثَةُ "3 slaves."
4	٤	أَرْبَعَةٌ	أَرْبَعٌ	
5	٥	خَمْسَةٌ	خَمْسٌ	
6	٦	سِتَّةٌ	(سِدْسٌ سِدْتٌ) سِتٌّ	
7	٧	سَبْعَةٌ	سَبْعٌ	
8	٨	ثَمٰنِيَةٌ ثَمَانِيَةٌ	(ثَمَانِي) ثَمَانٍ	
9	٩	تِسْعَةٌ	تِسْعٌ	
10	١٠	عَشَرَةٌ	عَشْرٌ	
11	١١	أَحَدَ عَشَرَ	إِحْدَى عَشْرَةَ	
12	١٢	اِثْنَا عَشَرَ	اِثْنَتَا عَشْرَةَ	The numerals compounded with ten are indeclinable, both
13	١٣	ثَلَاثَةَ عَشَرَ	ثَلَاثَ عَشْرَةَ	

		Masculine.	Feminine.
14	١٤	أَرْبَعَةَ عَشَرَ	أَرْبَعَ عَشْرَةَ
15	١٥	خَمْسَةَ عَشَرَ	خَمْسَ عَشْرَةَ
16	١٦	سِتَّةَ عَشَرَ	سِتَّ عَشْرَةَ
17	١٧	سَبْعَةَ عَشَرَ	سَبْعَ عَشْرَةَ
18	١٨	ثَمَانِيَةَ عَشَرَ	ثَمَانِيَ عَشْرَةَ
19	١٩	تِسْعَةَ عَشَرَ	تِسْعَ عَشْرَةَ
20	٢٠	عِشْرُونَ	
21	٢١	أَحَدٌ وَ عِشْرُونَ	إِحْدَى وَ عِشْرُونَ
22	٢٢	اِثْنَانِ وَ عِشْرُونَ	اِثْنَتَانِ وَ عِشْرُونَ
23	٢٣	ثَلَاثَةٌ وَ عِشْرُونَ	ثَلَاثٌ وَ عِشْرُونَ
24	٢٤	أَرْبَعَةٌ وَ عِشْرُونَ	أَرْبَعٌ وَ عِشْرُونَ
25	٢٥	خَمْسَةٌ وَ عِشْرُونَ	خَمْسٌ وَ عِشْرُونَ
26	٢٦	سِتَّةٌ وَ عِشْرُونَ	سِتٌّ وَ عِشْرُونَ
27	٢٧	سَبْعَةٌ وَ عِشْرُونَ	سَبْعٌ وَ عِشْرُونَ
28	٢٨	ثَمَانِيَةٌ وَ عِشْرُونَ	ثَمَانٍ وَ عِشْرُونَ
29	٢٩	تِسْعَةٌ وَ عِشْرُونَ	تِسْعٌ وَ عِشْرُونَ
30	٣٠	ثَلَاثُونَ	
40	٤٠	أَرْبَعُونَ	
50	٥٠	خَمْسُونَ	
60	٦٠	سِتُّونَ	
70	٧٠	سَبْعُونَ	
80	٨٠	ثَمَانُونَ	

taking *fetḥah* in all cases. The ten thus used in the compound follows the ordinary rule for masculine and feminine, while the units reverse it, as stated above.

From 11 *to* 99 *the numerals take an accusative singular of the thing numbered.*

ثَلَاثُونَ عِشْرُونَ, etc., are common to both genders, and are declined like ordinary sound plurals.

In compounding numerals with 20, 30, etc., and a unit, the unit is placed first, the two are connected by the conjunction وَ *and*, and both are declined.

		Masculine.
90	٩٠	تِسْعُونَ
100	١٠٠	مِائَةٌ
200	٢٠٠	مِائَتَانِ
300	٣٠٠	ثَلَاثُ مِائَةٍ
400	٤٠٠	أَرْبَعُ مِائَةٍ
500	٥٠٠	خَمْسُ مِائَةٍ
600	٦٠٠	سِتُّ مِائَةٍ
700	٧٠٠	سَبْعُ مِائَةٍ
800	٨٠٠	ثَمَانِ / ثَمَانِي } مِائَةٍ
900	٩٠٠	تِسْعُ مِائَةٍ
1000	١٠٠٠	أَلْفٌ
2000	٢٠٠٠	أَلْفَانِ
3000	٣٠٠٠	ثَلَاثَةُ آلَافٍ
4000	٤٠٠٠	أَرْبَعَةُ آلَافٍ
5000	٥٠٠٠	خَمْسَةُ آلَافٍ
6000	٦٠٠٠	سِتَّةُ آلَافٍ
7000	٧٠٠٠	سَبْعَةُ آلَافٍ
8000	٨٠٠٠	ثَمَانِيَةُ آلَافٍ
9000	٩٠٠٠	تِسْعَةُ آلَافٍ
10000	١٠٠٠٠	عَشَرَةُ آلَافٍ

The word مِائَةٌ mi-at*un* "hundred" is common to both genders.

From 100 *to* 1000 *the numerals govern the singular of the noun numbered, which they put in the oblique case*, as مِائَةُ رَجُلٍ "a hundred men."

When the *hundreds* are compounded with units, they are put in the oblique case of the singular.

[مِائَةٌ is pronounced as if written مِئَةٌ *mi-atun.*]

أَلْفٌ "a thousand" is common to both genders.

Thousands compounded with units follow the rules above given, *i.e. they are treated as a thing numbered.* Thus for 3000 to 10000 the broken plural آلَافٍ is used in the oblique case; from 10000 to 99000 the accusative singular أَلْفًا is used; and from 100000 upwards the oblique singular أَلْفٍ.

		Masculine.	
11000	١١٠٠٠	أَحَدَ عَشَرَ أَلْفًا	
12000	١٢٠٠٠	اِثْنَا عَشَرَ أَلْفًا	
13000	١٣٠٠٠	ثَلَاثَةَ عَشَرَ أَلْفًا	
100000	١٠٠٠٠٠	مِائَةُ أَلْفٍ	
200000	٢٠٠٠٠٠	مِائَتَا أَلْفٍ	
300000	٣٠٠٠٠٠	ثَلْثُمِائَةِ أَلْفٍ	In these cases the hundred and unit are written as one word.
400000	٤٠٠٠٠٠	أَرْبَعُمِائَةِ أَلْفٍ	
1000000	١٠٠٠٠٠٠	أَلْفُ أَلْفٍ	
2000000	٢٠٠٠٠٠٠	أَلْفَا أَلْفٍ	
3000000	٣٠٠٠٠٠٠	ثَلَاثَةُ آلَافِ أَلْفٍ	

Ordinal Numbers.

The ordinal numbers for the units (except the first) are formed on the measure of the agent, masc. فَاعِلٌ, fem. فَاعِلَةٌ; the tens, hundreds and thousands do not differ from the cardinal numbers.

Masculine.	Feminine.	
أَوَّلُ	أُولَى	1st
ثَانٍ	ثَانِيَةٌ	2nd
ثَالِثٌ	ثَالِثَةٌ	3rd

and so on up to عَاشِرٌ.

Masculine.	Feminine.	
حَادِى عَشَرَ	حَادِيَةَ عَشْرَةَ	11th
ثَانِى عَشَرَ	ثَانِيَةَ عَشْرَةَ	12th
etc.		
عِشْرُونَ		20th
حَادٍ وَ عِشْرُونَ	حَادِيَةٌ وَ عِشْرُونَ	21st
ثَانٍ وَ عِشْرُونَ	ثَانِيَةٌ وَ عِشْرُونَ	22nd
etc.		
تِسْعُونَ		90th
حَادٍ وَ تِسْعُونَ	حَادِيَةٌ وَ تِسْعُونَ	91st
etc.		

Other classes of Numerals.

1. Adverbial numerals :—مَرَّةً , نَوْبَةً "once" (*lit.* "one time," "one turn," etc.) ; ثَانِياً or ثَانِيَ مَرَّةٍ or مَرَّةً ثَانِيَةً "twice" , ثَالِثاً or مَرَّةً ثَالِثَةً "thrice" ; and so on.

2. Distributive :—أُحَادَ or مَوْحَدَ "one by one" ; ثُنَاءَ or مَثْنَى or اِثْنَيْنِ اِثْنَيْنِ "two by two" ; and so on.

These are imperfectly declined.

3. Multiplicative :—مُفْرَدٌ "single" ; مُثَنًّى "double, two-fold" ; and so on.

4. Adjectival :—ثُنَائِيٌّ "dual, consisting of two"; ثُلَاثِيٌّ "treble, consisting of three"; and so on.

PARTICLES.

Under the head Particle the Arabs include Prepositions, Conjunctions, Adverbs, and Interjections.

Prepositions.

The prepositions are either inseparable (*i.e.* are written as one word with the following noun) or separable.

The inseparable prepositions are five in number, namely:

بِ in, by, with, etc. This, when joined with the affixed pronouns هُ, هُمْ, هُمَا, changes their *ḍhammah* into ـِ, *e.g.* بِهِ, بِهِمْ.

تَ by (a particle of swearing).

وَ by (ditto).

لِ to (with pronouns this is pointed with *fetḥah*).

كَ like.

All prepositions take the following nouns in the dependent case.

Conjunctions.

The conjunctions are also either inseparable or separable.

The inseparable conjunctions are:

وَ and.

فَ and so (as a consequence of what has gone before).

Adverbs.

The adverbs are also either inseparable or separable. The first are:

أَ interrogative.

سَ or سَوْفَ expresses future time.

لَ certainly.

مَا "what?" after an indefinite noun is equivalent to the English "a certain," or "any whatever," as

رَجُلٌ مَّا خَرَجَ يَوْمًا مِنَ ٱلْأَيَّامِ "A certain man went out one day."

مَا رَأَيْتُ رَجُلًا مَّا "I did not see any man whatever."

The *n* of the *tenwín* in this case always coalesces with the م of مَا, which is then doubled; thus رَجُلٌ مَّا pronounced *rajulu mmá*.

Interjections.

The principal interjections are:

وَيْ وَا وَاهًا آهًا آهٍ أَ ah! alas!

أَلَا أَيَا يَا oh! ho! etc., etc.

A great many other words are used as interjections, but are in reality verbs or nouns, and are therefore not included amongst the particles.

All particles are indeclinable.

SECTION II.—SYNTAX.

The Principles of Arabic Syntax.

The following are the principal points of Arabic syntax, to which the attention of the student is directed.

1. Sentences are composed of nouns, verbs, and particles.

2. Arabic nouns are all *concrete*; that is, they are all what we should call substantives, and do not express *abstract* ideas.

3. The verbs contain a pronoun inherent in the form, which is their real agent.

Consequently, in analyzing the sentence جَآءَ زَيْدٌ ٱلْكَرِيمُ "Zeid the generous came," rather than say, as in European languages, that زَيْدٌ is the nominative or agent to the verb جَآءَ, and that ٱلْكَرِيمُ is an adjective agreeing with زَيْدٌ, I should prefer to say that the true explanation is—

جَآءَ "He came" (the agent *he* being contained in the word جَآءَ).

زَيْدٌ "I mean Zeid" (Zeid being the *name* of the agent اِسْمُ ٱلْفَاعِلِ, and therefore in apposition with it).

ٱلْكَرِيمُ "The generous one" (also in apposition with the agent or with the name).

4. One noun may define or determine another; such a state of dependence is indicated by the dependent case, as كِتَابُ ٱلرَّجُلِ "the book of the man."

THE *indefinite* NATURE OF A NOUN IS EXPRESSED BY *tenwín*.

THE DEFINITE NATURE OF A NOUN BY THE LOSS OF THE *tenwín*; and, if it stand by itself, except it be a proper name, by the addition of the article.

The absence of both *tenwín* and article shows that the noun, unless it be a proper name, is connected with that which immediately follows it.

5. A sentence naturally consists of a subject and predicate, that is, the thing about which we are going to speak, and some statement concerning it, as

Subject. Predicate.
زيدٌ قائمٌ "Zeid (is) standing.'

BOTH SUBJECT AND PREDICATE ARE PUT IN THE SUBJECTIVE CASE WITH ḌHAMMAH.

The simple logical copula "*is*," is generally omitted; if emphasis be required, the pronoun is used to supply its place, as زيدٌ هو قائمٌ "Zeid *he* (is) standing."

The predicate may consist of or contain a verb, as ضرب زيدٌ "Zeid struck." This is properly "*He struck*," namely "*Zeid*." The agent "he" being contained in the verb, and the *name* of such agent being subsequently mentioned for the sake of clearness, hence it follows that the natural order of words is to place the *so-called* agent after the verb.

But if the verb is active or transitive, there must be also an object on which the action falls, as ضرب زيدٌ عمرًا "Zeid struck 'Amr."

THE OBJECT IS PUT IN THE OBJECTIVE CASE WITH FETḤAH.

If it is neuter or intransitive, further explanation may

be needed as to the *state or condition* of the agent, as قَامَ زَيْدٌ مُسْرِعًا "Zeid rose hastily."

STATE OR CONDITION IS ALWAYS EXPRESSED BY THE OBJECTIVE CASE.

I have said that both subject and predicate are put in the direct case, as in the sentence "Zeid (is) standing," in which the logical copula "is," and a noun or a verb with its true inherent pronominal nominative, form the predicate.

If, however, we wish to express *existence in a state of*—or, *the fact of becoming*, that is, *of assuming a certain condition*—it is clear that by the rule above given, such state must be expressed by the objective case, as

كَانَ زَيْدٌ قَائِمًا "Zeid was standing."

صَارَ زَيْدٌ خَيَّاطًا "Zeid became a tailor."

HENCE THE RULE THAT كَانَ AND SIMILAR VERBS PUT THE PREDICATE IN THE OBJECTIVE CASE.

6. Particles modify the sentence by extending or restricting the action of the verb. Some few, إِنَّ and the like, are exactly the reverse of كَانَ, putting the subject in the objective case, and the predicate in the nominative, thus إِنَّ زَيْدًا لَقَائِمٌ "verily, Zeid is standing." Here the predicate is introduced by a second or subordinate initial particle لَ. The explanation of this seems to be—

إِنَّ "I am going to speak of my subject."

زَيْدًا *quâ* "Zeid," *i.e.* in his *condition* of Zeid (*whence the use of the objective case*).

لَقَائِمٌ "Well—(لَ) he is standing" (which last becomes, as it were, a new predicate, and is therefore properly put in the nominative).

These principles will account for every possible phase of Arabic syntax. The following rules, however, should be studied.

The Tenses of Verbs.

I. *The Preterite.*

The Preterite denotes a completed act, but the time at which it took place is left indeterminate, unless defined by the context or by some particle.

So an Arab author, in citing a verse of poetry, employs the expression, كَمَا قَالَ ٱلشَّاعِرُ "as the poet *says*."

Or it may express a foregone conclusion, such as naturally occurs in hypothetical or conditional sentences, as إِنْ قُمْتَ قُمْتُ "if you rise, I will rise."

A similar idea seems to influence the English colloquial idiom, "if you do that, you are lost," or "are a dead man"; where "you are lost," "are a dead man," are apparent preterites.

From this use of the preterite results another very common use in Arabic, namely, in precative sentences, as أَدَامَ ٱللّٰهُ بَقَاءَكُمْ "may God perpetuate your existence!"

And with لَا "not," in averting anything undesirable, or in cursing, as لَا بَارَكَ ٱللّٰهُ فِيكَ "may God not bless you!"

The preterite of the verb كَانَ with the preterite of

another verb is equivalent to the pluperfect, as كَانَ زَيْدٌ قَامَ "Zeid had stood up."

But the perfect or pluperfect is more usually expressed by the preterite preceded by the particle قَدْ, with or without the conjunction وَ.

The particle قَدْ restricts the preterite to a time actually past, as قَدْ جَاءَكُمْ رُسُلٌ مِنْ قَبْلِي "Prophets have come to you before me."

II. *The Aorist.*

The Aorist denotes an act not yet completed. Like the preterite, it is somewhat indeterminate in respect of time, until defined by the context or by particles.

The Moods of Verbs.

The Indicative Mood.—In the direct or indicative mood, the aorist ends in ـُ; it is used in all direct narration.

Subjunctive Mood.—The aorist of a verb changes its final vowel ـُ into ـَ, to express the subjunctive mood.

This change takes place when the verb is preceded by any one of the following particles:

1. أَنْ "that."
2. لَنْ=(لَا أَنْ=لَا يَكُونُ أَنْ "it will not happen that")= "certainly not."
3. إِذَنْ (=إِذْ أَنْ) "then."

The Apocopation of the Final Vowel of the Aorist.

The aorist of the verb loses its final vowel altogether in the following cases:

1. After لَمْ "not," and لَمَّا "not yet," which always give a *past* negative sense to the aorist, as

لَمْ يَقُمْ "He did not stand."

جَاءَ وَلَمَّا يَطْلَعِ ٱلْفَجْرُ "He came, and the dawn had not yet appeared."

2. After the particle لِ used in an imperative sense, as لِيَضْرِبْ زَيْدٌ "let Zeid strike."

[*Note.*—This is the regular form of imperative for all except the second person. When preceded by فَ, لِ loses its vowel, as فَلْيَضْرِبْ "so let him strike."]

3. After لَا prohibitive, as لَا تَضْرِبْ "do not strike."

After إِنْ "if," and similar particles, both verbs lose their final vowel, as

إِنْ تَكْسَلْ تَخْسَرْ "If you are lazy you will come to want."

III. *The Imperative.*

The Imperative is used in precisely the same manner as in other languages. It exists only in the second person; for the other persons the apocopated form of the aorist with the affirmative لِ prefixed is employed.

The prohibitive is obtained in the same manner, by apocopating the aorist for all persons and prefixing لَا.

THE CASES OF NOUNS.

In Arabic short vowels are used as terminations to express the different cases.

ـُ is nominative, direct or subjective.

ـِ is genitive, oblique or dependent.

ـَ is accusative, conditional, or objective.

In nouns these are doubled to express further the *indefinite* nature of the thing.

When so doubled, they are pronounced with an *n* sound called تَنْوِينْ.

[In verbs only ـُ and ـَ are used, and the *aorist* is the only *tense* capable of being modified by them.]

The Subjective Case.

The following require the subjective or nominative case:

The agent or subject of a verb: ضَرَبَ زَيْدٌ "Zeid struck."

The nominative or subject of a passive verb; as ضُرِبَ زَيْدٌ "Zeid was struck."

Both the subject and predicate of a simple sentence in which the simple copula "*is*" is either omitted, or expressed by هُوَ in the singular masculine, هم in the plural, &c.; as

زَيْدٌ قَائِمٌ "Zeid is standing."

اَلْعِلْمُ نَافِعٌ "Knowledge is useful."

أَللّٰهُ هُوَ ٱلْحَىُّ "God is the living one."

أُولَائِكَ هُمُ ٱلْمُفْلِحُونَ "They are the prosperous."

Where the subject is a personal pronoun of the first or second person, the pronoun of the *third person* is used to form the copula, as أَنَا هُوَ ٱلرَّبُّ إِلٰهُكَ "I am the Lord thy God."

The Agent and the Verb.

The agent is put in the subjective case.

The agent follows the verb, and the object of the action follows the agent; as ضَرَبَ زَيْدٌ عَمْرًا "Zeid struck 'Amr."

Concord of the Verb and the Agent.

The agent is always in the subjective case, and is properly placed after the verb.

When the agent is, grammatically speaking, masculine, of no matter what number, the verb is put in the masculine singular, as

قَامَ زَيْدٌ "Zeid stood."
قَامَ ٱلزَّيْدَانِ "The two Zeids stood."
قَامَ ٱلزَّيْدُونَ "The Zeids stood."

With a feminine agent the verb is properly put in the feminine singular, as

قَامَتْ هِنْدٌ "Hind stood."
قَامَتِ ٱلْهِنْدَانِ "The two Hinds stood."
قَامَتِ ٱلْهِنْدَاتُ "The Hinds stood."

But if the agent be not really feminine, but only feminine from a grammatical point of view, either the masculine or feminine verb may be used, *according as the speaker keep the feminine idea in his mind, or not, from the first*, as

طَلَعَ ٱلشَّمْسُ }
طَلَعَتِ ٱلشَّمْسُ } "The sun rose."

For the same reason, even when the agent is really feminine, provided a word intervenes between it and the verb, either form may be used.

قَامَ ٱلْيَوْمَ هِنْدٌ }
قَامَتِ ٱلْيَوْمَ هِنْدٌ } "Hind stood to-day."

When the intervening word is إِلَّا "except," the verb is more elegantly put in the masculine, as مَا قَامَ إِلَّا هِنْدٌ "there rose not save Hind."

When a second verb occurs referring to the same agent, such verb agrees with it logically in gender, number, and person, as اِجْتَمَعَتِ ٱلرِّجَالُ فَقَالُوا "the men assembled and (they) said," the broken plural requiring the grammatical construction with the feminine singular in the first verb; but in the second verb قَالُوا, which refers to the same agent, the logical agreement is preserved.

The Subject of a Passive Verb.

The same rules which apply to the agent of an active verb apply to the subject of a passive verb.

ضُرِبَ زَيْدٌ "Zeid was struck."

The following examples will illustrate the construction of the passive:

Active.	Passive.
آتَى ٱللّٰهُ بَنِي إِسْرَآئِيلَ كِتَابًا	أُوتُوا بَنُو إِسْرَآئِيلَ كِتَابًا
"God gave a Scripture to the Children of Israel."	"The Children of Israel were given a Scripture."
أَعْطَى زَيْدًا دِرْهَمًا	أُعْطِيَ زَيْدٌ دِرْهَمًا
"He gave Zeid a drachma."	"Zeid was given a drachma."
أَمَرْتُ زَيْدًا بِقَتْلِ عَمْرٍو	أُمِرَ زَيْدٌ بِقَتْلِ عَمْرٍو
"I ordered Zeid to kill 'Amr."	"Zeid was ordered to kill 'Amr."
سَارَ بِزَيْدٍ مِنْ بَغْدَادَ إِلَى ٱلْمَدِينَةِ	سِيرَ بِزَيْدٍ مِنْ بَغْدَادَ إِلَى ٱلْمَدِينَةِ
"He escorted Zeid from Bagdad to el-Medina."	"Zeid was escorted from Bagdad to el-Medina."
لَمْ يَقْدِرِ ٱلسُّلْطَانُ عَلَى أَخْذِهِ	لَمْ يُقْدَرْ عَلَى أَخْذِهِ
"The Sultan could not take him."	"He could not be taken (his taking was impossible)."
جَآءَ عُمَرُ ٱلنَّبِيَّ بِنَاسٍ مِنَ ٱلْعَرَبِ	جِيءَ ٱلنَّبِيُّ بِنَاسٍ مِنَ ٱلْعَرَبِ
"'Omar brought the Prophet some Arabs."	"The Prophet was brought some Arabs."

When a verb which governs with a preposition is put in the passive voice, as بَحَثَ عَنْهُ "he disputed about it," the preposition with its case is still retained, as بُحِثَ عَنْهُ "it was disputed about." The verb is then strictly impersonal, and therefore, in forming the passive participle, the masculine form only is used, the *pronoun alone* being altered to express the gender, thus:

أَلْمَبْحُوثُ عَنْهُ "The thing (masculine) disputed about."

أَلْمَبْحُوثُ عَنْهَا "The thing (feminine) disputed about."

This idiom is almost parallel to the English vulgarism by which I have translated it: "The thing *disputed about.*"

The Objective Case.

The following require the objective case:

1. The object of the action of a verb.
2. Words defining or specifying the action.
3. Nouns used adverbially.
4. Tho cause or effect of the action.
5. Words expressing the state or condition.
6. Words following particles of exception, vocatives (not addressing a person present), and a few other instances of which details are given in the following paragraphs:

The object of a Verb.

The object of the verb is that upon which the action falls, as ضَرَبْتُ زَيْدًا "I struck Zeid."

A verb may have two objects, as أَعْطَيْتُ زَيْدًا دِرْهَمًا "I gave Zeid a dirhem"; or two objects and a word defining the nature or period of the action, or the state of the object, as أَعْلَمْتُ زَيْدًا عَمْرًا مُنْطَلِقًا "I showed to Zeid 'Amr in the act of going away."

Similarly all definitions of time, place, circumstance, &c. are expressed by the objective case, as—

سِرْتُ مِيلًا "I marched a mile."

جَلَسْتُ قَرِيبَ ٱلْأَمِيرِ "I sat near the Emír."

هَرَبْتُ خَوْفًا "I fled fearing."

ضَرَبْتُ ٱبْنِى تَأْدِيبًا لَهُ "I beat my son to correct him."

هَرَبْتُ خَوْفَ ٱلْقَتْلِ "I fled fearing slaughter."

جَآءَ زَيْدٌ رَاكِبًا "Zeid came riding."

طَلَعَ ٱلْقَمَرُ بَدْرًا "The moon rose full" (*lit.* "A full moon").

A sentence may be used as an adverb, as—

جَآءَ زَيْدٌ وَيَدُهُ عَلَى رَأْسِهِ "Zeid came to me (with) his hand on his head."

جَآءَ زَيْدٌ يَرْكُضُ "Zeid came running."

THE SYNTAX OF THE OBJECTIVE CASE MAY BE SUMMED UP BY SAYING THAT IT IS USED OBJECTIVELY AND ADVERBIALLY. The following sentence contains an example of each of the various uses of the objective case:

ضَرَبْتُ أَنَا وَعَمْرًا زَيْدًا أَمَامَ ٱلْأَمِيرِ يَوْمَ ٱلْجُمْعَةِ ضَرْبًا شَدِيدًا تَأْدِيبًا لَهُ

"I struck, conjointly with 'Amr, Zeid, before the Emír, on Friday, a severe blow by way of correcting him."

THE GENITIVE OR DEPENDENT CASE.

The genitive case is peculiar to nouns, and is employed in two instances.

1. After a preposition, as خَرَجْتُ مِنَ ٱلْبَلَدِ "I went out *from* the city."

2. When following another noun, the sense of which it defines or determines, and with which it is said to be in a state of construction, as جَاءَنِي غُلَامُ زَيْدٍ "Zeid's slave came to me."

Prepositions.

رُبَّ "many a," or, conversely, "but few," is used as a preposition. It must begin the sentence, and the noun which it governs must be indefinite and qualified by a subsequent adjective, as رُبَّ رَجُلٍ كَرِيمٍ لَقِيتُهُ "many a generous man have I met." Sometimes a pronoun is affixed to it, in which case the following word must be indefinite and in the accusative case, as رُبَّهُ رَجُلًا "many a man."

If the particle مَا be affixed to رُبَّ, it signifies "perhaps," "probably," and serves to introduce a sentence, as رُبَّمَا زَيْدٌ قَائِمٌ "perhaps Zeid is standing."

رُبَّ is often omitted after وَ, but the noun still continues in the genitive case, as وَلَيْلٍ كَمَوْجِ ٱلْبَحْرِ أَرْخَى سُدُولَهُ "and (many a) night like the waves of the sea has let down its curtain of darkness."

قَبْلَ and بَعْدَ, meaning respectively "before" and "after," are used as prepositions; the length of time by which they are defined is introduced by بِ, as

قَبْلَ وَفَاةِ زَيْدٍ بِيَوْمَيْنِ "Two days before the death of Zeid."

بَعْدَ طُلُوعِ ٱلشَّمْسِ بِسَاعَتَيْنِ "Two hours after sunrise."

Many other nouns are used as prepositions, such as غَيْرَ "except," فَوْقَ "over," etc. They have the accusative form without *tenwín*.

The Vocative.

The vocative particles are يَا , أَىْ , أَ , أَيَا , هَيَا , of which the first, يَا , is the more common. They usually govern the noun in the subjective case.

The vocative is put in the objective case—

1. When the noun is in construction, as يَا عَبْدَ ٱللّٰه "Oh 'Abdallah!" Or when it governs another noun in the accusative, as يَا طَالِعًا جَبَلًا "O thou who art ascending a mountain!"

2. When it is undefined, or not directly addressed, *e.g.* as when a blind man says, يَا رَجُلًا خُذْ بِيَدِى "Here somebody! take my hand." But if the noun is not in construction, but is indefinite, and not qualified by a subsequent adjective, being nevertheless directly addressed, it is put in the nominative case without *tenwín*, as يَا زَيْدُ "Oh Zeid!" يَا رَجُلُ "Oh man!" If, however, it be so qualified, it is more often put in the objective case, as يَا رَجُلًا كَرِيمًا "O generous man!"

When the noun has the article prefixed, the vocative is expressed by putting it in the nominative case and prefixing the word أَيُّهَا "masculine," and أَيَّتُهَا "feminine," for all numbers, as

أَيُّهَا ٱلْفَاضِلُ "Oh (thou) the accomplished!"

أَيَّتُهَا ٱلْمَرْأَةُ "Oh you woman there!"

The name of God اَللّٰهُ is seldom put in the vocative, but when it is, the *hemzet el-waṣl* may be either retained or elided, as يَا أَللّٰهُ *ya-allah,* or يَا ٱللّٰهُ *ya 'llah.* But the word more generally used in addressing the Deity is اَللّٰهُمَّ, without a vocative particle.

A proper name may be familiarly shortened in the vocative, as

فَاطِمَةُ, vocative فَاطِمَ "Oh! Fatima."

جَعْفَرُ, vocative جَعْفَ "Oh! Ja'afer."

صَاحِ for صَاحِبِى "Oh! my companion," is a rare exception.

Nouns in Construction.

Of the first of two Nouns in Construction.

Of two nouns in construction, the first invariably loses its *tenwín.*

The use and application of the construct arrangement of nouns will be best understood from a study of the following examples:

غُلَامُ ٱلرَّجُلِ "The slave of the man."

غُلَامُ رَجُلٍ "The slave of a man."

Here the loss of the *tenwín* makes the word غُلَام definite in both instances; it is not necessary therefore further to define it by prefixing the article. From this results the rule that *the first of two nouns in a state of construction does not require the article.*

Sometimes, however, when the two nouns in construction have come to be regarded almost as a single expression, the article may be prefixed, as

اَلْحَيٰوةُ ٱلدُّنْيَا The "life of this world."

اَلْحَيٰوةُ ٱلْحَيَوَانِ The book called "The life of animals" (name of a work on natural history).

If it be necessary to leave the first of two nouns indefinite, and yet to express the same relation between them as that implied by the state of construction, the preposition لِ "to," or "belonging to," must be used with the second noun, as اِبْنٌ لِلْمَلِكِ "a son of the king."

Other Modes of expressing the relation between Nouns.

The idea of possession, companionship, etc. is also expressed in Arabic by the use of the following words: ذُو masc. ذَاتُ fem. "possessor," صَاحِبٌ "companion," أَبٌ "father," أُمٌّ "mother," اِبْنٌ "son," اِبْنَةٌ or بِنْتٌ "daughter," أَخٌ "brother," أُخْتٌ "sister"

ذُو and صَاحِبٌ imply simple possession or endowment, as ذُو ٱلْعِلْمِ "learned," صَاحِبُ مَالٍ "wealthy."

أَبٌ and أُمٌّ imply that the thing expressed by the following noun proceeds from, or has an intimate connexion with, the person or thing so qualified. They are used in forming nick-names, and in the names of localities, as

أَبُو هُرَيْرَةَ "Abu Huraireh" ("father of the kitten," the name of one of the companions of Mohammed).

أَبُو شِيحٍ "Abu Shíah" ("father of Shíah," *i.e.* a sweet-scented desert-herb; name of a mountain in Sinai).

أُمُّ ٱلْخَبَائِثِ "Mother of vices" (wine).

إِبْنٌ and بِنْتٌ, or إِبْنَةٌ are the converse of أَبٌ and أُمٌّ, as

إِبْنُ ٱلسَّبِيلِ "Son of the road (a traveller)."

أَخٌ and أُخْتٌ also imply being endowed with a quality, as—

أَخُو ٱلصِّدْقِ "Sincere (the brother of sincerity)."

أَخٌ is also used for "fellow," as هٰذَا ٱلثَّوبُ أَخُو هٰذَا "this garment is the fellow one to this."

Concordance of Nouns and Epithets.

If the noun be definite, the qualifying epithet must also be definite, as

أَلْكِتَابُ ٱلْعَظِيمُ "The mighty Book."

إِبْرَاهِيمُ ٱلأَمِينُ "The faithful Abraham."

If the noun be in a state of construction with another noun, or have an affixed pronoun, the qualifying epithet is placed after such compound expression, and is also rendered definite by prefixing the article, as

كِتَابُ مُوسَى ٱلْعَظِيمُ "The mighty Book of Moses."

كِتَابُهُ ٱلْمُكَرَّمُ "His honoured Book."

But if the noun be indefinite, the epithet will also be indefinite, as كِتَابٌ عَتِيقٌ "an old book." The rules for the concordance of the noun and epithet in gender and number are the same as for the agent and verb.

Occasionally, however, a broken plural may take the epithet in the feminine plural, as

أُسُودٌ ضَارِيَاتٌ "Devouring lions."

The use of the Participles as a Verb.

The agent, intensive agent, or passive participle, may govern a noun in the objective case if they refer to a present or future time, as هَذَا ضَارِبٌ زَيْدًا "this is (a man who) is striking, or is going to strike, Zeid."

The passive participle may govern the nominative like its verb; thus, just as you say ضُرِبَ زَيْدٌ غُلَامُهُ "Zeid, his slave is beaten," so also you say, زَيْدٌ مَضْرُوبٌ غُلَامُهُ "Zeid whose slave is beaten"; construed with the genitive, as زَيْدٌ مَضْرُوبُ غُلَامِهِ, it would mean "Zeid with a beaten slave."

The Noun of Superiority.

If the noun of superiority have the article prefixed, it is considered as a superlative, and agrees in gender, number, and case with the noun qualified by it, as

زَيْدٌ ٱلْأَفْضَلُ "Zeid is the most accomplished."

هِنْدٌ ٱلْفُضْلَى "Hind is the most accomplished."

If it is to be used as a comparative, it takes مِنْ, and in this case remains always in the masculine singular, as

زَيْدٌ أَفْضَلُ مِنْ عَمْرٍو "Zeid is more accomplished than 'Amr."

Comparatives formed from transitive verbs take the object in the dependent case with لِ, as هُوَ أَطْلَبُ لِلْعِلْمِ مِنْكُمْ "he seeks more after knowledge than you."

Those formed from intransitive verbs require the same preposition after them as the verb from which they are derived, as

هُوَ أَزْهَدُ فِى ٱلدُّنْيَا وَ أَسْرَعُ إِلَى ٱلْخَيْرِ وَ أَبْعَدُ مِنَ ٱلْإِثْمِ وَ أَحْرَصُ إِلَى ٱلْحَمْدِ

"He is more abstinent in worldly things, prompter to good, farther from sin, and more eager for praising God."

Followed by مَا, the noun of superiority expresses the greatest possible degree of superiority, as

فَارَقَنَا أَحْوَجَ مَا نَحْنُ إِلَيْهِ فِى مَخَالِيبِ أَعْدَآئِنَا

"He left us, when we had most need of him, in the claws of our enemies."

Nouns expressing inherent Qualities.

Nouns expressing inherent qualities may govern like verbs, as

ٱلرَّجُلُ ٱلْحَسَنُ { ٱلْوَجْهُ / ٱلْوَجْهَ }

[In this example ٱلْحَسَنُ is considered as equivalent to ٱلَّذِى حَسُنَ, the conjunctive and the verb, and if pointed with ـُ, ٱلْوَجْهُ is either considered as the agent or nominative of such verb="who the face is handsome"; or if pointed with ـَ, ٱلْوَجْهَ, as the adverbial accusative="who is handsome as to the face."]

Other verbal forms.

There is an adverbial form derived regularly from the verb, and used as an interjection, namely فَعَالِ , as

نَزَالِ "Come down!" = اُنْزِلْ.
كَتَابِ "Write away!" = اُكْتُبْ.

Words of this kind are construed exactly like the verb.

Such verbs as كَانَ "he was," صَارَ "he became," أَصْبَحَ "he was or did something in the morning," لَيْسَ "he is not," put the subject in the nominative, and the predicate in the objective case, as كَانَ زَيْدٌ كَرِيماً "Zeid was generous," and لَيْسَ ٱلْجَاهِلُ مَحْبُوباً "an ignorant person is not liked."

لَيْسَ generally takes the preposition بِ with its predicate, as لَيْسَ زَيْدٌ بِجَاهِلٍ "Zeid is not a fool."

The noun of action and the agent of the verb كَانَ are frequently construed like the verb itself, as

لِكَوْنِكَ قَوِيًّا وَ كَوْنِ غَيْرِكَ ضَعِيفاً "From thy being strong and others weak."

Certain particles—

لَعَلَّ "probably."	لَيْتَ "would that."
لٰكِنَّ "but."	كَأَنَّ "as though."
أَنَّ "that" (emphatic).	إِنَّ "verily."

are exactly the reverse of كان in their mode of governing, for they put the noun or subject in the objective or accusative, and the predicate in the nominative case ; thus—

كَانَ زَيْدٌ قَائِماً "Zeid was standing."
إِنَّ زَيْداً قَائِمٌ "Verily Zeid is standing."

Negative Particles.

The particles of negation, مَا , لَا , لَاتَ and إِنْ , govern words in the same manner as the verb لَيْسَ .

The absolute Negative.

When the negative particle لَا denies the existence of a thing absolutely, it governs in the same manner as إِنَّ, *i.e.* it puts the noun in the objective case, and the predicate in the subjective case; provided only that both noun and predicate are undefined, and that لَا introduces the noun, as لَا رَجُلَ قَادِمٌ "there is no man coming."

If the noun be grammatically unconnected with any other word, the *tenwín* is dropped, as in the example. If the subject of the negation be immediately connected with any other word, the *tenwín* is retained, as

لَا طَالِعًا جَبَلًا عِنْدَنَا "There is no one with us going-up-a-mountain."

لَا مَارًّا بِزَيْدٍ حَاضِرٌ "There is no passer-by-Zeid present."

But if the noun be definite, or separated by any intervening word or words from the negative لَا, it is not governed by the latter, as

لَا زَيْدٌ فِي ٱلدَّارِ وَلَا عَمْرٌو وَ لَا فِي ٱلدَّارِ رَجُلٌ وَ لَا عِنْدَ نَا ٱمْرَأَةٌ

"Zeid is not in the house, nor 'Amr; and there is not in the house a man, and there is not with us a woman."

In such cases as the above لَا should be repeated with each separate negation.

When there are several nouns to be denied, and لَا is

repeated (such nouns being undefined, unconnected with any other word, and introduced by the لَا), either or both of the above constructions may be used; thus

لَا حَوْلَ وَلَا قُوَّةَ إِلَّا بِٱللّٰهِ لَا حَوْلٌ وَلَا قُوَّةٌ إِلَّا بِٱللّٰهِ لَا حَوْلَ وَلَا قُوَّةٌ إِلَّا بِٱللّٰهِ لَا حَوْلَ وَلَا قُوَّةً إِلَّا بِٱللّٰهِ لَا حَوْلٌ وَلَا قُوَّةَ إِلَّا بِٱللّٰهِ	"There is no strength and no power but in God."

Relative Sentences.

The relative sentence in Arabic consists of four parts—(1) The antecedent. (2) The relative or conjunctive noun, pronoun, or particle. (3) The qualificative clause. (4) The pronoun referring to the antecedent, thus

اَلرَّجُلُ ٱلَّذِى رَأَيْتُهُ

	(1)	(2)	(3)	(4)
literally,	The man	who	I saw	him.

Relatives or Conjunctives.

اَلَّذِي is for *definite* antecedents only; for *indefinite* مَنْ "who?" and مَا "what?" are used. In interrogation the demonstrative pronoun is added مَنْ ذَا "who is that?" مَا ذَا "what is that?"

The article أَلْ is regarded as a relative.

أَيٌّ "which" (of two or more) "the one who," etc., may be used in four ways, as

يُعْجِبُنِي أَيُّهُمْ هُوَ قَائِمٌ
يُعْجِبُنِي أَيٌّ قَائِمٌ
يُعْجِبُنِي أَيٌّ هُوَ قَائِمٌ
يُعْجِبُنِي أَيُّهُمْ قَائِمٌ
} "He of them who is standing pleases me."

The Pronoun which refers to the Antecedent.

The pronoun which refers to the antecedent agrees with it in gender, number, and person, as

جَآءَ ٱلَّذِى ضَرَبْتُهُ "He came whom I struck."

جَآءَ ٱلَّذَانِ ضَرَبْتُهُمَا "They two came, both of whom I struck."

Conditional Sentences.

In conditional or hypothetical sentences the apodosis is generally introduced by one of the particles وَ and فَ.

The aorist subjunctive, pointed with *fetḥah*, and introduced by وَ or فَ, is used in the apodosis of a conditional proposition, as

زُرْنِي فَأُكْرِمَكَ أَوْ وَأُكْرِمَكَ "Visit me and I will honour you."

If, however, the protasis be an aorist, and the apodosis a preterite, the former must be apocopated, as إِنْ تَصْبِرْ ظَفِرْتَ "if you have patience, you will win" (*lit.* "have won," *i.e.* as we should say, "as good as won").

If the protasis be a preterite, and the apodosis an aorist, the latter may be either apocopated or not, as إِنْ صَبَرْتَ تَظْفَرْ ـ تَظْفُرُ "if you have patience, you will win."

If both be preterite, there can, of course, be no apocopation, as إِنْ قُمْتَ قُمْتُ "if thou standest, I stand."

The introduction of فَ prevents the apocopation of the aorist.

Particles of Exception.

اِلَّا takes the objective case, if the preceding *clause* is neither negative nor interrogative, as قَامَ ٱلْقَوْمُ إِلَّا زَيْدًا "the people rose—except Zeid." Otherwise it is put in simple apposition with the noun, as مَا قَامَ أَحَدٌ إِلَّا زَيْدٌ "no one rose but Zeid."

غَيْر and سِوَى, being nouns, place the thing excepted in a state of construction.

سِوَى is indeclinable, but غَيْر is declined, and follows the same rules as those given for the noun following اِلَّا.

عَدَا, خَلَا, and حَاشَا, are generally construed with the objective case, عَدَا and خَلَا having for the most part the particle مَا prefixed.

جَآءَ ٱلْقَوْمُ مَا عَدَا زَيْدًا
جَآءَ ٱلْقَوْمُ مَا خَلَا زَيْدًا
"The people came except Zeid," *lit.* what is beside (or free from) Zeid.

لَا سِيَّمَا "especially," may take either the nominative or genitive after it, as أَعْجَبَنِى ٱلنَّاسُ لَا سِيَّمَا زَيْدٌ أَوْ زَيْدٍ "all the people pleased me, especially Zeid."

Corroboration.

If it be required to repeat the affixed pronoun corroboratively, the word to which it is affixed must also be repeated, as مَرَرْتُ بِكَ بِكَ "I passed by thee, by thee" [not بِكَكَ].

It may, however, be repeated separately in its nominative form, as مَرَرْتُ بِكَ أَنْتَ "I passed by thee—thee." So, too, the initiative إِنَّ cannot be repeated without its noun, as إِنَّ زَيْدًا إِنَّ زَيْدًا "verily Zeid" [not إِنَّ إِنَّ زَيْدًا].

If the pronoun be inseparable from the verb or pre position, etc., it must be repeated in its detached form, as

ضَرَبْتَ أَنْتَ "Thou hast struck—thou."

ضَرَبْتَنِي أَنَا "Thou hast struck me—me."

مَرَرْتُ بِهِ هُوَ "I passed by him—him."

My—thy—him—her—its—self, etc. are expressed by the words نَفْسٌ "self" or "soul," and عَيْنٌ "eye" or "essence," with the affixed pronouns. نَفْسٌ agrees in number with the noun, as

Masculine.

زَيْدٌ نَفْسُهُ	جَآءَنِي	Zeid himself	came to me
اَلزَّيْدَانِ أَنْفُسُهُمَا		The two Zeids themselves	
اَلزَّيْدُونَ أَنْفُسُهُمْ		The Zeids themselves	

Feminine.

هِنْدٌ نَفْسُهَا	جَآءَتْ	Hind herself	came
اَلْهِنْدَانِ أَنْفُسُهُمَا		The two Hinds themselves	
اَلْهِنْدَاتُ أَنْفُسُهُنَّ		The Hinds themselves	

عَيْن is used in the singular only, as

ٱلزَّيْدُونَ عَيْنُهُمْ "The Zeids themselves."
ٱلْهِنْدَاتُ عَيْنُهُنَّ "The Hinds themselves."

We may also say بِنَفْسِهِ "*in propriâ personâ*," as جَاءَ زَيْدٌ بِنَفْسِهِ "Zeid came *in propriâ personâ*," and so on.

"Each other," "one another," are expressed by بَعْضٌ "a portion," repeated for each of the two parties to the mutual action, as

ٱهْبِطُوا بَعْضُكُمْ لِبَعْضٍ عَدُوٌّ "Go down, enemies to each other."

Admiration.

There are many forms of expressing admiration in Arabic, as

لِلّٰهِ دَرُّهُ فَارِسًا "God bless him (*literally* "To God his milk flow") for a horseman!" = "what a fine horseman!"

وَاهًا لِسَلْمَى ثُمَّ وَاهًا وَاهَا "Bravo! Selma! bravo! bravo!"

Such as these are of course irregular; but there are two forms which may be derived regularly from any verb, viz. (1) مَا أَفْعَلَ, and (2) أَفْعِلْ بِ.

(1) مَا أَفْعَلَ takes the accusative of the thing admired, as

مَا أَحْسَنَ زَيْدًا "How handsome is Zeid!"
مَا أَحْسَنَهُ "How handsome he is!"

(2) أَفْعِلْ بِ governs the thing admired in the genitive by the preposition ب , as

أَحْسِنْ بِزَيْدٍ "How handsome is Zeid!"
أَكْرِمْ بِهِ "How noble he is!"

The thing admired must immediately follow the forms مَا أَفْعَلَ and أَفْعِلْ بِ , and cannot occur in any other position in the sentence.

Particles.

The following are the most important:

لَوْ "if," used in conditional sentences, and followed by ل in the complement, as لَوْ جَآءَ زَيْدٌ لَأَكْرَمْتُهُ "if Zeid had come, I would have honoured him."

أَمَّا "as for," followed by ف , as أَمَّا زَيْدٌ فَمُنْطَلِقٌ "as for Zeid, (he is) going away."

أَ interrogative, as

أَقَامَ زَيْدٌ "Did Zeid stand up?"

When an alternative follows, it is introduced by أَمْ , as

أَ دِبْسٌ فِى ٱلْإِنَآءِ أَمْ عَسَلٌ "Is it *dibs* (syrup of raisins) in the vessel or honey?"

هَلْ asks a direct question, and is never used in alternative questions, as

هَلْ قَامَ زَيْدٌ "Did Zeid stand up?"

حَيْثُ "where," "since."

أَيْنَ "where?"

Indeclinable Words.

The compound numerals from 11 to 19.

جَاءَ أَحَدَ عَشَرَ "Eleven came."

Both portions of the compound are pointed with *fetḥah* throughout.

اِثْنَا عَشَرَ is, however, an exception, the first portion being declined as an ordinary dual noun.

Compound adverbs of time and place, as

صَبَاحَ مَسَاءَ "As morning and evening."

بَيْنَ بَيْنَ "Middling."

فُلَانٌ جَارِى بَيْتَ بَيْتَ "So and so is my next door neighbour" (*lit.* house house=house to house).

كَيْتَ كَيْتَ }
ذَيْتَ ذَيْتَ } "So and so."

كَمْ "How many?"

كَأَيِّ "How many!"

كَذَا "So and so," "so many."

SECTION III.—READING EXERCISES.

Classical and Grammatical Arabic.

ٱلرَّحِيمِ	ٱلرَّحْمٰنِ	ٱللّٰهِ	بِسْمِ
'rraḥím	'rraḥmáni	'lláhi	bismi*
the compassionate	the merciful	of God	In the name

ٱلرَّحِيمِ	ٱلرَّحْمٰنِ	ٱلْعَالَمِينَ	رَبِّ	لِلّٰهِ	اَلْحَمْدُ
'rraḥími	'rraḥmáni	'álamína	rabbi	lilláhi	El ḥamd
the compassionate	the merciful	of the worlds	lord	to God	Praise

نَعْبُدُ	اِيَّاكَ	الدينِ	يوم	مالك
na'budu	iyyáka	'ddíni	yaumi	máliki
we serve	thee	of Judgment	the day	the ruler of
1 per. pl. aor. of عبد	See p. 62.			

ٱلْمُسْتَقِيمَ	ٱلصِّرَاطَ	اِهْدِنَا	نَسْتَعِينُ	وَ اِيَّاكَ
'lmustaḳíma	'ṣṣiráṭa	ihdina	nasta'ínu	iyyáka wa
the straight	the way	guide us	we ask for aid	thee
Agent 10th conj. from قام accus. case		imp. هدى	1 p. pl. aor. 10th conj. of عان	

---

* For بِٱسْمِ.

ٱلْمَغْضُوبِ	غَيْرِ	عَلَيْهِمْ	أَنْعَمْتَ	ٱلَّذِينَ	صِرَاطَ
’lmaghḍhúbi	ghairi	‘alaihim	an‘amta	’lladhína	ṣiráṭa
the angered	not (other than)	to them	thou art gracious	of those	the way
See pp. 81–82.			2 sing. pret. 4th conj. نعم		

	ٱلضَّالِّينَ	وَلَا	عَلَيْهِمْ
[*Ḳor’án, Chapter* 1.]	’ḍhḍhálína	wa la	‘alaihim
	the erring	not and	against them
	pl. gen. agent of ضلّ		See pp. 81–82.

ٱلْقَيُّومُ	ٱلْحَىُّ	هُوَ	إِلَّا	إِلٰهَ	لَا	ٱللّٰهُ
’lḳaiyyúm	al ḥaiyyu	húwa	illá	iláha	lá	alláhu
the subsistant	the living	Him	except	God	no	God
root قوم				See p. 92.		

مَا	لَهُ	نَوْمٌ	وَلَا	سِنَةٌ	تَأْخُذُهُ	لَا
má	lahu	naum	walá	sinatun	ta’khudhuhu	lá
what	to him	sleep	and not	slumber	takes him	not
				root وسن	2 sing. aor. اخذ	

ذَا	مَنْ	ٱلْأَرْضِ	فِى	وَمَا	ٱلسَّمٰوَاتِ	فِى
dhá	man	’l arḍhi	fi	and what	essamawáti	fi
that	who is	the earth	in	and what	the heavens	in
					pl. of سَمَآء	

يَعْلَمُ	بِإِذْنِهِ	إِلَّا	عِنْدَهُ	يَشْفَعُ	ٱلَّذِى
ya‘lamu	bi idhnihi	illá	‘indahu	yashfa‘u	’lladhí
he knows	by-his-permission	except	with him	intercedes	which
3 sing. aor. علم				aor. 3 sing. شفع	

خَلْفَهُمْ	وَمَا	أَيْدِيهِمْ	بَيْنَ	مَا
khalfahum	wamá	aidíhim	baina*	má
behind them	and what	their hands pl. of يد pronoun	between	what

عِلْمِهِ	مِنْ	بِشَىْءٍ	يُحِيطُونَ	وَلَا
'ilmihi	min	bishai'in	yuhíṭúna	walá
his-knowledge	from	(with) anything (the preceding verb requiring the prep. بِ)	they comprehend 3 pl. aor. 4th conj. حاط	and not

كُرْسِيُّهُ	وَسِعَ	شَآءَ	بِمَا	اِلَّا
kursíyuhu	wasi'a	shá'a	bimá	illá
His throne (nom.)	extends over	He please	(with) what	except

حِفْظُهُمَا	يَؤُدُهُ	وَلَا	وَ ٱلْأَرْضَ	ٱلسَّمٰوَاتِ
ḥifdhuhumá	ya'úduhu	walá	wa'l ardha	'ssamawáti
the guarding them both	tires him 3 sing. aor. أود	and not	the earth	the heavens (accus.)

ٱلْعَظِيمُ	ٱلْعَلِىُّ	وَهُوَ
'l'adhímu	'l'alíyu	wahúwa
the mighty	the exalted	and He

[The "Áyat el Kursíy," *Kor'án, ch.* 2, *v.* 256.]

---

* بين ايديهم always means "before them."

The Caliph Mo‘áwiyeh and his Desert Bride.

مَجْدَلٍ	بِنْتُ	مَيْسُونُ	اتَّصَلَتْ	وَلَمَّا
Majdalin	bintu	Maisúnu	’ttaṣalat	lamma wa
——	daughter of	——	united	and when

نَقَلَهَا	وَ	عَنْهُ	اللّٰهُ	رَضِيَ	بِمُعَاوِيَةَ
naḳalahá	wa	(‘anhu	’allah	raḍhiya)	bi Mu‘áwiyatin
transferred her	and	from= with him	God	be pleased	with ——

تَكْثُرُ	كَانَتْ	الشَّأْمِ	اِلَى	الْبَدْوِ	مِنَ
takthuru	kánat	’shshá’m	ila	’lbadwi	mina
great at	she was	Damascus	to	the desert	from

لِمَسْقَطِ	وَالتَّذَكُّرِ	نَاسِهَا	عَلَى	الْحَنِينَ
li masḳaṭi	wa’ttadhakkura	násiha	‘ala	lḥanín
to the falling place سقط	and remembrance noun of act. 8th conj. of ذكر	her-people	for	yearning

يَوْمٍ	ذَاتَ	عَلَيْهَا	فَاسْتَمَعَ	رَأْسِهَا
yaumin	dháta	‘alaihá	fa’stama‘a	ra’sihá
day	a certain	to her	and he listened (8th سمع)	of-her-head*

وَ تَقُولُ	تُنْشِدُ	فَسَمِعَهَا
wa takúlu	tunshidu	fasami‘ahá
and saying	reciting poetry 3 fem. sing. aor. of 4th conj. of نشد	and heard her

---

* =birth-place.

فيهِ	الأَرياحُ	تَخفِقُ	لَبَيتٌ
fíhi	'l aryáḥu	takhfiḳu	la-baitun
in it	the winds pl. of ريح	flutter	certainly a tent

مُنِيفِ	قَصرٍ	مِنْ	إلَيَّ	أَحَبُّ
munífí	ḳaṣrin	min	ilaiya	aḥabbu
lofty	a palace	than	to me	is dearer

بَيتي	قَعرِ	مِنْ	كُسَيرَةٍ	وَأَكلُ
baití	ḳa'ri	min	kusairatin	wa aklu
my tent	the bottom of (floor)		a crust (dim. from كسى)	eating

الصُّنُوفِ	أَكلِ	مِنْ	إلَيَّ	أَحَبُّ
'ṣṣunúfí	akli			
sorts (various dishes) pl. of صنف				

فَجٍّ	بِكُلِّ	الرِّياحِ	وَأَصواتُ
fajjin	bikulli	'rriyáḥi	wa aṣwátu
hollow, pass	in every	the winds pl. ريح	and sounds pl. of صَوت

الدُّفُوفِ	نَقرِ	مِنْ	إلَيَّ	أَحَبُّ
'dúfúfí	naḳri			
of drums pl. of دَفّ	the beating			

عَيْنِي	تَقَرُّ	وَ	عَبَاءَةٍ	وَلُبْسُ
'ainí	taḳirru	wa	'aba'tin	lubsu wa
my eye	it is cool *i.e.* comfort-able	and =while	an abba*	wearing and

الشُّفُوفِ	لُبْسِ	مِنْ	اِلَيَّ	اَحَبُّ
shshufúfí				
gauze pl. of شف from شف to be transparent.				

دُونِي	اَلطُّرَّاقَ	يَنْبَحُ	وَكَلْبٌ
dúní	'ṭurráḳa	yanbaḥu	kalbun wa
in front of me	the nightly visitors (pl. of طارق)	barks at	a dog and

اَلُوفِ	قِطٍّ	مِنْ	اِلَيَّ	اَحَبُّ
alúfí	ḳuṭṭin			
familiar	a tom cat			

ظَعْنًا	اَلْاَظْعَانَ	يَتْبَعُ	بَكْرٌ	وَ
ṭha'nan	'laṭhána	yatba'u	bakrun	wa
departing	the departing ones	follows	a young camel	and

رَفُوفِ	بَغْلٍ	مِنْ	اِلَيَّ	اَحَبُّ
rafúfí	baghlin			
nibbling	a mule			

---

* A cloak of goats' or camels' hair worn by the desert Arabs, pronounced in modern Arabic '*abaiyeh*.

ضَعِيفٌ	عَمِّي	بَنِي	مِنْ	خِرْقٍ	وَ
ḍha'ífun	'ammí	baní	min	khirḳin	wa
weak	my-uncle	the sons pl. of بنو	from	a brave fellow	and

عَنُوفِ	عِجْلٍ	مِنْ	اِلَيَّ	اَحَبُّ
'anúfí	'ijlin			
rampant	a calf			

مُعَاوِيَةٌ	سَمِعَ	لَمَّا	وَ	اَلرَّاوِي	قَالَ
Muá'wiyetun	sami'a	lamma	wa	'rráwí	ḳála
	heard	when	and	the relator	said

اَبْنَةُ	رَضِيَتِ	مَا	قَالَ	اَلْأَبْيَاتَ
'bnatu	raḍhiyati	ma	ḳála	il abyát
the daughter of	was content	not	said	the verses pl. of بيت

عَنِيفاً	عِجْلاً	جَعَلَتْنِي	حَتَّى	مَجْدَلِ
'anífan	'ijlan	ja'alatní	ḥattá	Majdalin
rampant	a calf	she made me	until	

The Moḥaddeth and the Christian.*

النصرانى	فَأَخْرَجَ	سَفِينَةٍ	فى	وَنَصْرَانِيٌّ	مُحَدِّثٌ	اِجْتَمَعَ
	4th of خرج to go out.	boat		Christian		8th جمع to collect.

* *Moḥaddeth,* an authority for the *ḥadíth* or traditional sayings of Mohammed which make up the Sunneh or legal and ceremonial code of the Muslims. These people

زَكَرَة من خَمْر كانت مَعْه وصَبَّ منها فى كأْس وشَرِبَ

drank cup poured wine leathern bottle

ثم صب ثانياً وعَرَّض على المحدث فتَنَاوَلَهُ من غير

without took it in his hand (6th of نال) to offered a second time

فكْرَة و لا مبالاة فقال النصرانى جُعِلْتُ فِدَاك اِنَّها

thy ransom may I be made caring (3rd of بال) thought

خمرة فقال من اَيْن عَلِمْتَ ذلك قال اشتراها غُلامى

my slave bought it (8th شرى) that know where wine

من يَهُودِيّ فشَرِبَهَا المحدث سَرِيعًا و قال للنصرانى ما

quickly Jew

رَأَيْتُ احمق منك نَحْنُ اَصْحَابُ اَلْحَدِيثِ

tradition companions, masters we a more foolish fellow I have not seen

نَتَكَلَّمُ فى مِثْلِ سُفْيَانِ بْنِ عُيَيْنَةٍ وَيَزِيدِ بْنِ هَرُونِ

like speak, discuss (5th of كلم)

---

profess to be able to give the whole chain of authorities by whom these sayings are handed down, thus Z had it from Y, who had it from X, and so on up to A, who heard it from the Prophet's own mouth. The citation of these authorities is called اسناد Isnád.

أَنُصَدِّقُ نصرانياً عن غلامِهِ عن يهودى والله ما شربتها

from — shall we believe (2 of صدق)

إِلَّا لِضُعْفِ الإِسْنَاد

the authority — for the weakness of — except

Haroun al Raschid and Abu Nawwás the Jester Poet.

و نظيرُ ذٰلك ما اتَّفَقَ لأَبِي نوّاس و قد أَمَرَ

ordered — to Abu Nawwas — happened (5th of وفق) — like

الرَّشِيدُ بِقَتْلِه فقال أَتَقْتُلُنِي يا اميرَ المؤمنين

of believers prince — dost thou kill me? — for his slaughter — al Raschid

شَهْوَةً لِقَتْلِي قال لا بَلِ اسْتِحْقَاقًا قال ابو نواس

deservedly (noun of action, 10th from حق) — for my slaughter — lusting

إِنَّ اللّٰهَ تَعَالَى يُحَاسِبُ ثُمَّ يَعْفُو و يُعَاقِبُ

and punishes (3rd عقب) — pardons — them — calls to account (3rd حسب) — most high — but verily

فَبِمَ اسْتَحْقَقْتُ القَتْلَ قال بِقَوْلِك

for thy saying — have I deserved — and for what

الا فَاسْقِنِي خَمْرًا وَ قُلْ لِي هِيَ ٱلْخَمْرُ

say wine then give me to drink oh!

imper. سقى

ولا تَسْقِنِي سِرًّا إِذَا أَمْكَنَ ٱلْجَهْرُ

publicity is possible when in secret and do not give me to drink

قال يا أَمِيرَ ٱلْمُؤْمِنِينَ افَعَلِمْتَ أَنَّهُ سَقَانِي و

gave me to drink whether he do you know

شَرِبْتُ قال أَظُنُّ ذٰلك قال اتقتلنى على ظَنٍّ

suspicion I suspect so I drank

وَ بَعْضُ ٱلظَّنِّ إِثْمٌ قال قد قُلْتَ أَيْضًا ما تَسْتَحِقُّ بهِ

thou dost deserve also a sin* some

ٱلْقَتْلَ قال ما هو قال قلت فى ٱلتَّعْطِيلِ

atheism

مَا جَاءَنَا أَحَدٌ يُخْبِرُ بِأَنَّهُ

inform us came

aor. 4th خبر

فِي جَنَّةٍ مُذ مَاتَ أَوْ فِي ٱلنَّارِ

(hell) fire he died since Paradise

---

* Ḳor'án, ch. 49, v. 12.

قال أَفَجَاْنَا أَحَدٌ يا اميرَ المؤمنين قال لا قال

and did there come

اتقتلنى على ٱلصِّدْقِ قال أَلَسْتَ القَائِلَ

The sayer art thou not truth

لَيْسَ

يَا أَحْمَدُ ٱلْمرتَجَى فى كُلِّ مُلِمَّةٍ

accident trusted in Ahmed oh

fem. agent 4th from لمّ 8th رجا hope =Mohammed

قُمْ سَيِّدِى نَعْصِ جَبَّارَ ٱلسَّمٰوَاتِ

of the heavens the mighty one let us rebel against my lord rise

1st pl. apocopated aor. of عصى

قال يا اميرَ المؤمنين أَوَصَارَ ٱلْقولُ فِعْلاً قال

a deed and did it become?

صار with interrog. part. ا and conj. و

لا أَعْلَمُ قال يا اميرَ المؤمنين اتقتلنى على ما لا

know

تَعْلَمُ قال دَعْ هٰذَا كُلَّهُ قد ٱعترفتَ فى

thou hast confessed all of it this leave

8th عرف imp. ودع

مَوَاضِعَ كَثيرَةٍ من شِعْرِكَ بِمَا يُوجِبُ ٱلْقَتْلَ وهو

makes incumbent thy poetry many places

aor. 4th of وجب pl. of موضع

ٱلزِّنَا قال ابو نواس قد عَلِمَ ٱللّٰه هٰذا من قَبْلِ

before knew fornication

عِلْمِ امير ٱلْمؤمنين فَأَخْبَرَ أَنِّى اَقولُ ما لا أَفْعَلُ قال

and informed
4th of خبر

تَعَالَى و ٱلشُّعَرَآء يَتَّبِعُهُمُ ٱلْغَاوُونَ أَلَمْ تَرَ أَنَّهُمْ

seen the erring there follow them the poets

2nd sing. aorist from رأى apocopated after لم*

فى كُلِّ وَادٍ يَهِيمُونَ وَأَنَّهُمْ يَقُولُونَ ما لا يَفْعَلُونَ

do not do wander valley

فقال الرَّشِيد خَلُّوا سَبِيلَهُ

his way let him go

The next extract is from the pen of M. Francis Merrash, of Aleppo, and is an imitation of the موشحات or "Ornate Lyrics" invented by the Arabs of Spain. It is written in good classical Arabic, and the student is recommended to learn it by heart, as the rhythm, which is particularly flowing, will teach him to observe the proper accent of the words.

---

* Ḳor'án, ch. 26, v. 224.

Metre " *Raml.*"

فَاعِلَاتُنْ فَاعِلَاتُنْ فَاعِلَاتُنْ فَاعِلَاتْ

fāïlātun | fāïlātun || fāïlātun | fāïlat

—́ ◡ —́ — || —́ ◡ —́ — |||| —́ ◡ —́ — || —́ ◡ —́

أَيُّهَا ٱلظَّبْىُ ٱلْمُفَدَّى أَنْتَ لِلْبَدْرِ شَقِيقْ

own-brother full-moon whose ransom I am fawn oh!

(past part. from 2nd conj. فدى)

لَكَ عِيسُ ٱلْحُبِّ تُحْدَا وَعَلَى قَلْبِى ٱلطَّرِيقْ

road my heart are driven (حدو) love yellow camels (pl. of أَعْيس)

دَوْر

strophe

خَدُّكَ ٱلْقَانِي أَرَانِى مَآءَ وَرْدٍ فِي لَهِيبْ

conflagration of rose water showed-me (4th of رأى) crimson thy cheek

وَمُحَيَّاكَ سَبَانِى بِسَنَى ٱلْحُسْنِ ٱلْعَجِيبْ

wondrous beauty with flash captivated me thy face

أَنتَ مَا بَيْنَ ٱلْحِسَانِ بَدْرُ تَمٍّ لَا يَغِيبْ

sets (goes away غيب) full amongst

وَغَزَالٌ رَاحَ عَمْدًا لِدَمِ ٱلْأَسْدِ يُرِيقْ

shed lion to the blood deliberately goes ghazelle

aor. 4th of ريق

ثِغْرُكَ ٱلْبَاسِمُ أَبْدَى لُؤْلُؤًا بَيْنَ عَقِيقْ

ruby pearl displays smiling thy mouth

4th of بدى (row of teeth and gums)

درر

بِٱلَّذِي أَنْشَا قَوَامَكْ فِتْنَةً بَيْنَ ٱلْأَرَاكْ

the *Arák* trees a source of trouble stature caused to grow by Him who!

4th of نشأ

زُرْ أَخَا ٱلشَّوْقِ غُلَامَكْ لَا تَخَفْ عَيْنًا تَرَاكْ

sees thee eye fear thy servant longing of brother visit

apoc. aorist of خاف used as prohibitive.

imp. of يزور زار

حَمَلَ ٱلصُّبْحُ إِمَامَكْ وَحَمَى ٱللَّيْلُ وَرَاكْ

behind thee night defends before thee morning advances to attack

وَغَدَا ٱلْعَنْبَرُ عَبْدًا لَكَ وَ ٱلْمِسْكُ رَفِيقْ

companion musk slave ambergris was

(lit. was in the morning.)

وَٱلْمُعَنَّى لَكَ مَدًّا يَدَ مِيثَاقٍ وَثِيقْ

firm of compact hand stretched captive

(the alif is for the sake of the rhyme)

pass. part. 2nd from عنى

دور

تميلْ	عنّى	لمتى	رِفقاً	ٱلأعطافِ	لَيِّنَ
turn	from me	till when	be kind!	sides	soft
aor. 2nd from مال				pl. of عطف	gentle

أسيلْ	ٱلخدِّ	ناعمُ	رشقاً	ٱلأحشاءَ	أتلفَ
soft cheek	cheek	soft of	by a shot	heart (bowels)	destroyed
				pl. of حشو	4th conj. تلف

ٱلمحيقْ	ٱلعِشقِ	مِن لَظَى	وجْداً	دمْعِي	فَجَرَى
encompassing	love	flame	through passion	my tears	and run
agent 4th conj. حاق					

حرِيقْ	وَ	لغرِيقٍ	قَدْ تَصَدَّا	لِصَبٍّ	مَنْ
burning		drowning	is exposed to	for a lover who	who (sc. brings help)
			5th of صدى		

دور

ٱستقرّ	فِيَّ	هوىً	عَنْ	أسْلو	لا وٱللهِ	لَسْتُ
is settled	in me	love		be consoled	no! by God	I am not (will not)
10th of قرّ						

وَ مرّْ	جفَّ	كُلّ مَا	ويحلو	يندو	فالهوى
is bitter	gets dry	whatever	sweetens	wets	love

ٱستمرّْ	وٱلغالي	فيهِ	يغلو	ٱلسّعرُ	ورخيصُ
keeps so	the dear		grows dear	price	and cheap
10th conj.					

رَشِيقْ	اَلْعِطْفِ	لَدِنَ	قَدًّا	يَهْوَ	لَمْ	مَنْ	بِئْسَ
straight	sides	soft	stature	loves apocop. after لم			has ill luck

يُفِيقْ	لَا	وَنُوَّمٌ	يُهْدَى	لَيْسَ	غَاوٍ	فَهُوَ
awakes, revives aor. 4th of فاق		sleeper	get guided aor. pass. of هدى	does not	erring agent of غوى	

PART II.—THE MODERN DIALECT.

THE modern or vulgar dialect differs from the classical language in—1, Pronunciation ; 2, Simplifying grammatical forms ; 3, Vocabulary, especially in the introduction of foreign words ; 4, The use of local idioms.

PRONUNCIATION.

The long vowel اَ is often pronounced, especially in Syria, like our *ay* in *pay*, as كلاب pronounced *K'layb*, "dogs."

A short vowel at the beginning of a word is frequently omitted in the pronunciation, as in the example, *K'layb* for *Kiláb*.

ث is pronounced by Syrians and Egyptians sometimes as *t*, as in ثلاثة *t'láté*, "three," and sometimes as *s*, as حديث *ḥadíṣ*. The Bedawín Arabs generally give it the proper sound of *th* in *thing*.

ج is pronounced in Egypt like our hard *g* in *go*; in Syria it approaches to the French *j* in *journal*. Some Arabs, as those of Zanzibar, pronounce it almost as *y*, as جبل, *yebel*. The proper sound is *j* in *John*.

ذ is sometimes pronounced like *d*, as هٰذا *háda*, sometimes like *z*, as الذى *ellazí*. The proper sound is that of *th* in *that*, and is used by the Bedawín.

ظ is pronounced sometimes like a strong *z*, as عظيم *'azím* "grand," sometimes like ض, as ظُهر *dhohr*, "mid-day."

ق properly pronounced like a very guttural *ck* in *stick*, is often confounded, especially in Syria and Egypt, with the *hemzah*, as قال, pronounced *'ál*. The Bedawín almost always pronounce it like *g* in *go*, as قُم *gum* for *ḳum*, "get up."

ك is pronounced in some parts of Palestine and by some of the Arabs of the Syrian desert like our *ch* in *church*, as كلب *chelb* "a dog." But elsewhere it is sounded as *k* in *kiss*.

The diphthong وَ is pronounced in certain words nearly like our *o*, as يوم *yóm*.

ىَ is more often pronounced like *ai* in *wait*, than properly, like *i* in *wine*, e.g. بيتك *baytak* "thy house."

The short vowels ـَ ـِ ـُ are very indistinctly pronounced, and are modified greatly by the strong consonants; thus, in فهمت *fehEmt*, "I understand," الحمد لله *el hAmdu lillah*, and ضربة *dhUraboh*, the *fethah* is pronounced respectively as *e* in *let*, *a* in *lamb*, and *u* in *luck*. So *kesrah* hovers between *i* and *e*, and *dhammah* between *u* and *o*, according to the consonant which it follows. In the first syllable of words, as has been said above, the short vowels are scarcely sounded.

In words beginning with م *mim*, the first syllable, *mu*, is changed to *em*, as *emkaddem*, مُقَدّم "commander."

The long vowels ا , و and ى are not pronounced long at the end of a word, the penultimate taking the accent, as يرجو *yérju*, not *yerjú*.

THE VERB.

The final short vowels of the preterite and aorist are dropped; the second person fem. singular ends in long *í*, and the termination *tum* of the 2nd plural masc. of the preterite becomes *tú*.

The following is the modern conjugation of the verb كتب "to write."

Preterite.

	Singular.		Plural.	
	Masc.	Fem.	Masc.	Fem.
3.	kéteb	kétebet	kétebú	ketébú
2.	ketébt	ketébti	ketébtú	ketébtú
1.	ketébt		ketébna	

Aorist.

	Singular.		Plural.	
	Masc.	Fem.	Masc.	Fem.
3.	yéktub	téktub	yéktubú	yéktubú*
2.	téktub	téktubí	téktubú	téktubú
1.	éktub		néktub	

Imperative.

	Masc.	Fem.	Plural.
2.	éktub	éktubí	éktubú

---

* The Bedawín often use *yéktubin*.

Agent.

Singular.		Plural.	
Masc.	Fem.	Masc.	Fem.
kátib	kátibeh	katibín	kátibát

Verbal Noun.

Kitábeh

The dual is very rarely employed in modern Arabic.

In Egypt and Syria the syllable ب *b'* is prefixed, to all persons of the aorist except to the first plural, when *m'* is substituted. The aorist becomes—

	Singular.		Plural.	
	Masc.	Fem.	Masc.	Fem.
3.	b'yéktub	b'téktub	b'yéktubú	b'yéktubú
2.	b'téktub	b'téktubí	b'téktubú	betéktubú
1.	béktub		m'néktub	

With *doubled* verbs, the *bi* and *m'* form a syllable with the first letter of the word; thus, بتمد *bet-mudd*, "thou extendest," منمد *men-mudd*, "we stretch," &c. In verbs of this class the form مديت is always used in the preterite instead of مددت.

To define more exactly the time expressed by the aorist as present or future, the following means are employed:

In Egypt and Syria the present is expressed by prefixing the word عمّال "doing," declined according to gender and number, to the aorist, thus :—

húwa 'ammál b'yéktub, "he is writing."

híya ammálé b'téktub, "she is writing."

hum ammálín b'yéktubú, "they are writing" (masc.).

hum ammálát b'yéktubú "they are writing" (fem.).

Sometimes the agent form of the verb راح "to go" is used with a similar signification, as انا رايح *ana ráïḥ*, "I am going to . . . . ."

The future is expressed by the word بدّ *bidd* or *bedd*, with the affixed pronouns, followed by the aorist, as

بدّه يكتب *biddo yéktub*, "he shall or will write."

بدّها يكتب *biddhá téktub*, "she shall or will write."

بدك تكتب *biddak téktub*, "thou wilt write."

بدكِ تكتبى *biddik téktub*, "thou (fem.) wilt write."

بدهم يكتبوا *biddhum yéktub* , "they will write."

بدى اكتب *biddí éktub* "I will write," &c.

The ب and م are not prefixed to the aorist after بد , and the alif of the 1st person is elided, as بدى اروح *biddí 'rúḥ*, not *biddí arúḥ*.

The imperfect is made with كان declined throughout, followed by the aorist without the prefixes ب and م , as

كان يكتب *kán yektub*, "he was writing."

كانت تكتب *kánat tektub*, "she was writing."

كنت اكتب *kunt ektub*, "I was writing," &c.

The agent may be used with كان as in English, *e.g.* كان رائح "he was going."

The pluperfect is formed as in the classical language by كان, followed by the preterite, the short vowels being of course omitted.

كان كتب *kán kéteb*, "he had written."

كانت كتبت *kánat kétebet*, "she had written."

كنت كتبت *kunt ketébt*, "I had written," &c.

The past-future is formed by the aorist of كان with the preterite, as

يكون كتب *yekún kéteb*, "he will have written."
تكون كتبت *tekún kétebet*, "she will have written."
تكون كتبت *tekún ketébt*, "thou wilt have written," &c.

The tenses are used in the same manner as in the classical language.

In conditional sentences, for instance, the preterite is employed, even although past time may not be referred to, as اذا اردت *ízá 'radt*, "if you wish," ان كتب لى رديت له جواب *in kéteb lí raddeit loh jewáb*, "if he writes to me I will send him back an answer"; the apodosis may be, however, in the aorist, and we may say ان كتب لى ارد له جواب *in kéteb lí arudd loh jewáb.*

The agent of a verb signifying something done, of which the effect remains is sometimes used in a past sense, as انا حاط الصحون فى الخرستان *ana ḥáṭiṭ es s'ḥún fi'l kheristán*, "I have put plates in the cupboard."

The Passive voice is very rarely used in modern Arabic, except in the past participle of the form مَفْعُول, as مضروب *madhrúb*, "beaten"; موجود *maujúd* (*au* as *ow* in "cow"), "existing," "at hand." This form is of very common occurrence. Instead of the passive, one of the other derived forms is used, as انكسر *enkésser* "to be broken," تزوّج *etzawwaj* "to be married."

The derived conjugations are used much the same as in classical Arabic, some few verbs undergoing slight phonetic changes, as استأنى *esta'ná*, "to wait for," becomes *esténna*; استراح *esteráḥ* becomes occasionally استريّح *esteraiyyeḥ*.

In feminine passive participles derived from defective verbs, the termination اة becomes اية *aiyeh*, as مخلاة *mukhallát*, pronounced *m'khallaiyé*, "left."

The rules for the conjugation of the Irregular verbs are precisely the same as in classical Arabic.

The verb جاء "to come," is pronounced *édja* in the preterite; the imperative is *édji*, for which, however, تعال *ta'ál*, is almost always substituted.

From رأى "to see," the second conjugation becomes يروى , روّى, and sometimes ورّى, "to show."

The verb جآء "to come," when followed by the preposition ب, signifies in classical Arabic "to come with," "to bring." This in the modern dialect becomes جاب *jáb*, which is treated as a single word, and regularly conjugated: جاب "he brought," *jibt* "I brought," *bitjíb* "thou bringest," *jíb* "bring," and so on.

NOUNS.

The diminutive is of very common occurrence in the modern dialect, especially in adjectives as صغير *sogheiyír*, "little," كويّس *kwaíyis*, "pretty," شوية *shuweíyeh*, "a little."

Feminine nouns in اة are pronounced as if that termination were written اية, as عصاة "a stick," pronounced *'aṣúyeh.*

The plurals are formed as in classical Arabic, except that occasionally the sound feminine plural in ات is used even for masculine objects, as حصان "a horse," pl. حصانات.

The plurals of Turkish titles, such as باشا *Básha*, "Pasha," آغا *Agha*, &c., are formed in وات *e.g.* باشاوات,

اَغاوات ; sometimes the plural of بيك *Bek* "Bey," is similarly formed بيكوات *békawát.*

The form اَفعَل signifying *colour*, &c., makes its plural فُعْل, as احمر *aḥmar*, "red," حُمْر ابيض *abyadh*, "white," pl. بيض *bídh* (for بُيْض).

Adjectives in ى, make their plurals by adding ة, as انكليزى "an Englishman," pl. انكليزية *inkilíziyeh.*

In addition to the classical style of placing two nouns in construction, كتاب الرجل *kitáb ar rajul* (pronounced *rájil*), "the book of the man," the modern Arabs employ different locutions, as—

In Egypt بتاع, and in Syria متاع, "belonging to," are used; thus, الكتاب بتاع الراجل *el kitáb b'tá' er rajil.* متاع and بتاع are declined, fem. *b'tá't* pl. *b'tú'* e.g. العصاة بتاعته *el 'asáyeh b'tá'toh*, "his stick," الكتب بتوعه *el kutub b'tú'oh*, "his books."

In Arabia proper, حق *hakk* is used in the same sense as الكتاب حقى *el kitáb hakkí*, and in Bagdad مال, الكتاب مالى *el kitáb málí*, "my book"; these words are not declined.

PRONOUNS.

The personal pronouns are nearly the same as in the Classical:

ana "I."
ent or *ente*, masc., *enti* or *entí*, fem. "thou."
húwe or *hú*, "he," *hí* or *híye*, "she."
entum or *éntu*, "you."
hum, masc., *hunne*, fem. "they."

The affixed fem. pronoun becomes *ik* after a consonant,

and *kí* كى after a vowel, as *kitábik* "thy book," ضربوكى *dharabúkí*, "they struck thee."

The affixed masc. pronoun ك becomes *ak* after a consonant, and *k* after a vowel; thus, *kitábak*, "thy book," *dharabúk*, "they struck thee."

هُ becomes *o* or *oh* or *h*, as ضربه *dharabo*, "he struck him," ضربوه *dharabúh*, "they struck him."

The affixed pronouns are sometimes used instead of the isolated ones, as ما دامك هون *má dámak hón*, "whilst thou art here."

When a verb takes two pronouns for its complements, as, "he brought it me," the first may be affixed to the verb, and we may say, جابه لى, *jáboh lí* or it may be put last and introduced by the word ايا, as *jáb lí íyyáh*, "he brought me it."

This word ايّا, preceded by the conjunction و, is used for "with," as رح واياه *roḥ wa iyyáh*, "go with him."

For the reflexive pronouns, the words ذات روح نفس and حال are used with the affixed pronouns, as—

شفته بذاته *shifto b'záto*, "I saw him himself."

قتل حاله *katal ḥálo*, "he killed himself."

The isolated pronoun is used for emphatic repetition, as in the classical language,

هذا كتابى انا *háda kitábí ana*, "this is *my* book."

The preposition لِ used with pronouns is often pronounced *il*, like "ill" in English, as *ílo*, "to him," *íli*, "to me."

The demonstrative pronouns are slightly different from the classical.

The ه is often dropped from the beginning of هذا and its compounds, as ذا "this," ذاك "that," and in Egypt these are placed after the word الكتاب ذا *el kitáb da* (or *dí*).

When هذا and هذى or هذ are used, and followed by the article, it is shortened into *hal*, as هلكتاب *hal kitáb*, for هذا الكتاب , هلبنت *hal bint* for هذه البنت , هررجل *harrájil* for هذا الرجل "this man."

The plural of هذا and ذا is *hádól* and *dol*.

The relative pronouns, الذى , &c., become الّى *elli.* الذى is often used for "since," "inasmuch as," *e.g.* الحمد لله الذى شفتك "thank God that I have seen you."

مَنْ "who" becomes *mín.*

"What" is expressed by ماذا , ايش , or اى , as ما ذا بتريد *má dhá b'tríd,* ايش بتريد *aish b'tríd,* بتريد اى *b'tríd ay,* all meaning "what do you want?" (ايش is for اى شئٍ *aiyyu shaiïn,* "what thing?")

"Which" or "what" is in Syria اينا , and in Egypt انا , as انا كتاب *ana kitáb,* "which book."

NUMERALS.

The numerals are the same as in classical Arabic, except that from 10 to 19 they are contracted as follows:

أحد عشر	11	becomes	حدعش	*ḥadd'ash.*
أثننا عشر	12	„	أثنعش	*etn'ash*
ثلاثة عشر	13	„	ثلثعش	*t'lét'ash.*
اربعة عشر	14	„	اربعتعش	*arba't'ash.*
خمسة عشر	15	„	خمستعش	*khamst'ash.*

ستة عشر	16	becomes	ستعش	*sitt'ash.*
سبعة عشر	17	„	سبعتعش	*seba't'ash.*
ثمانية عشر	18	„	ثمانتعش	*t'mánt'ash.*
تسعة عشر	19	„	تسعتعش	*tisa't'ash.*

These are used for both genders.

TO HAVE.

The verb "to have" is expressed by prepositions; the following examples will show their use:

ايش بك *aish bek,* "what is the matter with you (what have you)?"
لى اراضى هناك *ĭlí arádhí hunák,* "I have lands there."
عندى كتاب *'andi kitáb,* "I have a book."
معى فلوس *ma'í f'lús,* "I have money."

A debt is expressed by ل for the creditor and عند for the debtor, as

لى عنده فلوس *ĭlí 'ando f'lús,* "he owes me money."

TO BE.

This is expressed by the preposition فى "in," or فيه "in it," *e.g.* فى عند كم موية *fí 'andkum moiyeh,* "have you water (is there with you water)?" *ma físh* or *ma fí andná,* "we have not," "there is not." كان فى موية "there was some water." يكون فى "there will be."

NEGATION.

The negation is formed by prefixing ما and adding ش (=شَيْأً "at all"), like the French "ne—pas," as ماشفتوش *má shiftúsh*, "I have not seen him," where the affixed pronoun هُ "him" becomes و or *ú* for *ó*, as above.

In Syria, especially, ما followed by انّ is used with the personal pronouns, as

مانى رائح *manní* (for *ma anní*) *ráyeḥ*, "I am not going."

مانك رائح *mannek ráyeh*, "thou art not going," &c.

The final ش without the preceding ما is sometimes used in asking a question, as

معكش من مصر عباره *ma'aksh min maṣr 'ebárah*, "have you any statement (news) from Cairo?"

MODERN LOCUTIONS.

The following are a few other locutions in common use in Modern Arabic:

آدى behold!

آدِينِى جِيْت here, I have come.

أَبّ جَرَم really, as أَبّ جَرَم أَنْت عَاوِز تَرُوح must you *really* go?

أَبْصر let 's see! who knows?

أَبْصَرْ مَا جَاش لِيه *abṣar má jásh li-ey*, who knows why he has not come?

ازّ آى how?

الَّذى اَللِّى who, that, as

كَتَّرْ خَيْرَك اِللِّى تَعَبْت مِنْ هَانِى كَذا I am much obliged to you for taking so much trouble on my account.

أنبارح *embáreḥ* = ألبارح yesterday.

إمّا — وإمّا or أمّا either . . . or, as

أمّا تقعد و امّا تروح either sit down or else go.

أمّالى or أمّال then, in that case, as تعال أمّالِ come, then!

أنجق *anjak*, scarcely, hardly.

آيا (وايّا) as

رح وايّاه go with him.

أيمتى when?

أيوه yes.

اى واللّه yes, indeed (also used for "good-bye").

بخت luck.

يا بختك how lucky for you.

بدّ or بدّ necessity, as

من كلّ بدّ تعال come without fail.

لا بدّ ما يجى he is sure to come.

انكان بدّك تجى تعال if you must come, come!

بدرى early.

برّا out, as

ان كنت طالع برّا if you are going out.

برضه the same still, as

هو برضه it is he himself.

برضه شابّ he is still young.

بسّ enough, only,

تلاتة بسّ only three.

تعال بسّ come, that will do.

بشقة other, separate, as

دا بشقة that is quite another thing.

بشويش gently.

بعد "after," is also used to express "yet," "still," like the French *encore*.

بقا then!

تعال بقا come, then.

بقا ما انتاش جاى are not you coming, then?

تا=حَتَى as تَأْنروح let 's go then.

قوَام at once (frequently used in the desert).

قوِى very, as

أَلْعَالِمَه دِي كوِيسَه قوِى this singing girl is very pretty.

كَامْ or كَمْ how much?

كمانِ or كَمَان again.

كَيْف how, as.

بِكَيْفَك as you like.

تومّا or تَوّ just now, as

تَوَّمَا نَام he has just gone to sleep.

تَوَّه فَايِت he has just gone by.

جِدًّا very, as

قوِى جِدًّا very strong.

جُوّا inside (the opposite of بَرَّا).

خُوش مَا كَان whatever happens, under any circumstances.

دُغْرى دوغْرِى *doghrí*, straight, exact, as

رُوح دوغرى go straight on.

أَلسَّاعَة تلاَتَه دُغرى three o'clock precisely.

ريت or يا ريت as

يا ريت يِطيب would that he might get better!

يَا رَيْتِنِي مَا كُنتْ عرفتْه وَاصل would I had never known him. (ريت is for ليت.)

سَوَا together, equal, as

نَرْكَب سَوَا للصَّيْد we will ride to the chase together.

كُلُّه عَنْدُه سَوا it is all the same to him.

ش —— at the end of a word is used as an interrogative, as

حَدَش جا has anyone come.

شُوْ بَش (Persian ها باش) bravo!

شُوَيَّه a little.

عِظيم certainly!

قَدْ أَيْش how much?

قُصْره in short.

على خاطر , على شان for the sake of.

عُمرى in my life, never.

للسَّاعَة=لسّة yet, not yet, as

لسَّة مَا جَاش he has not come yet.

مَا فِيش there is not, I have not.

مِنْ شَان for the sake of.

كثير=مَشْوَار much (in Syria).

نصْف=نُصّ half.

هَلْ ترى or هَنْترى let us see, who knows!

يعْنى that is to say.

It also asks a question:

يعنى ما نكونش نافعين shall not we profit?

Besides the above, there are a few words that differ from those used in classical Arabic, such as—

يشوف شاف instead of راى "to see";

حَاجَة (in Egypt) instead of شىء "a thing";

وِش (pl. وشوش) *wish* (pl. *w'shûsh*) for وجهة "a face."

and purely local idioms, such as—

بالزّف (in Algiers) instead of كثير "very much";

هَلْقَيْت (in Palestine)

هذا الوقت=هل وَقْيت "this time"="now."

These, however, must be learnt by practice.

READING EXERCISES IN COLLOQUIAL ARABIC.

Extract from رَحْلَةُ ابى نظارة زرقآء *Rahlat Abi Nadhdhára Zerká* (The journey of Father Blue-Spectacles), a political and satirical journal, published in Paris by Professor James Sanú'a, an exile from Cairo.

[The dialect is Arabic, as spoken in Egypt; the words are all to be read without final vowels, except where these are put in. The spelling represents the vulgar pronunciation, as نضارة for نظارة, and so on.]

Conversation between Abu Khalíl and Abu Naddára Zarká at the Café Riche on the Boulevart des Italiens, on the evening of the 14th of July 1878, in Paris.

محاورة بين ابى خليل وابى نظارة زرقا على قهوة ريش فى بولفار ديزيتليان فى ليلة اربعة عشر لوليو سنه ٧٨ فى پاريز

Abu Khalíl.—O, James; oh father of spectacles, we are glad to see you in Paris, you clever fellow! Have you any news of Egypt to cheer up my soul with?

ابو خليل

ياجِمْس يَابُو نَضَّاره

آنَسْت پَارِيز يَاشاطِرْ

مَعَكْش مِنْ مَصْر عِبَارَه

تُنعِش بهاَ مِنّى ٱلْخَاطِرْ

Abu Naddara.—If you like me to tell you, I will tell you about Egypt, oh, brilliant of aspect! After joy it has returned to weeping from the fire of its grievous accidents,

ابو نضاره
إن رُدْت أَحكيلَك أَحكي
عَنْ مصْر يا باهِي الطَّلْعه
بَعْد الفَرْح عادَتْ تبكي
مِن نار حَوادِثْها الْوَلْعَه

Egypt the happy, the protected, was joyful in honour; but to-day you see her sad, angry at the abasement of her lot.

مَصْر السَّعيدَه الْمَحْميَّه
بالعِزّ كانَتْ فرحانه
والْيوم تشوفها مَحْميه
مِن ذِل حالها زَعْلانَه

There is no freedom in Egypt, and tyranny has left her crushed. If you want to know the particulars, look through my "blue spectacles."

فِى مَصْر مافيش حُرِّيه
و الظّلم خَلّاها دُقَّه
وانْ رُدْت تَدرِى الكيفيَّه
أُنظُرْ بِنَضارتى الزرقَه

In Egypt the tyranny of the *Sheikh el Ḥárah** is as manifest as the shining sun; he ordered the shutting up of the Spectacles, suppressed them for

فى مصر جَوْر شَيْخ الحاره
ظاهر كمَا الشَّمْس الْواضِحه
أَمر بِقفْل النَّظاره
أكْمَنْهَا لِحالَه فاضِحه

---

* *Lit.* "the elder of the quarter," but it also signifies "a pimp." The ex-Khedive is meant.

showing up his circumstances.

I have travelled from Cairo, but my nightingale is singing there. He has taken hold of my bright spectacles, but Paris is full of (*lit.* exhales) them.

سافرت من مصر القاهره
وبلبلي فيها صايح
ومسك نضارتي الباهره
منها لباريز صار فايح

If I live I will go back again to Egypt and see my friends. And if I do, my brethren will keep on having pity on me, together with my friends.

ان عشت ارجع بالتاني
لمصر وانظر احبابي
وان بت تبقي اخواني
يترحموا مع اصحابي

Abu Khalîl.—Alas, for these! oh, Abu Naddara, alas! oh dear! By God, your words desolate me, oh Sheikh! Praise to God for your safety. O day fortunate in your arrival. What did you keep away so for. I travelled from Egypt on the same day that you travelled yourself, only in the afternoon. And I left you in Alexandria to take breath, and enjoy yourself, and associate with the youth of the city of "the two-horned one" (Alexander), who, according to what I hear (reaches me), love you like their two eyes. But I turned my back on it, my boy, and embarked

ابو خليل—بوسه على دول يا بو
نضاره بوسه * اخ * والله وحشني
كلامك ياشيخ * الحمد لله
بالسلامه يانهار مبارك بوصولك
انت غبت كدا لايه انا سافرت
من مصر يوم ما سافرت انت
انما بعد الضهر وخليتك في
اسكندريه تشم نفسك وتشطح
وتانس شبان مدينة ذي القرنين
اللي على ما بلغني بيحبوك زي
عينيهم وانا حطيت كتف ياوليد
وركبت بابور البرندزي اللي

(rode) on the Brindisi steamer which they talk about, and I came here quicker than lightning. And here I have been more than a fortnight waiting for you. How long did you stay in Alexandria? And how long in Malta? And how long in Marseilles? For God's sake tell me it at length, and let me share (present me with) those rare (stories) of yours; I cannot console myself (without) your charming speeches. Now here is the reason for my starting from my dear home, and coming to (being present in) these parts. Come! now then! what is it? Give something which you have, give! and refresh the ears of your friend Abu Khalíl.

يقولوا عليه وجيت هنا أسرع من
البرق وآهو مارلى فى انتظارك
يجى زياده من جمعتين انت
قعدت كم يوم فى اسكندريه وكم
يوم فى مالطه وكم يوم فى
مرسيليا بالله تحكى لى بالتطويل
وتتحفينى بنوادرك دا انا ما
اسلاش اقوالك الظريفه وادى
سبب ارتحالى من وطنى العزيز
وحضورى لهذا الطرف *يا الله
يقا امال هات من عندك هات
ورطب مسامع صديقك ابوخليل*

Abu Naddára.—Upon the eye and the head (with pleasure), oh Lord of men! If I don't tell my rare stories to you, who am I going to tell them

ابو نضاره—على العين والراس
ياسيد الناس اذا ما حكيتش
نوادرى لك رايح احكيها لمين
احسن منك والله ان القلوب

---

* This expression يالله is used for "come in," or, "let us go," it is probably from the Persian يليدن, and not the Arabic "oh God!"

to better than you? By God! verily hearts are with each other, and "from heart to heart (there is) a messenger." Only you have turned out more sagacious than me, and he spoke the truth who said, "I showed him the way, and he got to the door before me." Because you started after me and arrived before me. And what did you do, oh delight (coolness) of my eyes! in the few days that you were here?

عند بعضها ومن ٱلقلب الى
ٱلقلب رسول * إنما أنت طلعت
أفرس منى وصدق من قال علمته
على ٱلشحاته سبقنى على
ٱلبيبان لكونك سافرت من بعدى
ووصلت قبلى وعملت أيه ياقرة
عينى فى ٱلكم يوم اللى أنت
هنا *

Abu Khalíl.—No business, and nothing to occupy me. Keeping my eyes open. Oh sheikh! a man here in Paris *must* be pious.

ابو خليل—لا شغله ولا مشغله *
بصبصه منف عين * ده يا شيخ
الانسان هنا فى پاريز لا بد أن
يكون تقى *

Abu Naddára.—For God's sake explain yourself! "pious," how, while he is in a land of infidelity?

ابو نضاره—بالله عليك تفسر تقى
ازاى وهو فى بلاد ٱلكفر *

Abu Khalíl.—Excuse me. Now look, Sir; one of us in this great city keeps on thinking all the day, because wherever he turns, right or left, there is nothing before him but sweet faces, like rose-petals, and eyes that enchant, and their hair, too,

ابو خليل—أحلم بقا شوف ياسيدى
ٱلواحد منا فى ٱلبلد العظيمه ده
يفضل يذكر طول ٱلنهار لأن اذا
ٱلتفت يمين أو شمال ما قدامه
الا وشوش حلوه زى طبق الورد
وعيون يسحروا والشعور اياها

that comes down on to their marble shoulders like molten gold, and their wrists, too, the colour of silver, and quivering shoulders, and then he is obliged to scream out and say, "Allah! Allah!" and keep on thinking so all the while he is walking. By God, oh sheikh! most of the Houries of Paradise must be settled in Paris. Here, now, look at this one who is sitting beside us. Allah! Sir, Allah! Why! to-morrow, when the sun rises, one of the angels of heaven will rub his eyes and see our friend, and immediately seize her and take her straight to the Harem on high.

اللى ينزلوا على الكتاف المرمر زى سبابك الذهب والمعاصم اياها لون الفضه والكتاف الملظلظه فاذا يلتزم يصيح ويقول الله الله ويفضل يذكر كده طول ماهو ماشى * والله ياشيخ ان اغلب حوريات الجنه لا بد انهم وارد پاريز اهو شوف ده اللى قاعده جنبنا الله ياسيدى الله آهى ده بكره لما تشرق الشمس ملاك من ملايكة السما يضرب عينه ويشوف صاحبتنا وحالا يخطفها ودغرى يضيفها على الحريم العالى *

Abu Naddára.—No profanity, Sir! Don't go mad, or, by Allah, I will write to your people.

ابو نضاره — بلا كفر ياشيخ ما تتجننش والا والله اكتب لجماعتك *

Abu Khalíl.—No, my boy! do not disturb them! I have been all over the world for your sake.

ابو خليل — لا يا وليد ما تدقهاش انا سبت الدنيا على شان خاطرك *

Abu Naddára—God reward you (=I am much obliged to you).

ابو نضاره — جزاك الله خير *

Abu Khalíl.—Good! As for

ابو خليل — طيب احنا يرجع مرجوعنا

us, we come back to your journey. Mr. Joseph Ramleh wrote to me from Alexandria that you started, on the first day of this month, in the steamer of the Company Ferisina by way of Malta. So, now tell me, in detail, what happened to you from the day you set out from Alexandria until to-night.

لرحلتك * الخواجا يوسف رمله كتب لى من اسكندريه انك سافرت فى أول يوم من الشهر ده فى بابور من كمپانية فريسينه على طريق مالطه بقا احكى لى بالتفصيل كل اللى جرا لك من يوم ما خرجت من اسكندريه الى الليله ده *

Abu Naddára.—Fortunately, the steamer had not in it many passengers, and the captain was a friend of ours. So, as soon as he had saluted me and learnt the particulars, he at once told the waiter (garçon) and the steward and all the servants to take care of me, and introduced me to the ladies in the first and second class, and said to them, "This is Abu Naddára, who has opened the eyes of all the world, and shown to high and low the oppression and tyranny of the Rulers, and has awakened the Felláh from his carelessness to a sense of his rights and his strength."

ابو نضاره — بالبخت البابور ما كانش فيه ركاب كتير والقبطان كان من اخوتنا فاول ما سلم على ورسى على الكيفيه حالا وصى على الجرسون والسفرجى وجميع المستخدمين وقدمنى الى الستات بتوع اول وتانى درجه وقال لهم آهو ده ابو نضاره اللى فتح عيون العالم واظهر للخاص والعام جور وظلم الحكام وايقظ الفلاح من غفلته وعرفه بحقوقه وقوته *

Abu Khalíl.—Bravo! and

ابو خليل — ما شاء الله وانت

you did not believe it could be true when you found yourself amongst the ladies (*madámát*). Really, Abu Naddára, you are lucky in these affairs.

ماصدّقت لمّا وجدت نفسك بين المضامات حقًّا أنت يا ابو نضاره مبخت فى الأمور ده *

Abu Naddára.—Praise be to God. But the only enjoyment I had was during the first two days of the voyage. It left my eyes on the next day and the next night.

ابو نضاره—لله الحمد انّما الانبساط اللى انبسطته فى اوّل يومين السفر طلع من عيونى فى آخر يوم وآخر ليله *

Abu Khalíl.—What for? What happened? God forbid!

ابو خليل—لايه جرا ايه لا سمح الله

Abu Naddára.—Hold your tongue! Every time I think of that my hair stands on end and my flesh creeps.

ابو نضاره—اسكت دا ياشيخ انا كلّ ما افتكر شعرى يقبّ وجسدى ينمّل *

Abu Khalíl.—Then there must have arisen over you a storm, and the sea ran high, and the waves beat, and the ship pitched and tossed, and the hearts of the passengers trembled and felt faint.

ابو خليل—لا بدّ ان قامت عليكم فرتونه والبحر هاج وتلاطمت الامواج وصار البابور يغطس ويقبّ وقلب الركّاب يرجف ويطبّ *

Abu Naddára.—Just so! By Allah, to hear you describe it, one would say you had been present. I was sleeping in my first sleep, when I heard screaming and crying and lamentation, and the

ابو نضاره — تمام والله اللى بيسمعك توصف الوصفه دى ليقول عليك كنت حاضرها دا انا كنت نايم فى غرّ نومى واسمع لك صريخ وصياح وتولويل

water spoiling the seat, and dripping from my suspended locker, and the water was up to my knees: and I said, No doubt the Sheikh el Ḥarah has sent for the most skilful astrologers, and has let them cause the sea-demons to control us, so that the steamer may be wrecked and Abu Naddára may go to feed the fishes.

ومياه تشرّ فى المقعد فنطيت من خزنتى المعلّقه وكانت الميه للركب فقلت لاشك ولاريب ان شيخ الحاره احضر اشهر المنجّمين وخلاهم يسلّطوا علينا عفاريت البحر حتى ان البابور ينكسر وابو نضاره يروح خرا سمك *

Abu Khalíl.—Only the Lord saved you, because you had got the best sheikhs in Egypt praying for you.

ابو خليل—انّما ربّنا نجّاك لكون وراك افضل مشايخ برّ مصر بدعوا لك بالخير *

Abu Naddára.—God preserve them, and accept their prayers, and raise from the necks of our compatriots the yoke of oppression and tyranny, and bless them with some one who will rule them with justice and clemency.* Because, for certain, tyranny in our land has reached its last stage. If you look at people here in France, they are happy and joyful, and making money, and what does all that come from?

ابو نضاره—ربنا يحفظهم ويقبل دعاهم ويرفع عن عنق ابناء مصر الجور والظلم وينعم عليهم بمن يحكم بالعدالة والحلم لان يقينا الظلم فى بلادنا حصل لآخر درجة ان تشوف العالم هنا فى فرنسا مبسوطين ومسرورين وربحانين ودا كلّه من اية

---

* حلم an allusion to Halím Pasha, whose cause the writer of the journal espoused.

Abu Khalíl.—From Freedom. Here, if what has happened to us had happened to them, they would soon have silenced these people. Ah, how their kings have disappeared !	ابو خليل—من الحرّيه * هو اذا كان اللى بيحصّل عندنا كان يحصّل هنا كانوا يسكّتوا العالم دول * دول ياما فنوا ملوك *
Abu Naddára. — Time is going fast, oh Abu Khalíl, and I—to tell you a secret—am getting hungry. After we have eaten, I will tell you the rest of my voyage.	ابو نضاره—الوقت راح يابو خليل وانا الكلام فى سرّك جيعان بعد ما ناكل احكى لك بقيّة الرحلة *

The following is a satire on a convert to Mohammadanism, written in Arabic as spoken in Syria :

مضروب دقماق ركب جمل	طف الساقيه مفتون
شلح قبعه ارى بدعه	وساق على ساق ملتفون
بارخ مورّ عل شبقونو	وشلوم عل كلخون *

Madhrúb doḳmáḳ rakab jemel
Taffe 'ssáḳiyeh maftún
Shalaḥ ḳub'oh árá bid'oh
Wa sáḳ álá sáḳ multaffún
Bári<u>kh</u> moro 'al shubḳonû
Weshlom 'al kulkhûn.

---

* This is the Syriac benediction :
ܒܪܟ ܡܪܝܐ ܠܫܘܒܩܢܗ ܘܫܠܡ ܥܠ ܟܠܟܘܢ

A stupid dolt (*lit.* "struck on the head with a mallet") rode on a camel (*i.e.* adopted Arab ways) and jumped over the gutter (=passed the rubicon); took off his red skull-cap (which Christians wear), displayed heresy, and sat with one leg crossed over the other (like a Turk).—"*The Lord bless your ancestors, and peace be on us all.*"

An Egyptian popular love-song (from Lane's "Modern Egyptians"). The translation is from "Meister Karl's Sketch Book," by Ch. G. Leland (Hans Breitmann), Trübner & Co., London :—

1.

مَعْقُولْ مَنْ نَا مَتْ عُيُونُهْ   يَحْسِبْ ٱلْعَاشِقْ يِنَامْ

وَٱللّٰهْ أَنَا مُغْرَمْ صَبَا بِهْ   لَمْ عَلَى ٱلْعَاشِقْ مَلَامْ

دُوسْ يَا لَلِّي دُوسْ يَا لَلِّي   عِشْقِي مَحْبُوبِي فَتَنِّي

2.

يَا شَيْخْ ٱلْعَرَبْ يَا سَيِّدْ   تَجْمَعْنِي عَلْخِلّ لَيْلَه

وان جَاءنِي جِيبَ قَلْبِي   لَاعْمَلْ لُهْ الكَشْمِير طُلَيْله

دُوس يَا لَلِّي دُوس يَا لَلِّي   عِشْقِي مَحْبُوبِي فَتَنِّي

3.

كَامِلَ ٱلْأَوْصَاف فَتَنِّي   وَٱلْعُيُونَ ٱلسُّود رَمُونِي

مِن هَوَا هُم صِرْت أَغَنِّي   وَٱلْهَوَى زَوِّد جُنُونِي

دُوس يَا لَلِّي دُوس يَا لَلِّي   عِشْقِي مَحْبُوبِي فَتَنِّي

4.

جمعهم جمع العواذل   عن حبيبى يمنعونى

والله انا ما افوت هواهم   بالسيوف لو قطعونى

دوس يا للى دوس يا للى   عشقى محبوبى فتنى

5.

قم بنا يا خل نسكر   تحت ظل الياسمينة

نقطف الخوخ من على امه   و العواذل غافلين

دوس يا للى دوس يا للى   عشقى محبوبى فتنى

6.

يا بنات جو المدينه   عندكم اشيا ثمينة

تلبسوا الشاتح بلوله   و القلادة عنهد زينه

دوس يا للى دوس يا للى   عشقى محبوبى فتنى

7.

يا بنات اسكندرية   مشيكم علفرش غيه

تلبسوا الكشمير بتلى   و الشفائف سكارية

دوس يا للى دوس يا للى   عشقى محبوبى فتنى

8.

يا ملاح خافوا من الله   و ارحموا العاشق لله

حبكم مكتوب من الله   قدروا المولى على

دوس يا للى دوس يا للى   عشقى محبوبى فتنى

1.

Although your slumber may be deep,
Think not that love can yield to sleep;
By ALLAH wild with love I flame!
And he who loves is ne'er to blame.
    Step, O my joy!*
    Step, O my joy!
Mad love has stung with sore annoy.

2.

Sheyk of the Arabs! Seyed the free!
Oh! give her but one night to me!
I'll give her if she come to me,
My cashmere for a canopy.
    Step, O my joy!
    Step, O my joy!
Mad love hath stung with sore annoy.

3.

From all her charms my grief has grown,
By her black eyes I'm overthrown;†
They made me love, love made me sing,
And every word doth madness bring.
    Step, O my joy!
    Step, O my joy!
Mad love has brought me sore annoy.

---

* *lella*, in the Egyptian patois, means "lady," "sweetheart."

† In the Arabic it is "her black eyes have shot me."

4.

To keep me from her love the crew
Who blamed our love together drew;
By ALLAH! she my love shall be,
Although with swords they mangle me!
Step, O my joy!
Step, O my joy!
Mad love hath wrought me sore annoy.

5.

Up love! let us be drunk with wine!
Beneath the spreading jessamine!
We 'll cull the dripping apricot,
While those who blame us know it not.
Step, O my joy!
Step, O my joy!
Mad love hath wrought me sore annoy.

6.

Ye city damsels, rich and fair!
Ye 're jewels bright of value rare!
Ye wear the *shateh,* pearl encrest,
And the *kiladeh* on your breast.
Step, O my joy!
Step, O my joy!
Mad love hath wrought me sore annoy.

7.

Girls of Iskendereéyeh, all,
Ye wear with grace the cashmere shawl,
Ye walk with grace on tiny feet,
And oh, your lips are sugar sweet!
    Step, O my joy!
    Step, O my joy!
Mad love hath wrought me sore annoy.

8.

Ye lovely girls, fear God above!
And for His sake love all who love!
To love you is what God ordains;
He willed that I should wear your chains.
    Step, O my joy!
    Step, O my joy!
Mad love hath wrought me sore annoy.

EXERCISES FOR TRANSLATION.

Exercise 1.

a daughter, girl, بنْت	house, بيْت	large, كبير
merchant, تاجر	leaf, ورقة	garden جنينة
good, طيّب	tree, شجرة	son, child, ولد
	modest, متواضع	pretty, كويسة

The merchant's daughter. The leaf of the tree. The window of the house. The two trees of the garden. The merchant's children. The merchant's daughters are modest. The garden is pretty. A large window. Large houses. Pretty girls. A leaf of a tree. A son of the merchant. A merchant's daughter.

Exercise 2.

father, اب	the Nile, نيل	white, ابْيض
good, حسن	river, نهر	enough, بالكفاية
broad, عريض	paper, ورقة	weather, هوا

bad, رَدِى — next, adjoining, مُجَاوِرَة — book, كتاب

horses خيل — to place, حَطّ

street, حارة — table, سُفرة

Better than a father. A river broader than the Nile. The paper is not white enough. The weather is too bad. The best of the gardens. The prettiest horses. In their houses. The merchant whose house is in the next street. The table on which you placed the book. My house has no garden. My book is larger than yours.

Exercise 3.

broad, عَرِيض — more than, اكثرمن — mufti, مُفْتِى

useful, نافع — judge, قاضٍ — learned, عَالِم

industrious, مُجْتَهِد

A good father. The good father. The father is good. A pretty girl. The pretty girl. The girl is pretty. A large garden. The large garden. The garden is large. Two large (كُبار) houses. The two houses are large. Two broad (عراض) streets. The books are useful. More industrious than the son of the merchant. The judge is more learned than the mufti.

Exercise 4.

fathers, آبَهات — door, باب — pound, رطل

small, صَغير — day, يَوْم — piastre, غِرش

camel, جَمَل — an hour, سَاعَة — tumbler, كباية

horses, خَيْل

The best of the fathers. The prettiest of the horses. The two most beautiful horses. The horse is much smaller than the camel. The most beautiful horses. The first day. The second book. The third door. The fourth tree. A quarter of an hour. A half a pound. Two hundred and thirty-four piastres. Two tumblers of water.

Exercise 5.

book, كِتَاب, pl. كُتُب — white, أَبْيَض
I have, عِنْدِى — all, كُلّ
tall, طويل

These books are mine. My book is larger than yours. I have the large books. The books which he has are larger than mine. This horse is prettier than your two horses. The three white camels were the tallest of all. The second house in the broad street is very large. The three industrious sons of the merchant of Bagdad.

Exercise 6.

good, حسن — too, بزيادة — to speak of, to speak about, تَكَلَّمَ فى خُصُوص
brother, اخو , اخ — enough, بالكفاية
to buy, اشترى — next adjoining, مُجَاوِر
sister, أخت

Which is the best book? It is the largest of your brother's books. The house which your father has bought is better than that which my sister is going to buy for her son. The door is too large. The horses are too tall. The street is not broad enough. I have a pretty house, but it is too small for me and my children. The merchant whose house is in the next street to ours The man you spoke of. The children you came with.

Exercise 7.

who, مَن
to see, نظر , رأى
to see (modern Arabic), شاف , يشوف
to want, أَرَادَ
to want (modern Arabic), عَاوِز
what, ما
which, أيّ

self, نَفْس , pl. أَنْفُس
each other, بَعْضُهُم بَعْضاً
each other (modern Arabic), بعض
to say, tell, قَالَ , يَقُول
to touch, مَسّ
dear, غالى
cheap, رخيص

to enter, دَخَلَ
to enter (modern Arabic), خش , يَخُوش
to reside, أَقَامَ , نُقِيمُ
there, هناك
to sell, بَاعَ , يبيع
apple, تُفاحة

Who is there? Who has come? What do you want? What did you say? Did you tell the merchant's son who came in at the door? Go in and see who has been touching my books. The house is too dear, but it is large enough. The man you spoke of sells apples cheaper than the merchant who resides in our street. They told each other to go in. They spoke of each other to the merchant. I have the book the merchant spoke to me of.

Exercise 8.

youth, فَتًى	life, حَيَوٰة	another, آخر
to tell a lie, كَذَبَ	length, طُول	a lie, كِذْبَة

A youth said, "I have never told a lie in my whole life" (my life in its length). Another answered, "Then this is your first lie."

Exercise 9.

to ask, سَأَلَ	to eat, أَكَلَ	poor, فَقِير
physician, طَبِيب	to answer, أَجَابَ	whenever, حِينَمَا
time, وَقْت	rich, غَنِيّ	to be possible for
proper, مُنَاسِب	to please, أَعْجَبَ	أَمْكَنَ

Some one asked a physician about the proper time in which to eat. He answered, "If you are rich, the time that pleases you; but if you are poor, the time that is possible for you."

Exercise 10.

to stand, وَقَفَ على	to see, رَأَى	beauty, جَمَالٌ , حُسْنٌ
crow, غُرَابٌ	jackal, ابن آوى	feather, رِيشٌ
branch, غُصْنٌ	to hasten, اِبْتَدَرَ, أَسْرَعَ	to exceed (go fur-
tree, شَجَرَةٌ	shade, ظِلٌّ	ther), زَادَ
beak, مِنْقَارٌ	to begin, أَخَذَ فِى	say, يَقُولُ , قَالَ
cheese (a piece of)	gross flattery, مَدِيح	voice, صَوْتٌ
جُبْنَةٌ	الْمُنَابَ	beautiful, جَمِيلٌ

like, نظير	to wish, أراد	to fall, سقط
to call, يدعو , دعا	to hear, سمع	to go off,
bird, طير , pl. طيور	to hesitate, لبث	مضى في سبيله
to glory, افتخر	to open, فتح	

A crow stood on the branch of a tree with a piece of cheese in his mouth. A jackal saw him and hastened to the shade of that tree, and began grossly to flatter the beauty of the crow's feathers. Then he went further, and said to him, "If your voice were beautiful, like your feathers, I should call you the sultan of birds." So the crow gloried, and wished to let the jackal hear the beauty of his voice, and did not hesitate to open his beak till the cheese fell out, and the jackal hurried to it and went off.

Exercise 11.

stranger, poor man, غريب	Egypt, بر مصر	young man, جدع
	whilst, بينما	what is the matter with? ما بال
ride, ركب	gallop, يجول , جال	
ass, حمار	bray, نهق	home-sick, مفارق

A certain (*One of the strangers*) stranger was riding an ass in Egypt, and while he was galloping in the street the ass brayed, and a man asked its master "Young man! what is the matter with the ass that he brays?" Said he, "He is a stranger and home-sick."

Exercise 12.

to faint, أغْمى
wife, امرأة , زوجة
Ireland, ارْلَندا
to order, أمَرَ
servant, خادم
to prepare, هَيَّأ , أعدّ
horse, حِصَان

search, طَلَب
physician, طَبيب
after, بعْد
note, تَذْكِرَة
to come to, revive, اِسْتَفَاق

margin, postscript, حَاشِيَة
following, آتى
to cure, شَفَى
necessity, حَاجَة
presence, حُضُور
to send, أرْسَلَ

The wife of a man from Ireland fainted. So her husband ordered his servant to get a horse ready that he might go in search of the doctor. But when the horse was ready and the note written to the doctor, the wife came to. So he wrote on the note the following postscript: "My wife is quite cured, so there is no need for your presence," and sent it off by the servant to the doctor.

Exercise 13.

student, تِلْميذ
to spend, صَرَفَ
time (extent) مُدَّة
to open, فَتَحَ
door, بَاب

cupboard, مِخْدَع
to be able, قَدَرَ
bother! . . . تَبًّا لِـ
to steal, سَرَقَ

keyhole (*lit.* lock-hole), ثَقْبُ الغال
would that, يالَيْتَ
to give rest, أرَاحَ
torment, عَذَاب

A student, after he had spent a long time in trying to open the door of his cupboard without being able to do it, said, "Bother him who stole the key-hole; would that he had stolen the lock as well, and given me rest from this torment."

Exercise 14.

to be used, عَادَ, يَعُودُ	to marry, تَزَوَّجَ	to grow up, to get big, كَبِرَ
beating, ضَرْب	to provide, bless, رَزَقَ	to reach, وَصَلَ
father, أب	a son, وَلَد	to stop, كَفَّ
to drag, جَرَّ	to grow old, شَاخَ	grandfather, جَدّ
door, بَاب	an old man, شَيْخ	

A man was accustomed to beat his old father, and drag him to the door of the house. At length he married, and was blessed with a son, and when he grew old and his son grew up, his son used to beat him as he had been used to beat his own father, until he reached the door, when the old man used to cry out, "Stop, my boy! this is where I used to drag your grandfather to."

Exercise 15.

to stand before, مَثَلَ	sage, حكيم, plural, حكماء	presence, حَضْرَة
		some, بَعْض

money (dinars, drachms) دَنَانِير, دَرَاهِم

you used to (*lit.* it preceded to you), سَبَقَ لَك

to be in need of, احْتَاجَ

to give, أَعْطَى

at first, أَوَّلاً

to speak, تَكَلَّمَ

matter, أَمْر

king, مَلِك, pl. مُلُوك

to see, رَأَى

not, other than, غَيْر

One of the sages stood in the presence of a certain king, and asked him for some money. The king said to him, "You used to tell me that sages never wanted money." The sage replied, "Give me first what I ask, and after that we will speak of this matter." So the king ordered it to be given to him. Then he said to the king, "Do you not see that I do not want money now?"

Exercise 16.

lamp, سِرَاج

alight, مُشْتَعِل

pottery, earthenware, فَخَار

to open, فَتَح

wood, stick, عُود, pl. عِيدَان

sulphur, كِبْرِيت

to trim, أَصْلَح

being requisite, اقْتِضَاء

at, عِنْد

to find fault with, لَام

to visit, زَار, يَزُور

master, صَاحِب.

to place, put, وَضَع

needle, اِبْرَة

instead of, عِوَضًا

to absorb, امْتَصّ

grain, قَمْحَة

oil, زَيْت

A man visited one of his friends at night, and saw a lamp alight. It was one of the open earthenware lamps;

and he saw in the lamp a lucifer match (*a stick of sulphur sticks*), to trim the lamp with as required. The visitor blamed the master of the house for that, and said to him, "Put a needle there instead of a match, because it absorbs every night two or three grains of oil, and a needle absorbs nothing."

Exercise 17.

to boast, افتخر	to see, رَأَى	ground, earth, أَرْض
family, عائلة	foot, قَدَم	to mean, أَرَاد
high, عالى	to touch, مَسّ	hanged, مَشْنُوق
to be right, حَقَّ لِ		

A certain man was boasting that he came of a very high family, and one of those who were present answered, "You are quite right to boast so, for I have seen some one of your family so high that his feet could not touch the ground." (He meant that he had seen him hanged.)

Exercise 18.

to claim to be a prophet, تَنَبَّأ	yes, نَعَم	fool, سَفِيه
day, يَوْم, pl. أَيَّام	to send, بَعَث	stupid, أَحْمَق
before him, بَيْنَ يَدَيْه	to bear witness, شَهِد	like, مِثْل
a prophet, نَبِى		reward, جَائِزَة

A man claimed to be a prophet in the days of a certain king, and when he came before him the king said, "Are you a prophet?" "Yes," said he. "And to whom are you sent?" again asked the king. "To thee," answered the other. "I bear witness," said the king, "that you are a stupid fool." He replied, "There is only sent to every people one like unto themselves."* And the king laughed and ordered him a reward.

Exercise 19.

near to, بِٱلْقُرْبِ مِنْ
'Abd el Melik, عَبْدُ ٱلْمَلِك
time, when, حِين
to draw nigh, اِقْتَرَبَ
end, term of life, أَجْل
to blame, لَامَ , يَلُوم
self, نَفْس
hand, يَد

head, رَأْس
to desire, تَمَنَّى
to earn, اِكْتَسَبَ
to feed, قَاتَ , يَقُوتُ
slave, عَبْد
tend, رَعَى
flocks, غَنَم
to occupy oneself, اِشْتَغَلَ
obedience, طَاعَة

be He exalted (most high), تَعَالَى
to rebel, to be a sinner, عَصَى
to hear, سَمِعَ
to praise, حَمِدَ
to make, جَعَلَ
death, مَوْت

A poor man was near to 'Abd el Melik when he drew nigh to his end, and 'Abd el Melik was blaming himself,

* See Ḳor'án, *passim*.

and beating on his head with his hand, and saying, "I would desire to earn day by day what would feed me, or to be the slave of a man and tend his flocks, and occupy myself with obedience to God most high (rather) than be a sinner." And the poor man heard him, and said, "Praise be to God, who makes them at their death desire the state that we are in, while we do not at our death desire the state that they are in."

Exercise 20.

to go, ذهب
bull, ثَور
market, سُوق
to sell, باع
to crowd about, اِجْتَمَعَ الى
people, قَوْم
to offer, عَرَضَ عَلَى
piastre, غِرْش
to take, begin, أَخَذَ
to be angry, اِغْتاظ
to increase, run up, يَزيد زَادَ
to be worth, سَاوَى
little by little, شيئاً فشيئاً
to buy, اِشْتَرَى
to pay, دَفَعَ
amount, مَبْلَغ
to lead, قَادَ
joy, delight, فَرَح
to undo, حَلّ
purse, كِيس

A man took his bullock to market, to sell it; and people came round him and offered him a hundred and fifty piastres, and then began to run it up (*increase*) little by little to two hundred and fifty piastres. Then he got angry, and said, "It is worth more than three hundred, and I will buy it myself for that." Then he undid his purse and paid them the amount, and led the bull off, and went away delighted.

Exercise 21.

to dispute, تجادل
clergyman, قسيس
on account of, about لجهة
drinking, شرب
intoxicating drink, مسكرة
smoking, تدخين
to find fault with, to carp at, طعن فى

unlawful, محرم حرام
to begin, شرع
to try, حاول
agreement, contenting, اقناع
without, بدون
result, نتيجة
bishop, أسقف

to be present, حضر
to be right, أصاب
it is said, قيل
to enter, دخل
to defile, نجس
man, إنسان
to go out, خرج

A man disputed with a clergyman about drinking intoxicating things and smoking. And the clergyman found fault with smoking, and said that it was unlawful. Then he began to try and persuade the man that drinking intoxicating things was not unlawful, like smoking, but without success. A bishop who was present said, "The priest is right in his opinion. Have you not heard what is said, 'It is not what entereth the mouth that defileth a man, but that which goeth out of his mouth, that defileth a man.'"

Exercise 22.

to be present, حضر
a desert Arab, أعرابى

El Hejjáj, ألحجاج
to bring forward, قدم

food, طعام
pudding, sweetmeat, حلوى

to leave, تَرَك
until, حَتَّى
morsel, لُقْمَة
to be beheaded, ضُرِبَتْ عُنُقُه
to refrain, اِمْتَنَع
to remain, بَقِى

at one time . . . and at another time, طَوْرًا وتَارَةً
prince, أَمِير
to leave as a legacy, or in one's care, أَوْصَى بِ

to laugh, ضَحِك
to roll over, اِسْتَلْقَى
back of the neck, قَفَا
a reward, صِلَة

A desert Arab was present with some people at (عند) El Hejjáj's, and the food was brought and they eat of it. Then the pudding was brought, and El Hejjáj let the Arab alone until he had eaten a morsel of it, when he said, "Whoever eats of the pudding shall be beheaded," so they all refrained from eating it. But the Arab remained looking one time at El Hejjáj and another at the pudding, and then said, "O Prince, I leave my children to your care," and began to eat. El Hejjáj laughed until he rolled over on his back, and ordered him a reward.

Exercise 23.

preacher, وَاعِظ
to incite to, حَرَّض عَلَى
soldier, جندى, pl. جنود

to fight, تَقَاتَل
enemy, عَدُوّ
bravery, شُجَاعَة
lion, أَسَدٌ, pl. أُسُود
until, at length, الى أنْ

war, حرب
supper, عَشَاء
evening, مَسَاء
Paradise, فِرْدَوْس
to be delighted with, سَرَّ بِ كلام

to grow hot or fierce (a fight), أَنْتَشَب
battle, combat, قِتَال
to shake, تَزَعْزَع
rank, صَفّ, pl. صُفُوف

army, عَسْكَر, pl. عَسَاكِر
returned, رَجَع
back, عَلَى عَقِبِهِ
to seek, طَلَب
flight, فِرَار
to stop, أَوْقَف

to promise, وَعَد بِ
to forget, نَسِيَ, يَنْسَى
habit, عَادَة
to take supper, أَتَعَشَّى

A preacher was once inciting the soldiers to fight the enemy with the valour of lions; at length he said, "any one of you who is killed to-day in the war, his supper this evening shall be in Paradise." The soldiers were delighted at his words, but when the combat grew fierce, and the ranks of the army were shaken, the preacher turned back, seeking flight; but a soldier stopped him, and said, "Have you forgotten the supper which you promised us in Paradise to-night?" Said the priest, "I have not forgotten, my son, I have not forgotten, but I am not in the habit of taking supper myself!"

Translation of a ballad from "Alice in Wonderland":—

1.

"You are old, father William," the young man said,
"And your hair has become very white;
And yet you incessantly stand on your head,
Do you think at your age it is right?"

"In my youth," the old man replied to his son,
"I feared it might injure the brain,
But now that I 'm perfectly sure I have none,
I do it again and again."

2.

"You are old," said the youth, "as I mentioned before,
And have grown most uncommonly fat;
Yet you turned a back somersault in through the door!
Pray what is the reason of that?"
"In my youth," said the sage, as he shook his white locks,
"I kept all my limbs very supple
By the use of this ointment, one shilling the box;
Allow me to sell you a couple."

3.

"You are old," said the youth, "and your jaws are too weak
For anything tougher than suet;
Yet you eat up the goose with the bones and the beak!
Pray how did you manage to do it?"
"In my youth," said the old man, "I took to the law,
And argued each case with my wife,

And the muscular strength which it gave to my jaw
Has lasted the whole of my life."

4.

"You are old," said the youth, "one would hardly suppose
That your eye was as steady as ever;
Yet you balanced an eel on the end of your nose!
What made you so wonderfully clever?"
"I have answered three questions, and that is enough,"
Said the old man; "Don't give yourself airs.
Do you think I will listen all day to such stuff?
Be off, or I'll kick you down stairs."*

---

* In the following translation of this trifle I have imitated the rhyme and metre of the well-known poem by Omar ibn el Fâridh beginning—

سائق الاظعان يطوى البيد طى * منعماً عرج على كثبان طَىّْ

Zeid and 'Amr are the fictitious personages used as illustrations in all works of grammar and jurisprudence: they are the John Noakes and Thomas Stiles, or the John Doe and Richard Roe of the Arabs.—*E.H.P.*

1.

رَاحَ زَيْدٌ طَاعِنًا فِى سِنِّهِ   وَٱنْبَرَى عَمْرٌو يُنَاجِيهِ فَتَىّْ
قَالَ شَيْخَ ٱلْحَارَةِ ٱلْهَمُّ ٱلَّذِى   شَهِدَ ٱلشَّيْبُ عَلَيْهِ بِٱلْفَنَىّْ
مَا ٱحْتِيَالِى فِيكَ مَقْلُوبًا عَلَى   رَأْسِكَ ٱلْمَنْكُوبِ نِكْسًا لِلثَّرَىّْ
أَفَشَيْخٌ شَائِبٌ مِثْلُكَ يَرْ   ضَى بِأَمْرٍ مِثْلِ ذَا جَرَّ ٱلْخِزَىّْ
قَالَ يَا ٱبْنِى عَادَةٌ مَرَّ شَبَا   بِى بِهَا قَدْ بَقِيتُ مُنْذُ ٱلصِّبَىّْ
بَيْدَ أَنِّى كُنْتُ قَبْلًا خَائِفًا   مِنْ فَسَادٍ فِى دِمَاغِى أَوْ ضَنَىّْ
طِبْتُ نَفْسًا عَارِفًا مَا إِنْ حَوَى   قَحْفُ رَأْسِى مِنْ دِمَاغٍ قَطُّ شَىّْ

2.

قَالَ عَمْرٌو وَٱنْثَنَى يَعْذِلُهُ   أَنْتَ شَيْخٌ شَائِبٌ هَىٌّ بْنُ بَىّْ*
مِثْلَمَا قَدْ مَرَّ قَوْلِى سَابِقًا   بَدَنٌ كَٱلْبَدَنِ مَنْفُوخُ ٱلْحَشَىّْ
أَبُوَيْبٌ طَافِرًا تَدْخُلُهُ   لَيْسَ كَهْلٌ فِى نَشَاطٍ كَصَبِىّْ
قَالَ قَدْ أَلْفَيْتُ يَا ٱبْنِى حِيلَةً   تُنْعِشُ ٱلْجِسْمَ مَزِيدًا فِى ٱلْقُوَىّْ
خُذْ حُبُوبِى† ذِى وَأَعْطِ دِرْهَمًا   فَهْىَ لِلْقُوَّةِ مِنْ أَجْدَى دُوَىّْ

---

* Haiy 'ibnu Baiy=" anybody, the son of nobody!"
† Literally " pills."

3.

قَالَ عَمْرٌو يَا كَبِيرَ ٱلسِّنِّ لَا   سِنَّ فِي فِيهِ تَبَقَّى مِنْ ثُنَى
غَيْرَ شَحْمِ ٱلْكِرْشِ لَا تَمْغُضُهُ   مَنْ رَأَى ٱلطَّحَّانَ مِنْ غَيْرِ ٱلرَّحَى
تَبْلَعُ ٱلْوَزَّةَ مَعْ مِنْقَارِهَا   وَٱلْعِظَامَ الصُّمَّ مِنْهَا كَٱلْعَصَى
لَمْ أُحِطْ عِلْمًا بِهٰذَا فَأَبِنْ   لِي جَلِيَّ ٱلْأَمْرِ مِنْ غَيْرِ مِرَى
قَالَ مُذْ كُنْتُ صَبِيًّا قَدْ تَفَقَّهْتُ حَتَّى صِرْتُ أَقْضِي مَنْ قَضَى
وَٱحْتِجَاجِي كُلُّهُ مَعْ زَوْجَتِي   حِينَمَا تَشَبَّهَ ٱلْفَتْيَا عَلَيَّ
نَشَأَتْ بِي قُوَّةُ ٱلْبَلْعِ مِنَ ٱلْ   هِرْفِ بِٱلتَّحْرِيكِ فِيهِ حَنَكِي

4.

عَادَ عَمْرٌو قَالَ وُقِّيتَ ٱلرَّدَى   بِئْسَ شَيْبٌ يُورِثُ ٱلنَّاسَ ٱلْعَمَى
أَيُّهَا الشَّائِبُ إِنَّا قَدْ عَهِدْ   نَا عَلَى عَيْنَيْكَ قَدْ غَشَى ٱلْعَشَى
تَنْصُبُ ٱلْأَفْعَى عَلَى ٱلْمَارِنِ مِنْ   أَيْنَ وِجْدَانُكَ لِلْعَيْنِ ٱلضُّوَى
يَدُكَ ٱلْبَيْضَاءُ حَسْبِي مُعْجِزًا   هَلْ لِمُوسَى مِثْلُ هٰذِي مِنْ عَصَى *
هَا ثَلَاثٌ مِنْ سُؤَالَاتٍ مَضَتْ   لَا تَزِدْنِي بَعْدُ مِنْ حَيٍّ وَلَيّ †
مَلَّ سَمْعِي ٱنْتِهَارِي كُلُّهُ   أَسْمَعُ ٱلْهَذْيَ بِإِصْغَاءٍ لَغَى
ايهِ عَنِّي وَٱنْحَدِرْ مِنْ دَرَجٍ   هَاكَ مِنْ رِجْلِي تَعْجِيلًا لِذَى

---

* In allusion to Moses' miracle of the white hand, and of the rod which became a snake, as described in the Kor'ân, vii. 104–105.

† Ḥaiyun wa laiyun = nonsense.

THE BLACK CAT.

FOR the most wild yet most homely narrative which I am about to pen I neither expect nor solicit belief. Mad indeed would I be to expect it in a case where my very senses reject their own evidence. Yet, mad am I not; and very surely do I not dream. But to-morrow I die, and to-day I would unburden my soul. My immediate purpose is to place before the world, plainly, succinctly, and without comment, a series of mere household events. In their consequences, those events have terrified—have tortured—have destroyed me.

الهِرّة السوداء وعربدة سفّاك الدماء

EXTRACT from "The Black Cat," translated from the English of Edgar Poe by E. H. Palmer.

لى قِصّةٌ عجبٌ سأُخبركم بها   لغريب ما تجرى بهِ الاحوالُ
لو اقتضِى من سامعٍ تصديقها   لَغدوتُ ممّن يعتريهِ خَبَالُ
اذ كنت أُكذِبُ ما ترى عيناىَ او   سمعت به اذنى وذاك محالُ

ولست بمجنون ولا نائماً ارى اضغاث احلام لكننى فتّاكٌ قد دنا منى الاجل وارقب الموت فى الغد فاريد ان اضع اليوم عنى وقرى الذى انقض ظهرى معترفا بِاثْمِى مقرّا بكبير ذنبى ولا أُودّ الّا ان ابين ما جرى علىّ من الامور غير مضيف على ذلك كلمةً مّا تفسيرا او اعتذارًا فانها من الموادّ المُهوِلة المُخيفة لى المعذّبِة لقلبى الجالبة على الدمار

Yet I will not attempt to expound them. To me they have presented little but Horror; to many they will seem less terrible than *barroques*. Hereafter, perhaps, some intellect may be found which will reduce my phantasm to the common-place; some intellect more calm, more logical, and far less excitable than my own, which will perceive, in the circumstances I detail with awe, nothing more than an ordinary succession of very natural causes and effects.

From my infancy I was noted for the docility and humanity of my disposition. My tenderness of heart was even so conspicuous as to make me the jest of my companions.

وهوذا اشرع فى شرح سببها

وما كان لى فيها سوى العذاب والخوف ولئن تشابه على القارى بخزعبلات اللهو واللعب فربَّ ناظر فيها يخال هَوْلِى هزلا ويظن اضطرابى سهلا وذلك شأن من لم يَسًبْر غَوْر الامور غير ملتفت الى الطيش والزيغ والنفس الامَّارة بالسوء ولا يرى فيما يروعنى ايرادة الآ الاسباب الطبيعية او القيام بما يجب علىّ حقيقةً

فقد كنت منذ الحداثة مشتهراً بدماثة الاخلاق و مَحَّبة بنى جِنْسى حتّى صرت بين الخلان والاصحاب عبرة لرقة قلبى

I was especially fond of animals, and was indulged by my parents with a great variety of pets. With these I spent most of my time, and never was so happy as when feeding and caressing them. This peculiarity of character grew with my growth, and in my manhood I derived from it one of my principal sources of pleasure. To those who have cherished an affection for a faithful and sagacious dog I need hardly be at the trouble of explaining the nature or the intensity of the gratification thus derivable. There is something in the unselfish and self-sacrificing love of a brute which goes directly to the heart of him who has had frequent occasion to test the paltry friendship and gossamer fidelity of mere *Man.*

فاحببتُ فی الحیوانِ کُلَّ مؤانسٍ   تَآلَفَ والانسانَ من فرطِ صبْوتی

وتسامح لی ابوای فیما رغبت فیه من الحیوانات المؤتلفة علی اختلاف انواعها ولبثت اصرف غالب اوقاتی وایاها جاعلاً غایة انشراحی فی اطعامها وموانستها

وکلُّ مَنْ آلَفَ کلباً له   مؤتَمَنا فی الدار ربّاهُ حیْنْ
یعلمُ ما أُولِعَ قلبی به   فی حُبِّ حیوانٍ انیسٍ فَطِیْنْ

فلا حاجة ان اشرح له مقدار التسلّی وفرط الانبساط الذی یتأتّی من ذلك لانه یوجَد فی الفة الکلب الخالیة من الغرض شیٌّ یؤلّف قلبَ من قد مارس الودَّ الکاذب الخدّاع الذی یرآئی به البشر

I married early, and was happy to find in my wife a disposition not uncongenial with my own. Observing my partiality for domestic pets, she lost no opportunity of procuring those of the most agreeable kind. We had birds, gold-fish, a fine dog, rabbits, a small monkey, and *a cat.*

This latter was a remarkably large and beautiful animal, entirely black, and sagacious to an astonishing degree. In speaking of his intelligence, my wife, who at heart was not a little tinctured with superstition, made frequent allusion to the ancient popular notion which regarded all black cats as witches in disguise. Not that she was ever *serious* upon this point; and I mention the matter at all for no better reason than that it happens just now to be remembered.

تزوّجتُ وانا فتى وقد اسعفنى الحظ بزوجة موافقة لى لاسِيّما فى عاداتى السلف الايمآء اليها فلما آنسَتْ منى المحبة للحيوانات بذلت مجهودها فى تحصيل ما هو الالطف والاطرب تلهّياً من الحيوانات الموانسة فحوينا عصافير وسمكا وكلباً جيّدِا وارنبا صغيرا وقطًّا فطينا

فاما القط فكان كبير الحجم جميل المنظر حالك السواد ذا ذهن عجيب مدهش وكانت زوجتى تتخيّل قليلا من خرافات العجآئز فكلما صودف ذِكْر قطّنا تلمّح لتوهّم العوام ان كل قطّ اسود ساحر ممسوخ ولا اظنها تقول ذلك بالجد ولكننى ذكرت كلمتها ههنا لانها فى هذه الدقيقة خطرت على بالى

Pluto—this was the cat's name—was my favourite pet and playmate. I alone fed him, and he attended me wherever I went about the house. It was even with difficulty that I could prevent him from following me through the streets.

Our friendship lasted in this manner for several years, during which my general temperament and character, through the instrumentality of the fiend Intemperance, had (I blush to confess it) experienced a radical alteration for the worse. I grew, day by day, more moody, more irritable, more regardless of the feelings of others. I suffered myself to use intemperate language to my wife. At length, I even offered her personal violence.

ولّقبنا قطنا بابى مُرّةٍ فصار من اخص موانسىّ واشدهم لى التزاما ولا اطعمه الّا بيدى وكان لا يفارقنى البتة فى البيت حتى كِدْتُ لا امنعه من الخروج معى الى السوق

وبقينا على هذه الالفة والمودة حيناً بَيْدَ اننى فى اثنآء ذلك اعترتنى علّة شرعت تغير طبعى وتبدّل مزاجى وتوسمنى بخصال غير محمودة ليس مما وصفته واضحى ادمانى على الخمر واستغراقى فى النشوة سببا لمجلبة عارٍ علىّ طول المدى فما زلت ازداد يومًا عبوساً وشراسة وهيجانا سريعا غير مكترث باحد حتى رضيت لنفسى ان اخاطب زوجتى بالفحشآء والغضب ثم بعد هنيهة ابتدأْت اضربها

My pets, of course, were made to feel the change in my disposition. I not only neglected but ill-used them. For Pluto, however, I still retained sufficient regard to restrain me from maltreating him, as I made no scruple of maltreating the rabbits, the monkey, or even the dog, when by accident, or through affection, they came in my way. But my disease grew upon me—for what disease is like Alcohol?—and at length even Pluto, who was now becoming old, and consequently somewhat peevish—even Pluto began to experience the effects of my ill-temper. One night, returning home much intoxicated from one of my haunts about town, I fancied that the cat avoided my presence. I seized him; when, in his fright at my violence, he inflicted a slight wound upon my hand with his teeth.

واما موانسىّ المساكين فما نجْونَ من حدة خُلقى فغفلت عنهنّ بل ظلمتهنّ بالداهية والغريزة الاّ قطنا ابا مرة بقيت له فى قلبى بقيةٌ من المودّة القديمة تمنعنى ان اضربه او اطرده وان كنت اوجعت الارانب والقرد حتى الكلب ضربا مؤلما وطردتها وآذيتها ولم تأخذنى بها رأفة

لأنّنى احسست منهنّ ٱلقِلَى ينفرْنَ انْ صَدًّا وان تدلُّلاَ

لكنّ دآئى وناهيك من دآء كشرب الخمر قد ازداد بى حتى لحق غضبى بابى مرة وقد طعن فى السن وذلك اسرع للهياج عليه مما لوكان فى غَضّ شبابه

ففى ليلةٍ مّا اتيت البيت من الخمارة سكران فوسوست النشوة فى صدرى أنّ القط فار منى مجتنب مواجهتى فقبضت عليه امرص رقبته فلخوفه من شدّة غضبى عض باسنانه المسنونة يدى فضرجها دمًا

The fury of a demon instantly possessed me. I knew myself no longer. My original soul seemed at once to take its flight from my body; and a more than fiendish malevolence, gin-nurtured, thrilled every fibre of my frame. I took from my waistcoat-pocket a pen-knife, opened it, grasped the poor beast by the throat, and deliberately cut one of its eyes from the socket!

I blush, I burn, I shudder, while I pen the damnable atrocity.

When reason returned with the morning—when I had slept off the fumes of the night's debauch—I experienced a sentiment half of horror, half of remorse, for the crime of which I had been guilty; but it was at best a feeble and equivocal feeling, and the soul remained untouched.

فحملنى غضبٌ وجنونٌ لم اطق ان املك معهما نفسى وكأنّ روحى الاصلية انتزعت منى ونبض بديلا منها فى كل اعصابى ومفاصل بدنى روح داهية عنيدة اشبه بالابالسة متولّدة من سَورة الخمر على ان اعمد الى موسى مطوية فى جيبى فانتضيتها وعصرت رقبة الحيوانة المسكينة فعوّرت عينها

واحرّ قلباهُ من عارٍ ومن خجلٍ   اذ ليس ينفع قرع السنّ من ندَمِ
يكاد يكوى فوادى من لظى اَلَمٍ   اذا كتبتُ اجترامى الاثمَ بالقلمِ

ولما صحوت من سكرتى وقد اطار النوم الخمور عنى وعاودنى شعورى أرعدت فرآئصى و خامرنى الندم على ما فرّطت وقد كسبته يداى

وهيهات النزوعُ الى متابٍ   أاترك ههنا الصهباءَ نقدَا

واذ لم تكن توبتى نصوحا فما فتئتُ فى الغواية جامحا وعجت

I again plunged into excess, and soon drowned in wine all memory of the deed.

In the meantime the cat slowly recovered. The socket of the lost eye presented, it is true, a frightful appearance, but he no longer appeared to suffer any pain. He went about the house as usual, but, as might be expected, fled in extreme terror at my approach. I had so much of my old heart left, as to be at first grieved by this evident dislike on the part of a creature which had once so loved me. But this feeling soon gave place to irritation. And then came, as if to my final and irrevocable overthrow, the spirit of PERVERSENESS. Of this spirit philosophy takes no account. Yet I am not more sure that my soul

---

اعوم فى الخمور واستهوانى الغوص فى لجها فاغرقت نفسى فى خباثتها

وفى ذلك الحين برئَ القط من جراحته لكن موضع العين العائرة كان منظره شنيعا واذ زال الوجع عنه فطفق يطوف فى الدار كعادته السالفة غير انه لشدة فزعه كان يفرّ منى فرارًا كلما واجهنى فى ناحية مّا من البيت

فحزنت فى البدأة لما دهمنى من اجتنابه موآنستى وكراهته لى وقد كان يحبنى فيما مضى حبًّا شديدًا

وبعد ذا هاج صدّه غضبًا   متّقدا فى حَشايَ ملتهبا
وحلّ روح الاصرارفىّ لكى   يبيدنى بالدمار منقلَبا

امّا روح الاصرار فلا يبحث عنه فى كتب الحكمة ولا يعدّه الحكماء بين الحركات لقلوب الناس لكننى متيقّن كما ان روحى حية وابدية

lives, than I am that perverseness is one of the primitive impulses of the human heart—one of the indivisible primary faculties or sentiments which give direction to the character of man. Who has not, a hundred times, found himself committing a vile or silly action, for no other reason than because he knows he should *not?* Have we not a perpetual inclination, in the teeth of our best judgment, to violate that which is *law*, merely because we understand it to be such? This spirit of perverseness, I say, came to my final overthrow. It was this unfathomable longing of the soul *to vex itself*—to offer violence to its own nature—to do wrong for the wrong's sake only—that urged me to continue and finally to consummate the injury I had inflicted upon the unoffending brute. One

---

ان الاصرار هو من الخصال الغريزية بالملكة فى اصل الفطرة واحد القوى البسيطة الحاكمة طبع الانسان

مَن ذا الذى ما ساءَ قطّ   ومَن له الحسنى فقَطْ
كم فِعلَةٍ سيّئَةٍ   ورّطنا فيها الغلَطْ

افلا نميل الى مخالفة امر الشريعة على زعم عقلنا حال كوننا متيقنين اوامر الشرع فاقول ان رُوح الاصرار هذه قد حلت فىّ لهلاكى والبوار التام ونزعت نفسى نزوعا غير متناهٍ لتعذيب ذاتها واضطهاد طبعها واغرانى الاستمرار على ما تصدّيت اليه باتمام اغرارى وايذآئى للحيوانة البريئة

morning, in cool blood, I slipped a noose about its neck and hung it to the limb of a tree; hung it with the tears streaming from my eyes, and with the bitterest remorse at my heart; hung it *because* I knew that it had loved me, and *because* I felt that it had given me no reason of offence; hung it *because* I knew that in so doing I was committing a sin—a deadly sin that would so jeopardise my immortal soul as to place it—if such a thing were possible—even beyond the reach of the infinite mercy of the Most Merciful and Most Terrible God.

On the night of the day on which this cruel deed was done, I was aroused from sleep by the cry of fire. The curtains of my bed were in flames. The whole house was blazing. It was with great difficulty that my wife, a servant, and myself, made our escape from the conflagration.

فاصبحت فى احد الايام والقيت فى عنق الغط حبلا وشددت عليه الوثاق وعلقته مربوطا على غصن شجرة فاختنق خنقته وعيناى تفيض دموعا ومرارة الندامة فى قلبى خنقته لعلمى انه كان يحبنى فيما سلف ولاننى اعرف انه لم يسئ الى ابداً خنقته لاننى علمت انى مرتكب بذلك سيئة سوف تهلك روحى الابدية وتجعلنى لو امكن محروما من موفور رحمة الله الرحيم المهيب

وفى الليهة التالية بعد هذا الفعل القبيح ارّقنى صوتُ صاحٍ "النارَ النارَ" فنظرت واذا استار سريرى تلتهب والدار كلها تتأجّج ضرامًا وكدتُ انا وامراتى وجاريتى لا نجد النجاة من اللّهب

The destruction was complete. My entire worldly wealth was swallowed up, and I resigned myself thenceforward to despair.

I am above the weakness of seeking to establish a sequence of cause and effect between the disaster and the atrocity. But I am detailing a chain of facts, and wish not to leave even a possible link imperfect. On the day succeeding the fire, I visited the ruins. The walls, with one exception, had fallen in. This exception was found in a compartment wall, not very thick, which stood about the middle of the house, and against which had rested the head of my bed. The plastering had here, in great measure, resisted the action of the fire—a fact which I attributed to its having been recently spread.

جـآء البوارُ وادركتنى هلكةٌ   لم تُبقِ لى فى الارض شيئا يُملَكُ
اسلمتُ مذ يومئذ نفسى الى   يأس مبيدٍ بُتُّ فيهِ أُضْنَكُ

وما انا بأفينٍ حتى اخال الجرم علةً للحادث كأن بينهما اشتراك السبب بالمسبَّب لكننى اشرح ههنا كل ما قد جرى لى على التتابع ولا اغادر من ذلك شيئا مّا البتة

فلما اضوانى النهار طفقت اطوّف الخرآئب فرأيت الحيطان متهدّمة الّا جدارا لم يبرح قآئما وقد كان غير غليظ وموقعه وسط الدار وكان مستنداً اليه سريرى جهة راس مضجعى والجير هنالك قد كان يدفع تاثير النار لكونه على ما اخال مطلياً جديدا

About this wall a dense crowd were collected, and many persons seemed to be examining a particular portion of it with very minute and eager attention. The words "strange!" "singular!" and other similar expressions, excited my curiosity. I approached and saw, as if graven in *bas relief* upon the white surface, the figure of a gigantic *cat*. The impression was given with an accuracy truly marvellous. There was a rope about the animal's neck.

When I first beheld this apparition—for I could scarcely regard it as less—my wonder and my terror were extreme. But at length reflection came to my aid. The cat, I remembered, had been hung in a garden adja-

---

واجتمع حول هذا الحائط جماعة كثيرون يتاملون جزءاً منه بكمال الفحص والتدقيق فحثّنى استغرابهم وصراخهم "ياللعجب" وما اشبه ذلك الى الاطلاع على امرهم فلما دنوت منهم اذا بصورة كانها صورة قط ضخم مطبوعة فى صفحة الحائط البيضاء وكانت صورة مدهشة باستكمال الهيئة وفى عنق القط حبل مبين فلما رأيت هذا المنظر الهائل واستيقنت انه منقوش بيد عفريت فما كدت املك نفسى لفرط ما اعترانى من العجب وما نزل بى من الرهب

ثم اقبلت علىّ هواجس الافكار فى تأويل هذا السر الخفىّ فخطر لبالى ان القط مشنوق فى جُنَيْنة متّصلة بالدار ولما تصايح

cent to the house. Upon the alarm of fire, this garden had been immediately filled by the crowd, by some one of whom the animal must have been cut from the tree and thrown through an open window into my chamber. This had probably been done with the view of arousing me from sleep. The falling of other walls had compressed the victim of my cruelty into the substance of the freshly-spread plaster.

الناس بالنار امتلئت الجنينة بالخلق ازدحامًا فلا بدّ ان يكون احد
الناس قطع الحبل وانزل الحيوان من فوق الشجره فرمى به فى
شباك الحجرة المفتوح وذلك ليوقظنى من الكرى ولما وقعت الحيطان
لفّت قتيلى فنقشت صورته فى الجبس الطرىّ

FORMS OF ADDRESS, &c.

A person is seldom addressed directly unless he be an inferior or a very intimate friend, in which case the second person singular may be used. In speaking to equals or superiors some periphrasis such as "your excellency," or "your highness," must be employed with the second person singular or plural, according to the rank of the person addressed or the degree of familiarity between him and the speaker. Of these the most common are—

جَنَاب } presence.
حَضْرَة }

سِيَادَة lordship.

سعادة happiness (used only to a Prince or a Patriarch).

e.g. كَيْفَ حَال جَنَابَك how are you?

كَيْفَ حَال حَضْرَة ٱلسِتّ how is the lady (your wife)?

The following are some of the most common formulæ in conversation :—

ٱلسَّلَام عَلَيْك peace be on you.*

Answer.—وَعَلَيْك ٱلسَّلَام وَرَحْمَة ٱللّٰه وَبَرَكَاتُهُ and on you be peace and the mercy and blessings of God.

صَبَاح ٱلْخَيْر good morning.

Ans.—ٱللّٰه يُصَبِّحكم بِٱلْخَيْر God make your morning good!

مساء ٱلخير good evening.

Ans.—ٱللّٰه يُمَسِّيكُمْ بِٱلْخَيْر God make your evening good.

لَيْلَتَك سَعِيدَة good night.

Ans.—أَسْعَد ٱللّٰه لَيْلَتَك God make your night happy.

---

* This is only to be used by and to Muslims.

أَيْش حَالك } how do you do?
or كَيْف حالك }

Ans.—اَلحَمْدُ لله praise to God (*i.e.* I am well, thank you).

In Egypt زَيَّك or أزَيَّك is most commonly used for How are you? and in Aleppo they say—

اش لَوْم كيفيتك *ish-laum kéfíyetek,* what is the state (colour) of your condition?

Thanks are never given direct to an individual, but one must say—

كَتَّر خَيْرَك may (God) increase your goodness.

شكَّر الله فَضْلَك may God thank your kindness.

الله يِدِيم وُجُودَك God preserve you—or the like.

So, too, when any good wish or blessing occurs in any of the customary formulæ, the answer must be a prayer for the same blessing on the speaker, *e.g.*:

حَلَّت البَرَكَه بِقُدُومك I am glad to see you (*lit.* blessing has descended at your approach).

Ans.—ألله يُبَارِك فِيْك God bless you!

خاطرك good-bye! (*lit.* your mind.)

Ans.—الله يُسَلِّم خاطرك God save your mind.

سَلِّم على اخوك give my compliments (salaam) to your brother.

ألله يُسَلِّمك God salute you or keep you in peace.

No expression of direct admiration must be used; to do so is considered very unlucky, and it is customary to say when a thing pleases you—

ما شاء الله (it is) as God pleases!

or سُبْحَان اللّٰه Glory be to God!

If anything unpleasant or impolite must be mentioned, the speaker prefaces it with the remark اجلّك الله "God keep you clear of such a thing," or بعيد مِن السّامعِين "May it be remote from my hearers!"

أهْلاً وَ سْهلاً
مرحبا
مرحبا بك } welcome.

هنيًّا your health—said to a person who is about to eat or drink.

Ans.—الله يهنّيك

نَعيمًا in comfort!—said to one about to be shaved.

A future intention or a hope must be accompanied with the formula ان شاء الله "if God please."

ان شاء اللّٰه أروح بُكْرَه please God, I will go to-morrow.

مَا شَىْ شَرّ انْ شَاء الله (to a sick person) there is no harm, please God.

كُلّ عَام وَأنْت سَالم a happy new year to you! (*lit.* every year and you happy).

شرّفتنا I am glad you called (you do me honour).

Ans.—انا المشرّف it is I who am honoured.

مع السلامة good-bye!

Ans.—اَللّه يُسَلّم خاطرك God save you.

فِي امَانِ اللّه good-bye!

آنَسْتَنَا I am glad to see you (you have made us comfortable with your society).

Ans.—اَللّه يُوَانسك God comfort you with society.

أَوحَشْتَنَا we have not seen you for some time (you have made us lonely).

Ans.—الله لا يُوحِش فيك may God make no loneliness in your case.

أَعُوذُ بالله I seek refuge in God (when any calamity is mentioned).

Mohammedans say when in sudden danger or trouble—

لَا حَولَ وَلَا قُوَّةَ اِلَّا بِٱللّه ٱلعَلِيّ ٱلْعَظِيم there is no power or strength save in God the exalted and mighty!

and, when death seems imminent—

اِنَّا لِلّه وَاِنَّا اِلَيْهِ لَرَاجِعُون verily we belong to God, and unto him shall we return.

On beginning anything, they say—

بِسم ٱللّه in the name of God.

Thus, in Egypt and elsewhere, if a person knocks at a door, the occupant of the room calls out—

سَمّى "name," that is, "say بسم الله and enter."

When deprecating any course of action—for instance, on being asked not to divulge a secret—they say—

أَسْتَغْفِرُ ٱللّٰه I ask pardon of God!

When a person sneezes عند العطاس it is usual to say—

يَرْحَمُكُم ٱللّٰه God have mercy upon you!

but, as this suggests the formula for a deceased person, the person addressed averts the omen by saying—

رَحِمَ ٱللّٰهُ أَمْوَاتَكُم God have mercy on your dead ones!

or simply says—

آجَرَكُم ٱللّٰه God reward you.

A deceased person is spoken of as ٱلْمَرْحُوم "the late," *lit.* "on whom God has had mercy."

There are several formulæ of condolence, but to say ٱللّٰه يُعَوِّض عَلَيْك "God give you a substitute," is the most usual.

A beggar is met with a pious and courteous reply, such as—

ٱللّٰه يرزقك God provide for you!

ٱللّٰه يَفْتَح عَلَيْك God find an opening for you!

and if he exhibits some deformity as an appeal *ad misericordiam*, you say—

مكتوب "it is written," that is, "fated."

TRANSLITERATION AND NOTES.

As the reading exercises and translations in colloquial Arabic are not easy to read, I add a transliteration of them for the benefit of beginners, with an explanation of the difficult constructions and idioms. The student is recommended to practice reading the extracts in the native character, making use of this part only as a help or key.

p. 131.

Muḥáwarah bain Abí Khalíl wa Abí Naḍhḍhárah Zerḳá ‘ala Ḳahwat Rísh fí “Búlefár dezítalíyán” fí lailat arba‘t ‘ashar Lúliyú senneh 78 fí Paríz.

Abu Khalíl:

Yá Chéms [1] yá Bu Naḍhḍhárah
Ánast [2] Páríz yá sháṭir
Ma‘aksh [3] min Maṣr [4] ‘ibárah
Tun‘ish b’há minní ’l kháṭir

---

[1] James. [2] 4th of انس “to be social.” [3] مع “with,” ك “thee,” ش used as an interrogative, see p. 127.
[4] Properly Miṣr.

p. 132.

Abu Naḍhḍhárah :

In rudt[1] aḥkílak aḥkí
'An Maṣr yá báhi 'ṭṭala'
Ba'd al ferḥ 'ádat tabkí
Min nár ḥawádithhá 'l wula'.

Maṣr es sa'ídeh el maḥmíyeh[2]
Bi'l'izz kánat ferḥáneh
Wa'l yóm t'shúfhá maḥmíyeh[2]
Min dhill ḥálha za'láneh.

Fí Maṣr má físh ḥurríyeh
Wadh dhulm khalláha duḳḳah
Wa in rudt tadri 'l kaifíyeh
Unzur binaḍhḍhártí 'zzerḳah.

Fí Maṣr jaur Sheikh el Ḥárah
Dháhir kama 'shshams el wáḍhihah
Amar bi ḳufl en Naḍhḍhárah
Akmanhá lihálo fáḍhihah.

---

[1] For *aradtu*, from اراد. [2] The verb حمى means both "to protect" and "to be angry with." It is used here in both senses.

---

p. 133.

Safart min Maṣr el Ḳáhirah[1]
Wa bulbulí fíha sá-iḥ

---

[1] Miṣr el Ḳáhirah, "Egypt the Victorious," the name of which "Cairo" is a corruption.

Wa masak nadhdhártí 'l báhirah
  Minhá li-Páríz sár fá-iḥ.

In 'isht arja' bit-táni[2]
  Li Maṣr w' unzur aḥbábí
Wa in bitt tabḳí ikhwání[3]
  Yet'raḥḥemu ma' aṣ-ḥábi.

Abu Khalíl.—Búsa 'ala dól ya Bú Naḍhḍhárah búsa! akh! wallah! waḥḥashní k'lámek, yá Sheikh! Alḥamdu lillah bi'sselámeh! yá n'hár embárek[4] biwusúlek! ante ghibt kéde li-aiy? Ana safart min Maṣr, yóm-ma safart ante, innamá bád eḍh-ḍhohr,[5] wa khalleitak fi Iskanderíyeh t'shimm nafsak wa tashṭaḥ wa ta-ánas[6] shebbán medínat Zi 'l ḳarnain ellí[7] 'ala ma balaghní biḥabbúka[8] zaiy 'ainaihum; wa ana ḥaṭṭeit kitf, ya wuleid! wa rakébt bábúr (vapore) el Brindizí ellí

---

[2] For ثانياً or ثانى مرّة. [3] Pl. of اخ. [4] For *mubárak*. [5] الضهر vulgar for الظهر. [6] 6th conj. of انس. [7] For *elladhí*. [8] See p. 119.

---

p. 134.

yaḳúlu 'alaih wa ji't héne[1] asra' min al barḳ wa áhú ṣár lí fi intizárak yejí ziyádeh min jim'atain; ante ka'adt[2] kem yóm fí Iskanderíyeh, we kem yóm fí Málṭah, we kem yóm, fí Mársíliya? Billahi! taḥkí lí bit-taṭwíl wa tut-ḥifní binawádirak dá; ana má aslásh aḳwálak ezzarífeh!

---

[1] For *huna*. [2] قعد "to remain," *lit.* "to sit."

Wa á dí sebeb irtiḥálí min waṭaní 'lázíz wa ḥuḍhúrí li hádha 'ṭṭaraf. Yellah! baḳá ummáli[3] hát min 'andak hát! wa raṭṭib mesámi' ṣadíḳak Abu Khalíl!

Abu Naḍhḍhárah.—'Ala 'l 'ain wa'rrás! ya, seiyid en nás! iza ma ḥakeitsh nawádirí lak, rá-iḥ aḥkíha limín[4] aḥsan minnak? wallah anna 'l ḳulúb

[3] See p. 127. [4] For *liman* لمن.

---

p. 135.

'and ba'ḍhhá, wa "min al ḳalb ila 'l ḳalb rasúl." Innamá ante ṭala't afras minní; wa ṣadaḳ man ḳál "'allamto 'ala 'shshaḥaṭah, sabaḳní 'ala 'l bíbán," likaunak[1] safart min ba'dí wa waṣalt ḳablí. Wa 'amalt aiy, yá ḳurrat 'ainí, fi'lkem yóm elli ante héne?

Abu Khalíl.—Lá shughl wa lá mushghila; baṣbaṣa ṣanaf 'ain! Díh, ya Sheikh! el insán héne fí Páríz, lá budd an yakún taḳí.

Abu Naḍhḍhárah.—Billahi 'alaik, t'fassir[2]! takí izzai wa húwa fi b'lád el kufr?

Abu Khalíl.—Aḥlam! baḳa shúf, ya sídí! al wáḥid minna fi'l beled el 'azíma dih yafḍhal yazkur ṭúl an nihár, li-an iza altafat[3] yamín au shemál ma ḳaddámo illa wushúsh[4] ḥalwah zaiy ṭabak al ward, wa 'uyún yas-harú, wa 'shshu'úr iyyáhá

[1] "for your being," *i.e.* "because." [2] 2nd conj. 2nd pers. sing. imper. from فسر. [3] 8th of لفت. [4] Pl. of وِش vulgar for وَجْه "a face."

p. 136.

ellí yanzilú ‘ala ’l kitáf al marmar zaiy sebábek ed-deheb, wa’l ma‘áṣim iyyáha laun el fuḍhḍhah, [1] wa ’l kitáf el muladhla[illegible]a; fa-izan [2] yeltazem yaṣíḥ wa yaḳúl “Alláh, Alláh!” wa yafḍhal yazkur kéde ṭúl má húwa máshí! Walláhi, ya sheikh! an aghlab ḥúriyát el jenneh lá budd annahum wárid Páríz! Á hú, shúf dí ellí ḳá‘ideh jambaná; Alláh, ya sídí, Alláh! á hí dí bukra, lemma tushriḳ esh-shems malák min meláïk es-semá yadhrib ‘ainoh, wa yashúf ṣaḥibetná, wa ḥálan yakhṭifhá, wa doghrí [4] yuḍhífhá [5] ‘ala ’lḥarím al ‘álí!

Abu Naḍhḍhárah.—Belá kufr, ya sheikh! ma tet’jen-nensh, wa-illa, walláhi! ektub li-jamá‘atak.

Abu Khalíl.—Lá, ya wuleid! ma taduḳḳhásh! Ana subt ed dinyá ala shán [5] kháṭirak.

Abu Naḍhḍhárah.—Jazák Alláh khair!

Abu Khalíl.—Taiyib! aḥna yarja‘ marjú‘na

---

[1] For *fidhdhah*. [2] And then. [3] 2nd sing. fem. aor. of 4th conj. of هرق. [4] “direct,” from the Turkish طوغرو. [5] 3rd sing. masc. aor. of 4th ضاف. [5] “for the sake of.”

---

p. 137.

li raḥlatak. Al khawájah Yúsuf Ramleh keteb lí min Iskanderíyeh annak safart fí awwal yóm min ash-shahr díh, fí bábúr (vapore) min kumpaníyet Ferísínah ‘ala ṭaríḳ Málṭa; baḳá, aḥkí lí bittafṣíl kull ellí jará lak min yóm-má kharajt min Iskanderíyeh ila ’l leilah díh.

Abu Naḍhḍhárah.—Bi 'l bakht al bábúr má kánsh fíh rakkáb k'tír,[1] wa 'l ḳapṭán kán min ikhwatná[2]; fa-awwal ma sallam 'alaiya wa rusí 'ala 'l kaifíyeh, hálan waṣṣá 'alaiya 'l *garçon* wa 'ssufrají wa jamí' el mustakhdimín wa ḳaddamni ila 'ssittát b'tú'[3] awwal wa tání darajah, wa ḳál lahum " á dí Abu Naḍhḍhárah ellí fattaḥ 'uyyún al 'álam wa-aḍhhar li 'l kháṣṣ wa 'l 'ámm jaur u dhulm al ḥukkám, wa aiḳaz el felláḥ min ghuflatoh, wa 'arrafho biḥuḳúḳoh wa kúwwatoh.

Abu Khalíl.—Má shá'alláh! wa ante

[1] For *kathír*. [2] Pl. of أخ. [3] Pl. of *'btá'*, see p. 123.

---

p. 138.

ma saddaḳt lemma wajedt nafsak bain el maḍhamát. Haḳḳan, anta, ya Abu Naḍhḍhárah! mubkhit[1] fi 'l umúr díh.

Abu Naḍhḍhárah.—Lillahi 'l ḥamd! innamá 'l imbisáṭ elli embasṭuh fí awwal yómain essafr tala' min 'uyúní fí ákhir yóm wa ákhir laileh!

Abu Khalíl.—Li-aiy? jará aiy? lá samaḥ Alláh!

Abu Naḍhḍhárah.—Uskut! Dá, yá sheikh ana kullamá eftekir, sha'rí yaḳubb wa jisdí yanmall!

Abu Khalíl.—La budd an ḳámat 'alaikum fortúna wa 'l baḥr háj wa taláṭamat el amwáj, wa sár al bábúr yaghṭus wa yaḳubb, wa ḳalb ar rakkáb yarjiff wa yaṭabb.

[1] Agent from أبخت from بخت " fortune."

Abu Naḍhḍhárah.—Tamám! walláhi! elli b'yesma'ak túṣef el waṣfah dí, l'yakúl[2] alaik kunt háḍhirhá! dá ana kunt náïm fi ghurr nómí, wa asma' lak ṣarí<u>kh</u> wa ṣaiyáḥ wa tawalwíl

---

[2] "Would certainly say."

---

p. 139.

wa miyáh tashurr fi 'l maḳ'ad; fa naṭṭait min <u>kh</u>aznatí al mu'allaḳah[1] wa kánat al maiyah lirrukab faḳult lá shakk wa lá reib an Shei<u>kh</u> el Ḥárah aḥḍhar amhar al munajjimîn wa khalláhum yusalliṭú 'alainá 'afárít al baḥr ḥatta anna 'l bábúr yankasir, wa Abu Naḍhḍhárah yarúḥ <u>kh</u>ara samak.[2]

Abu Khalíl.—Innamá rabbuná najják likaun warák afḍhal masháï<u>kh</u> barr[3] Maṣr yad'ú lak bil-<u>kh</u>air.

Abu Naḍhḍhárah.—Rabbuná yaḥfuzhum, wa yaḳbul da'áhum, wa yarfa' 'an 'unḳ abná' Maṣr[4] al jaur wa 'zzulm, wa yan'am 'alaihim biman yaḥkum bi 'l 'adálat wa'l ḥilm! Lianna yaḳínan azzulm fí bládna ḥaṣṣal liá<u>kh</u>ir darajeh. In t'shúf al 'álam hene fí Fransá mabsúṭín wa masrúrín wa rubḥánín; wa dá kulloh min aiy?

---

[1] "I jumped from my bunk." By a misreading of the lithographed original, this sentence was mistranslated, and by an oversight left uncorrected in the text until the sheet was printed off. [2] *Lit.* stercor piscium. [3] The land of Egypt. [4] The sons of Egypt.

p. 140.

Abu Khalíl.—Min el Ḥurríyeh! Hú izá kán [1] ellí b'yaḥaṣṣal 'andná kán b'yaḥaṣṣal hene kánú biyuskitú 'l'álam dól! Dól yá má f'nú mulúk!

Abu Naḍhḍhárah.—Alwaḳt ráïḥ, ya Bú Khalíl? wa ana — al k'lám fi sirrak—jí'án. Bád ma na'kul aḥkí lak baḳíyat er raḥlah.

---

[1] *izá kán*=" if."

---

p. 141.

Ma'ḳúlu man námat 'uyúno
Yaḥsib el 'áshiḳ yanám
Walláh ana mughram ṣebábeh [1]
Lam 'ala 'l 'áshik malám
    Dús [2] yá lellí, dús yá lellí,
    'Ishḳe maḥbúbi fettaní!

Yá sheikh el 'Arab! ya Seiyid!
Tejma'ní 'al [3] khilli leileh!
W' in já'ní ḥabíbe ḳalbí
L' 'amal loh 'l Kashmír duleileh! [4]
    Dús yá lellí, dús yá lellí,
    'Ishḳe maḥbúbi fettaní!

---

[1] Excited by passion. [2] يدوس داس " to tread." [3] For على الخل 'ala 'l khilli, " to the friend." [4] " pay " or " brokerage."

Kámil el auṣáf fettaní
We 'l 'uyún es súd ramúní
Min hawáhum ṣirt ughanní [5]
Wa 'l hawá [6] zawwad j'núní [7]
    Dús yá lellí, dús yá lellí,
    'Ishḳe maḥbúbí fettaní!

---

[5] I began to sing. [6] hawá means both "love" and "air." [7] Increased my madness.

---

p. 142.

Jama'um [1] jam' al 'awázil [2]
'An ḥabíbí yamna'úní;
Wallah, ana ma afút [3] hawahum
Biss'yúf lau ḳaṭṭa'úní!
    Dús yá lellí, dús yá lellí,
    'Ishḳe maḥbúbí fettení!

Ḳum b'ná ya khillí nasker
Taḥta ẓill alyásmíneh
Naḳṭuf al-khókh [4] min 'ala ummoh [5]
Wa 'l 'awázil gháfilína!
    Dús yá lellí, dús yá lellí,
    'Ishḳe maḥbúbí fettení!

---

[1] For *jama'ú*. [2] Pl. of *'ázil*, "one who reproves." [3] يفوت فات "to pass away from," "leave." [4] Peach. [5] *lit.* from off its mother, *i.e.* native branch.

Ya b'nát júw'[6] el Medínah
'Andakum ashyá themíneh
Telbisú 'shsháṭiḥ[7] bilúleh[8]
Wa 'l ḳ'ládeh[9] 'ala 'nnahd zíneh
Dús yá lellí, dús yá lellí,
'Ishḳe maḥbúbí fettení!

Ya b'nát Iskenderíyeh
Mashykum ala 'l furshi jíyeh
Telbisú 'l Kashmír biṭalí[10]
Wa 'shshefáïf[11] sukkaríyeh
Dús yá lellí, dús yá lellí,
'Ishḳe maḥbúbí fettení.

Ya meláh k͟háfú min Alláh
Wa 'rḥamú 'l 'áshiḳ lillah[12]!
Ḥubbukum maktúb min Alláh
Ḳaddarú[13] 'l maulá 'alaiya.
Dús yá lellí, dús yá lellí,
'Ishḳe maḥbúbí fettení.

---

[6] "inside." [7] Properly شاطح "a band or necklace of coins." [8] With pearls. [9] A necklace. [10] With gold embroidery or fringe. [11] Lips. [12] For God's sake! [13] For ḳaddarahu, "He has decreed it."

p. 163.

Translation of the Ballad from "Alice in Wonderland."

The previous extracts are in the colloquial style, as *spoken* by the modern Arab-speaking peoples; in the present and following translations the style I have employed is that in use for literary composition.

They are intended to show how purely English ideas and expressions may be rendered into Arabic equivalents; and I have chosen them, especially Poe's "Black Cat," because of the very idiomatic English they contain, which makes the contrast between the two languages stronger.

1.

Ráḥa Zeidun ṭá'inan fí sinnihi [1]
Wa 'mbará [2] 'Amrun yunájíhí futaiy [3]
Ḳála, Sheikh el Ḥárat al himmu [4] 'lladhí
Sháhida 'shshaibu 'alaihi bi'l funaiy [5]
Ma 'ḥtiyálí fíka [6] maḳlúban 'alá
Ra'sika 'l mankúbi nikthan liththuraiy [7]
A-fa-sheikhun shá-ibun mithluka yar-
-ḍhá bi-amrin [8] mithli dhá jarra 'lkhuzaiy? [9]

---

[1] "Far advanced in years." [2] began. [3] dimin. of *fatan*, "a youth." [4] *himm*, "a decrepit old man." [5] "to whose decay his hoary locks bear witness," *funaiy* dim. of *faná*, "decay." [6] "What am I to do with you?" *lit.* "What is my device concerning you?" [7] dim. of *thará*, "the ground." [8] "be content (to do) a thing." [9] "(which) brings (*lit.* drags on) disgrace," dim. of *khazy*.

Ḳála ya ’bní, ‘ádatun marra shebá-
-bí bihá ḳad baḳiyat mundhu ’ṣṣubaiy [10]
Baida anní kuntu ḳablan kháïfan
Min fasádin fí dimághí au ḍhunaiy [11]
Ṭibtu nafsan [12] ‘árifan má in ḥawá [13]
Ḳaḥfu ra’sí min dimághin ḳaṭṭu shai.

---

[10] "a habit in which my youth has passed has endured since my childhood," *ṣubaiy*, dim. of *ṣaby*. [11] "sickness." [12] "I became easy in mind." [13] *má in ḥawá*="it did not contain"; *má in* is a strong form of negative.

2.

Ḳála ‘Amrun wa ’nthaná [1] ya‘ẓiluhu [2]
Anta sheikhun sháïbun haiyu ’bnu baiy
Mithlumá ḳad marra ḳaulí sábiḳan [3]
Badanun ka ’lbudni manfúkhu ’l ḥushaiy [4]
A-buweibun ṭáfiran tadkhuluhú
Laisa kahlun fí nisháṭin ka-ṣubaiy [5]
Ḳála ḳad alfaitu,[6] ya ’bní, ḥílatan [7]

---

[1] "and turned," 7th of ثنى. [2] to reproach him. [3] previously. [4] "a body like a bulky camel with puffed out belly," *ḥushaiy*, dim. of *ḥashá*. [5] "An adult is not like a boy (*ṣubaiy*, dim. of *ṣabíy*) in nimbleness." [6] "I have found." [7] "a device."

Tun'ishu [8] 'ljisma muzídan fi 'l ḳuwaiy
Khudh ḥubúbí dhí wa a'tí dirheman
Fahya lilḳúwati min ajda 'dduwaiy.[9]

---

[8] 3rd fem. sing. aor. of 4th conj. of نعش, "raising or recuperating the strength of the body"; *kuwaiy*, dim. of *kuwá*, pl. of *kúwatun*. [9] "The best of medicine," *duwaiy*, dim. of *dawá*.

3.

p. 164.

Ḳála 'Amrun ya kabíra 'ssinni [1] lá
Sinna [2] fí fíhi [3] tabaḳḳá min thunaiy [4]
G͟haira shaḥmi 'l kirshi la tamg͟huḍhuhú [5]
Man ra-á 'ṭṭaḥḥána min g͟hairi 'rruḥaiy [6]
Tabla'u 'lwazzata ma' minḳáriḥá
Wa 'l'id͟háma 'ṣṣammi minhá ka 'l'uṣaiy [7]
Lam uḥiṭ [8] 'ilman bihádha fa-abin [9]
Lí jalíya 'l-amri [10] min ghairi muraiy [11]

---

[1] *sinni*, "years." [2] *sinna*, "a tooth." [3] *fíhi*, "his mouth," from فم, see p. 54. [4] dim. of *thaniyatun*, "gums." [5] "Except the fat of the paunch you cannot chew (it)." [6] "Who has (ever) seen a miller without a mill-stone." *ruḥaiy*, dim. of *raḥá*. [7] "and the bones of it as hard as walking-sticks." [8] 3rd sing. masc. aorist, 4th conj. from حاط, apocopated after the negative *lam*. *lam uḥiṭ 'ilman bi* . . . "I comprehend not by (my) knowledge." [9] "so explain," imper. 2nd conj. of بان. [10] *jalíy al 'l-amri*=*al-amri 'l jalíyi*, "the important affair." [11] *muraiy*, dim. of *mary*, "strife and doubt."

Ḳála mudh kuntu ṣabíyan ḳad tafaḳ-
-ḳahtu [12] hatta ṣirtu aḳḍhá min ḳuḍhaiy [13]
Wa'ḥtijájí [14] kulluhu ma' zaujatí
Ḥínamá [15] tashabbaha [16] 'lfatya [17] 'alaiy
Nashsha-at [18] bí ḳúwata 'lbal'i [19] min al-
-hirfi bit-taḥríki fíhi ḥanakaiy.[20]

---

[12] "I have studied law" (*fiḳh*). [13] "till I became more of a cádhí than a cádhí is." Comparative أَقْضَى and dim. قُضَيّ of قاضٍ (for قَاضِيٌ, see p. 36), "a ḳáḍhí," which is the agent of قَضَى "to judge." [14] 8th conj. of حج "to argue," حجة *ḥujjatun*, "an argument." [15] Whenever, *ḥína* + *má*. [16] "was doubtful," 5th of (شبه) شُبْهَة, "doubt." [17] "the judicial sentence." [18] "caused to grow," 2nd of *nasha'a*. [19] The faculty of swallowing. [20] "my two jaws."

4.

'Áda [1] 'Amrun ḳála wuḳḳíta 'rradá [2]
Bi'sa shaibun yúrithu 'nnása 'l'umaiy [3]
Aiyuha 'shsháïbu inna ḳad 'ahid-
-ná 'alá [4] 'ainaika ḳad ghasha 'l'ushaiy [5]

---

[1] "He repeated." [2] "May you be guarded from evil," 2nd sing. preterite (used precatively) masc. passive of وقى. [3] *Lit.* Evil is old age which makes men inherit dimness of sight (*yúrith*, 3rd sing. masc. aor. 4th of ورث "to inherit;" '*umaiy*, dim. of '*umyun*, blindness). [4] '*ahidná 'alá*, "we have been accustomed to." [5] "purblindness has covered them."

Tansubu 'l-uf'á 'ala 'l márini[6] min
Aina wujdánuka lil'aini 'ḍhḍhuwaiy[7]
Yaduka 'lbaiḍhá'u ḥasbí mu'jizan[8]
Hal li Músa mithlu hádhí min 'uṣaiy
Há theláthun min suwálátin maḍhat[9]
La tazidní ba'du[10] min ḥaiyin wa laiy;
Malla sam'í[11] a nahárí kullahu
Asma'a 'lhadhyá[12] bi-iṣghäïn[13] li-ghaiy[14]
'Ihi 'anni[15] wa 'nhadhir[16] min derajin
Háka min rijlíya ta'jílan lidhaiy.[17]

---

[6] "you set up a snake on the tip-of-the-nose." [7] "where did you find (*lit.* is your finding) (this) light for the eyes," *ḍhuwaiy*, dim. of *ḍhaw*, "light." [8] These two lines are inserted: "Thy white hand is enough miracle for me (suffices me as a miracle)! had Moses a little rod like this?" see note, p. 164. [9] 3rd sing. fem. pret. of مضى "to pass away." [10] "Do not give me any more nonsense," *lit.* "do not increase me after of . . . ." [11] "my hearing is wearied." [12] "trifling." [13] Giving an attentive ear to. [14] "error," perverseness. [15] An idiomatic expression, "get thee gone from me!" [16] "descend," imp. of 7th conj. of حدر . [17] "here is my foot to hasten that," *dhaiy*, dim. of ذا "that."

p. 165.

Al Hirratu 'ssaudá' wa 'Arabdatu[1] saffáki 'damá'.[2]

(In reading the prose portion of this translation the rules given on pp. 6, 7, for the omission of the final vowels in pause must be observed.)

Lí ḳissatun[3] 'ajabun sa-ukhbirukum[4] bihá
Li-gharíbi má tajrí bihi 'l-aḥwálú[5]
Lau aḳtaḍhí[6] min sámi'in taṣdíḳahá[7]
Laghadautu[8] mimman ya'taríhi[9] khabálú
Idh kuntu ukzibu[10] ma tará[11] 'ainaiya au
Sami'at bihí udhní[12] wa dháka maḥálú.[13]

---

[1] "drunken frenzy." [2] A shedder of blood.
[3] The metre of these lines is *kámil*:

⏑ ⏑ –́ ⏑ –   ⏑ ⏑ –́ ⏑ –   ⏑ ⏑ –́ ⏑ –́

⏑ ⏑ –́ ⏑ –   ⏑ ⏑ –́ ⏑ –   ⏑ ⏑ –́ –́

The foot ⏑ ⏑ –́ ⏑ –́ may become – –́ ⏑ –́

[4] 1st. sing. aor. 4th of خبر with sign of future س prefixed. [5] Because of (*li*) the strange thing with which (*ma*) circumstances happen (from جرى) to me! [6] 1st pers. aor. from 8th of قضى "I require." [7] "the believing it," verbal noun of 2nd conj. of صدق. [8] "I should be in the morning," *i.e.* "I should become." [9] Attacks him, 8th of عرى. [10] 1st. sing. aor. 4th of كذب "if I should belie." [11] 3rd sing. fem. aor. راى "to see." [12] "my ear." [13] *wadháka maḥálu*, "then that were impossible."

Wa lastu bimajnúnin[14] wa lá náïman[15] ará[16] aḍh-g͟hátha 'l-aḥlámi.[17] Lákinnaní fattákun[18] ḳad daná minníy[19] al-ajalu[20] wa arḳubu[21] 'lmauta fi 'lg͟haddi[22] fa urídu an aḍha'a[23] 'lyóma waḳrí[24] 'lladhí anḳaḍha[25] d͟hahrí, mu'tarifan[26] bikabíri dhambí,[27] wa lá awaddu[28] illa an ubaiyina[29] má jará 'alaiya min al-umúri, g͟haira muḍhífin[30] 'alá dhálika kelimatam-má,[31] tafsíran aw i'tidháran fa-innahá mina 'lmuwáddi[32] 'lmuhwilati[33] 'lmuk͟hifati[34] líy, almu'adhdhibati[35] liḳalbíy aljálibati 'ala[36] 'l-idmári.[37]

---

[14] *lastu bi* . . . . "I am not," fr. لَيْسَ "not to be," *majnún*, "mad" (possessed by a *jinn* or "demon"). [15] Agent of نام ينام "to sleep." [16] 1st sing. aor. of رأى "to see." [17] "jumbles of dreams." [18] "a murderer." [19] *daná minní*, "has drawn nigh to me." [20] "doom." [21] I watch. [22] To-morrow. [23] 1st sing. aor. of وضع "to put off." [24] "my burden." [25] "weighed down," 4th of نقض . [26] Confessing, 8th of عرف , the verb requires the preposition ب with the following noun. [27] *bi-dhambíy alkabíri*, "my great sin." [28] ودّ "to be fain." [29] 1st sing. masc. aor. 2nd conj. of بان يبين . [30] أضاف 4th conj. "to add." [31] See p. 71. [32] pl. of مادّة "matter." [33] "terrible," fem. agent 4th conj. هال يهول . [34] "causing fear," fem. agent 4th conj. of خاف يخاف (خوف). [35] "tormenting," fem. agent 2nd عذب . [36] "conducing to." [37] "destruction," verb. noun 4th دمر .

p. 166.

Wa húdhá [1] ashra‘u fi [2] sharḥi [3] sebebihá wa ma kána lí fihá siwá ’l‘adhábi wa ’l khaufi wa la-in tashábaha [4] ‘alá ’l-ḳárí’i bi-khuza‘biláti [5] ’llahwi wa ’lla‘bi [6] fa rubba [7] názirin fíhá yakhálu [8] haulí hazalan wa yadhunnu ’ḍhtirábí [9] sahlan, wa dhálika sha’nu man lam yasbur ghaura [10] ’l-amúri ghaira multafitin ila ’ṭṭaishi wa ’zzaighi wa ’nnafsi ’l-ammárati bi’ssúï [11] wa la yará fímá yarú‘uni íráduhu [12] illa ’l-asbába ’ṭṭabí‘íyeta au alḳiyáma [13] bimá yajibu [14] ‘alaiya haḳíḳatan.

Faḳad kuntu mundhu ’lḥadáthati [15] mushtaheran [16] bidamáthati [17] ’l-akhláḳi [18] wa maḥabbati baní jinsí [19] ḥattá ṣirtu baina ’lkhulláni wa ’l-as-ḥábi ‘ibratan [20] li-riḳḳati [21] ḳalbí.

---

[1] “behold!” [2] I begin. [3] Explanation. [4] Resemble, 6th of (شبه) شبيه “like.” [5] “idle tales.” [6] “sport and play.” [7] “many a,” see page 84. [8] Will fancy. [9] “agitation,” 8th conj. from ضرب, the ت being changed to ط, see page 12. [10] “Does not fathom the depths of.” [11] “the spirit that bids evil” is the usual Arabic equivalent for “sensuality.” [12] “alleging,” “quoting,” verbal noun, 4th from ورد. [13] Consistence, =مقاومة 3rd from قام. [14] aor. of وجب “to be necessary.” [15] “youth.” [16] Well known, 8th of شهر (شهرة “renown”). [17] Gentleness. [18] pl. of خلق “disposition.” [19] “the sons of my race,” *i.e.* my fellow creatures. [20] “an example.” [21] Softness.

p. 167.

Fa-aḥbabtu[1] fi 'l haiwáni kulla mu-ánisin.[2]
Ta-allafa[3] wa 'l-insána[4] min farṭi ṣabwatí[5]

Wa tasámaḥa[6] lí abawaiya[7] fíma raghabtu[8] fíhi min al ḥaiwánati 'lmu-talifati[9] 'ala 'khtiláfi[10] anwá'ihá[11]; wa labithtu[12] aṣrufu[13] gháliba[14] auḳátí[15] wa-íyáhá[16] já'ilan gháyata[17] 'nshiraḥí[18] fí iṭ'ámihá[19] wa mu-ánasatiha.

Wa kullu man allafa[20] kalban laho
Mu'taminan[21] fi 'ddári rabbáhu[22] ḥín[23]

---

[1] "I loved," 4th conj. حبّ. [2] "tame," "sociable," 3rd conj. انس. [3] "becomes familiar," 5th of الف. [4] *wa* with the accusative="with." [5] The metre of this verse is *ṭawíl*

⏑ —́ — ⏑ —́ — — ⏑ —́ — ⏑ —́ ⏑ —

repeated. [6] Allowed, 6th of سمح. [7] "my two parents." [8] *raghaba fí*="to long for," *raghaba 'an*="to be averse from." [9] "familiar," 8th of الف. [10] "variety," 8th of خلف. [11] pl. of نوع "sort," "kind." [12] "I tarried." [13] "to spend." [14] "the most of," from غلب to overcome. [15] pl. of *waḳt*, "time." [16] "with them," see above, note [4]. [17] The extremity of. [18] "my joy,' '7th conj. from شرح "to expand," cf. Ḳor'án, ch. v. 1, *a lem nashraḥ laka ṣadraka*, "have we not expanded for thee thy breast?" [19] "feeding," 4th of طعم. [20] "has attached," 2nd of الف. [21] "trusty," 8th of امن. [22] Has brought it up. [23] For a time.

Ya‘lamu ma úli‘a [24] ḳalbí lahú
Fí ḥubbi ḥaiwánin anísin [25] faṭín.[26]

Falá ḥájata [27] an ashraḥa lahú miḳdára [28] ’ttasallí [29] wa farṭa ’l-imbisáṭi [30] ’lladhí yata-attá [31] min dhálik li-annahu yújadu [32] fí ulfati [33] ’lkalbi ’lkháliyati [34] min algharaḍh [35] shai-un [36] yu-allifu ḳalba man ḳad márasa [37] ’lwudda ’l-káziba [38] ’lkhaddá‘a ’lladhí yará-a [39] bihi ’l-insánu.

---

[24] passive of 4th of ولع, "passionately fond of." [25] "sociable." [26] "intelligent." The metre of these lines is 2nd *Basíṭ*

[27] "necessity." [28] "the amount," قدر. [29] "consolation," 8th of سلا (سلو). [30] Pleasure, from بسط "to spread," cf. *inshiráḥ*, note [18] above. [31] "proceeds." 5th of أتى. [32] "there is found," "exists," passive of وجد. [33] "familiarity." [34] "void of," خلا, agrees with الفة. [35] "ulterior motives." [36] Nominative to *yújadu*. [37] "experienced," 3rd of مرس. [38] "false," "lying." [39] Pretends, 3rd of رأى.

---

p. 168.

Tazawwajtu [1] wa ana fatan [2] wa ḳad as‘afaní [3] al ḥazzu [4] bizaujatin muwáfiḳatin [5] lí, lá-síyamá [6] fí ‘ádátí [7] ’ssalafi [8]

---

[1] "I married," 5th from زوج. [2] "while yet a young man." [3] "permitted me," 4th of سعف. [4] "fortune." [5] "suitable," 3rd of وفق. [6] "especially." [7] "my habit." [8] "former."

'l-ímá-i ilaihá.[9] Falemmá ánasat[10] minníy almaḥabbata lilḥaiwánáti bazalat[11] majhúdahá[12] fí taḥṣíli[13] má húwa 'l-alṭafu wa 'l-aṭrabu[14] talahhíyan[15] mina 'lḥaiwánáti lmuwánisati faḥawainá[16] aṣáfíra wa semakan wa kalban jaiyidan[17] wa arneban ṣaghíran wa ḳuṭṭan faṭínan.

Fa-amma 'lḳuṭṭu fa kána ḳabíra 'lḥajmi,[18] jamíla[19] 'l-manzari,[20] ḥálika[21] 'ssuwádi, dhá[22] dhahnin[23] 'ajíbin mudhishin[24] wa kánat zaujatí tatakhaiyala[25] ḳalílan min kharáfáti[26] 'l'ajáïzi,[27] fakullamá ṣúdifa[28] zikru kuṭṭina tulammiḥu[29] litawahhumi[30] 'l'awwámi[31] an kulla ḳuṭṭin aswadin sáḥirin[32] mamsúkhin[33] wa lá azunnuhá taḳúlu

---

[9] "referred to," *ímái*, 4th of ومى, verbal noun, dependent case, in apposition with *'ádati*, which is governed by *fí'*, *lit.* "in my habit of preceding-reference to it," *i.e.* "previously referred to." [10] "she perceived," 3rd of انس. [11] "she bestowed." [12] "efforts," from جهد. [13] "acquiring," 2nd حصل. [14] Comparatives of لطيف "fine," and طرب "pleasing," "merry." [15] "diversion," 5th from لهو لها sport. [16] "we held." [17] "excellent." [18] "bulk." [19] "handsome." [20] "aspect." [21] Of a deep black, حالك السؤاد "intensely black." [22] Accusative of *dhú*, "possessed of." [23] "sagacity." [24] "astonishing," 4th of دهشة. [25] "fancy," 5th of خال (خيال). [26] "nonsensical stories." [27] pl. of عجوز "an old woman." [28] "accidentally came up," pass. of صدف, to "come suddenly upon." [29] "she would hint at," or "refer to," 2nd of لمح. [30] "suspicion," 5th of وهم. [31] pl. of عامّ "the vulgar." [32] "magician," "wizard." [33] "metamorphosed," مسخ.

dhálika biljiddi wa lákinnaní dhakartu kalimatahá háhuná liannahá fi hádha 'ddakíkati[34] khaṭarat[35] 'alá bálí.[36]

[34] "moment." [35] "occurs." [36] "my mind."

---

p. 169.

Wa lakkabná[1] kuttaná bi-Abi Murratin[2] fa-sára min akhaṣṣi[3] mu-ánisíya[4] wa ashaddihim líya 'ttizáman[5] wa lá ut'imuhu[6] illa bi yadí wa kána lá yufárikuní[7] albattata fí 'lbaiti ḥatta kidtu lá amna'uhu[8] mina 'lkhurúji[9] ma'í ila 'ssúki wa bakíná 'alá hádhihi 'l-ulfati wa 'l-mawad-dati[10] hínan[11] baida[12] annaní fi ithná'i[13] dhalika ''ta-ratní[14] 'illatun[15] shara'at[16] tughaiyiru[17] ṭab'í wa tubaddilu[18] mizájí[19] wa túsimuní[20] bi khiṣálin ghairi

[1] "We entitled." [2] "Abu Murrati," "Father of Powers," is a nickname of the Devil. [3] Superlative of خاصّ "intimate." [4] pl. masc. of مؤانس "familiar," with the affixed personal pronoun, the final ن being lost, see p. 62, ي added. [5] "most attached to me." [6] 1st aor. of 4th of طعم "feed." [7] aorist, 3rd of فرق. [8] "I came near to not preventing him," "I could scarce prevent him." [9] "going out," from خرج. [10] "love." [11] "for a time." [12] "although." [13] "in the midst of," verbal noun, 4th of ثنى. [14] "attacked me." [15] "a malady." [16] "began." [17] "changed," 3rd fem. sing. aor. 2nd غير. [18] "altered," 3rd fem. sing. aor. 2nd بدل. [19] "my temperament," from مزج "to mix." [20] "marked me."

maḥmúdatin [21] laisa mimma waṣaftuhu [22] wa aḍhá idmání [23] ‘alá ’lkhamri wa ’stighráḳí [24] fi ’nnashwati [25] sebaban li majlabati ‘árin [26] ‘alaiya ṭúla ’lmadá [27] fa má ziltu [28] azdádu [29] yóman ‘abúsan [30] wa sharásatan [31] wa híjánan [32] sarí‘an ghaira muktarithin [33] bi-aḥadin ḥattá raḍhaitu linafsí an ukháṭiba [34] zaujatí bil-faḥshá’i wa ’lghaḍhabi thumma ba‘da hunaihatin [35] ibtada’tu [36] aḍhrubuhá.

[21] "laudable," passive participle fem. of حمد "praise." [22] "not such as I have described." [23] "my persistence," 4th of دمن. [24] "my immersion in," 10th of غرق "to drown." [25] "intoxication." [26] "disgrace." [27] "the time." [28] 1st sing. masc. aor. of زال يزال "to cease." [29] "increase," 8th of زاد, ازداد for ازتاد, see p. 12. [30] "scowling." [31] "peevishness." [32] "excitement." [33] "concerning oneself," 8th of كرث. [34] "to address," 3rd of خطب. [35] "A little time," dimin. of هنّ (هنو). [36] "I began," 8th of بدأ.

---

p. 170.

Wa amma muwánisíya ’lmasákína [1] fa ma najaună [2] min ḥiddati [3] khulḳí faghafaltu ‘anhunna [4] bal [5] zalumtuhunna biddáhiyati [6] wa ’lgharízati [7] illá ḳuṭṭaná Abá Murratin baḳiyat laho fí ḳalbí min al-mawaddati ’l-ḳadímati tam-

[1] pl. of مسْكين "poor." [2] pl. fem. pret. of نجا "to escape." [3] "sharpness." [4] "I neglected them." [5] "nay," "but rather." [6] "in accidental circumstances." [7] "naturally."

na'uní[8] an aḍhrubahu au aṭrudahu[9] wa-in kuntu auja'tu[10] 'l-aránibа[11] wa 'lḳirda ḥattá 'lkalba ḍharaban mú'liman[12] wa ṭaradtuha wa ázaituha[13] wa lem ta'khudhní bihá ra'fatun.[14]

Li-annaní aḥsastu[15] minhunna 'lḳilá
Yanfurnă[16] in ṣaddan[17] wa in tadallulá[18]

lákinna dáï[19]—wa náhíka min[20] dáïn ka-sharbi 'lkhamri —ḳad izdáda bí ḥatta laḥiḳa[21] ghadhabí bi-Abí Murrati, wa ḳad ṭa'ana fi 'ssinni[22] wa dhálika asra'u lilhiyáji 'alaihi mimma lau kána fí ghaḍhḍhi shabábihi.[23]

Fafí lailatim-má ataitu 'lbaita min al khammárati[24] sakrána,[25] fawaswasati[26] 'nnashwatu fi ṣadrí[27] ann al ḳuṭṭa fárrun[28] minní mujtaniban[29] muwájahatí[30] faḳa-

---

[8] "prevented me." [9] طرد "to push away." [10] "I gave pain to," 4th of وجع. [11] pl. of أرنب "a rabbit." [12] "painful," agent of 4th from ألم. [13] "I harmed them." [14] "kindness." [15] "I perceived," 4th of حسّ. [16] 3rd fem. pl. aor. of نفر "to flee." [17] "from aversion." [18] "from coquetry." [19] "my illness." [20] "where will you find a," *lit.* "prohibition to thee from . . . . !" [21] "caught up," "reached." [22] See note [1], page 195. [23] "the freshness of his youth." [24] "the wine-shop," "tavern." [25] "drunk." [26] "whispered," "suggested." [27] "my breast." [28] Agent of فرّ "to flee." [29] "avoiding," 8th of جنب. [30] "my presence," verbal noun, 3rd وجه (face).

baḍhtu ʻalaihi amruṣu [31] raḳabatahu [32] fa li<u>kh</u>aufihi [33] min shiddati [34] <u>gh</u>aḍhabí ʻaḍhḍh bi-asnánihi ʼlmasnúnati [35] yadí faḍharajahá [36] daman. [37]

---

[31] "to tickle." [32] "his neck." [33] "and for (because of) his fear." [34] "the severity." [35] "sharp." [36] "smeared it." [37] "with blood."

---

p. 171.

Faḥamalaní [1] <u>gh</u>aḍhabun wa junúnun [2] lem uṭiḳ [3] an amluka [4] maʻahuma nafsí wa ka-anna [5] rúḥí ʼlaṣlíyata [6] ʼntazaʻat [7] minní wa nabaḍha [8] badílan [9] minhá fí kulli ʻaṣábí [10] wa mafáṣili [11] badaní rúḥun dáhiyatun ʻanídatun [12] ashbahu [13] bil-ibálisati [14] mutawallidatun [15] min saurati [16] ʼl<u>kh</u>amri ʻalá an aʻamuda [17] ilá músí [18] ʼlmaṭwíyatí [19] fí jaibí fa'ntaḍhaituhá [20] wa ʻaṣartu [21] raḳabata ʼlḥaiwánati ʼlmiskínati faʻawwartu [22] ainahá.

---

[1] "and bore me," *i.e.* "induced me." [2] "madness," possession by a *jinn*. [3] 1st sing. aor. (apocopated after لم) 6th of اطاق 4th conj. "to be able," طاقة. [4] "to control." [5] "(it was) as though." [6] "original." [7] "was plucked out," 8th of نزع. [8] "pulsated." [9] "instead." [10] "nerves." [11] "joints." [12] "rebellious." [13] "resembling," compar. of شبيه "like." [14] pl. of ابليس "the devil." [15] "born of," 5th of ولد. [16] Violence, intoxicating effects. [17] "I made for," "purposely took." [18] "my penknife." [19] "closed" = clasp. [20] "opened," *lit.* "drew," or "unsheathed." [21] "wrung." [22] عور "to blind of one eye."

Wa ḥurra[23] ḳalbáhu[24] min ‘árin wa min khajalin
Iz laisa yanfa‘u[25] ḳar‘u ’ssinni[26] min nadamí[27]
Yakádu[28] yukwá[29] fu-ádí[30] min ladhá[31] alamin[32]
Izá ketebtu ’jtirámi[33] ’l-ithma[34] bilḳalamí.[35]

Wa lamma saḥautu[36] min sukratí waḳad aṭára[37] ’nnauma ’lkhumúra[38] ‘anní wa ‘áwadaní[39] shu‘úrí[40] ur‘idat faráïsí[41] wa khamaraní[42] ’nnadamu alá má farraṭtu[43] wa ḳad kasabat-hu[44] yadaiya.

Wa haiháta[45] ’nnuzú‘u[46] ilá matábin[47]
A atruku[48] ’háhuna ’ṣṣahbáa[49] faḳdá[50]

---

[23] "Oh, the heat of." [24] Vocative affix اه to قلب "heart." [25] "profit." [26] "gnashing the teeth." [27] "repentance." [28] "it almost." [29] "was branded with." [30] "my heart." [31] "fire of." [32] "pain," "grief." [33] Commission of a crime. [34] Sin. [35] "with the pen." The metre of these lines is *basîṭ*

—́ — ⏑ —́   —́ ⏑ —́   —́ — ⏑ —́   —́ ⏑ —́ repeated.

[36] "I became sober." [37] "caused to fly," 4th of طار. [38] "intoxication." [39] "returned to me." [40] "my senses." [41] "my joints trembled." [42] "overcame me," "affected me." [43] "I had exceeded." [44] "had committed." [45] "alas for!" this always implies a negative or impossibility. [46] "inclination." [47] "repentance." [48] Can I leave. [49] "wine." [50] "lacked," "missing." The metre of these lines is *wáfir*.

⏑ —́ ⏑ ⏑ —   ⏑ —́ ⏑ ⏑ —   ⏑ —́ — repeated, with the licence ⏑ — — — in one of the first two feet.

Wa iz lem takun taubatí naṣúḥan [51] famá fati'tu [52] fi 'lghawáyati [53] jámiḥan [54] wa 'ujtu [55]

---

[51] "sincere." [52] "I did not stop." [53] "error." [54] "headstrong." [55] "I turned aside."

---

p. 172.

a'úmu [1] fi 'lkhumúri wa 'stahwání [2] 'lghauṣu [3] fí lajjihá [4] fa-aghraḳtu [5] nafsí fí khabáthatihá [6]

Wa fí dhálika 'lḥíni barí-a [7] 'lḳuṭṭ min jaráḥatihi [8] lákin mauḍhi'a [9] 'l'aini 'l'á-irati [10] kána mandharuhu [11] shaní'an, [12] wa in zála [13] 'lwaj'u [14] 'anhu fa ṭafaḳa [15] yaṭúfu [16] fi 'ddári k'ádatihi [17] 'ssálifati [18] ghaira annahu li-shiddati faz'ihi [19] kána yafirru minní firáran kullamá wájahaní [20] fí naḥiyati-mmá [21] min al beiti.

Fa ḥazintu [22] fi 'lbedááti [23] limá dahamaní [24] min ijtiná-

---

[1] "swim." [2] 10th of هوا "seduced me." [3] "diving." [4] "its abyss." [5] "I drowned," 4th of غرق. [6] "its vileness." [7] "was healed." [8] "its wound." [9] "the place," noun of place from وضع. [10] "blinded," عور. [11] "its view," "aspect." [12] "ugly." [13] "ceased." [14] "the pain." [15] "began." [16] "to go round about." [17] "as (was) its custom." [18] "former." [19] "its fright." [20] "it met me face to face," 3rd of وجه. [21] "any part." [22] "I grieved." [23] "in the beginning." [24] "unexpectedly happened to me."

bihi mu'ánisatí wa karáhatihi[25] lí wa ḳad kána yuḥibbuní fímá maḍhá[26] ḥubban shadídan.[27]

Wa ba'da <u>dh</u>á hája ṣadduhu[28] <u>gh</u>aḍhaban
Muttaḳidan[29] fí aḥsháya multahibá[30]
Wa ḥalla[31] rúḥu 'l-iṣrári[32] fíya lakai.
Yubídaní[33] bi 'ddamári munḳalebá.[34]

Ammá rúḥu 'l-iṣrári falá yubḥathu 'anhu[35] fí kutubi 'lḥikmati[36] wa lá ya'udduhu[37] 'lḥukamá-u baina 'lḥarakáti[38] li-ḳulúbi 'nnási lakinnaní mutayaḳḳinun,[39] kamá anna rúḥí ḥaiyatun wa-abadíyatun,[40] anna 'l-iṣrára húwa min al-<u>kh</u>iṣáli 'l<u>gh</u>arízíyati bi 'lmilkati fí aṣli 'lfiṭrati[41] waḥidu

---

[25] "its aversion." [26] "in the time past." [27] "strong." [28] "its turning away." [29] "kindled," 8th of وقد, the و becoming ت by assimilation. [30] "flaming," 8th from لهب. [31] "alighted," "took up its abode." [32] "perversity." [33] "to destroy me." [34] 7th of قلب, "reversed." The metre of these lines is *munsarih*

— —́ ⏑ —   — — —́ ⏑   —́ ⏑ ⏑ —

[35] "discussed," passive aorist of بحث with preposition عن, see p. 81. [36] "metaphysics." [37] "number it." [38] "the motives." [39] "certain," 8th of يقن, the ى becoming ت by assimilation. [40] "immortal," "eternal." [41] "original constitution."

p. 173.

al kuwá [1] 'lbasíṭati [2] 'l ḥákimati [3] ṭab'a [4] 'l-insáni

Man dha 'lladhí má sá-a [5] ḳaṭṭ [6]
Waman lahu 'lḥusná faḳaṭṭ [7]
Kam fi'latin saiyí-atin
Warraṭana [8] fíhá 'l ghalaṭ.[9]

A falá numílu [10] ila makhálafati [11] amri 'shsharí'ati [12] 'ala raghmi [13] 'akliná [14] hála kauniná [15] mutayaḳkinína awámira [16] 'shshar'i fa aḳúlu anna rúḥa 'l-isrári hádhihi ḳad ḥallat fíya lihalákí [17] wa 'l bawári [18] 'ttámmi [19] wa naza'at [20] nafsí nuzú'an ghair mutanáhin [21] lita'zíbi zátihá [22] wa 'iḍhṭihádi [23] tab'ihá wa aghrání [24] 'l-istimrára [25] 'ala má tasaddaitu [26] ilaihi bi-itmámi [27] iḍhrárí [28] wa ídha'í li'lḥaiwánati 'lbarí-ati.[29]

---

[1] pl. of قوّة "faculty." [2] "simple." [3] "governing." [4] "nature." [5] "does evil." [6] at all." [7] "only." [8] "has plunged us." [9] "mistake." [10] 1st. pl. aor. of أمال "to incline," 4th conj. [11] "opposition to," 3rd خلف. [12] "lawful, legal." [13] "in spite of." [14] "our common sense." [15] "while we," *lit.* "in the condition of our being . . ." [16] "biddings," أمر. [17] "to destroy me," *lit.* "for my destruction." [18] "ruin." [19] "complete." [20] "incited." [21] "incontrollable," 8th from نهى "to deny;" *ghaira*= "negative." [22] "itself." [23] "persecute," 8th conj. ضهد. [24] "incited," "hounded me on," 4th conj. غرى. [25] "perseverance," 10th of صرّ. [26] "I had engaged in," or "exposed myself to." [27] "completion," 4th conj. تم. [28] "harm," 4th of ضرّ. [29] "innocent."

p. 174.

Fa aṣbaḥtu[1] fí aḥadi 'l-aiyámi wa alḳaitu[2] fi unḳi 'lḳuṭṭi ḥablan wa shaddadtu 'alaihi[3] 'lwitháḳa[4] wa-'allaḳtuhu[5] marbúṭan[6] 'alá ghuṣni[7] shajratin[8] fa 'khtanaḳa[9]—khanaḳtuhu[10] wa-'aináya tafíḍhu[11] dumú'an,[12] wa-marárratu 'nnadámati[13] fí ḳalbí—khanaḳtuhu li'ilmí annahu kána yuḥibbuní fímá salafa[14] wa li-annaní a'rifu annahu lam yasí'[15] ilaiya abadan khanaḳtuhu li-annaní 'alimtu anní murtakibun[16] bi-dhálika saiyí-atan saufa[17] tuhliku[18] rúhí 'labadíyata wa-taja'luní lau amkana[19] maḥrúman[20] min maufúri raḥmati[21] 'lláhi 'rraḥími 'l muhíbi.[22]

Wa fi 'llailati 'ttáliyati[23] ba'da hádha 'l fi'li 'lḳabíḥi[24]

---

1 "I was in the morning," 4th conj. صبح, see p. 20. 2 "I threw," 4th conj. لقى. 3 شدّ على "to bind." 4 pl. of وثيق, "a tight knot or bond." 5 "I hung it," 2nd conj. 6 "tied," from ربط. 7 "branch." 8 "of a tree." 9 "it was strangled," 8th conj. خنق. 10 "I stangled—hung—it." 11 "pouring," 3rd fem. aor. of فاض. 12 pl. of دمع, "a tear." 13 "repentance." 14 "formerly," *lit.* "in what had preceded." 15 "had not done harm," aor. apocopated after *lam*, from ساء. 16 "committed," 8th conj. ركب. 17 Sign of the future tense. 18 "destroy," fem. sing. aor. 4th of هلك. 19 "it were possible," 4th of مكن. 20 "excluded," حرم. 21 =*min er-raḥmati 'lmaufúrati*, "the ample mercy." 22 agent from اهاب, 4th conj. to cause "awe" or "terror" هيبة. 23 "next," from تلا "to follow." 24 "vile."

arraḳaní [25] ṣautu [26] ṣáïḥin [27] "annára! annára!" [28] fanadhartu [29] wa izá astáru [30] sarírí [31] taltahibu [32] wa'ddáru kulluhá tata-ajjaju [33] ḍharáman [34] wa kidtu ana wa 'mra 'tí wajáriyatí [35] lá najidu [36] 'nnajá'tu min allahebi.

---

[25] "awakened," 2nd conj. [26] "voice." [27] "one shouting." [28] "fire! fire!" expressions like these are always in the accusative, some such verb as "beware of" being understood. [29] "so I looked." [30] pl. of ستر "a veil" or "curtain." [31] "bedstead." [32] 8th from لهب "to flame." [33] "was blazing." [34] "conflagration." [35] "my maid-servant." [36] 1st pl. aor. of وجد "to find."

---

p. 175.

Já- albawáru wa adrakatní [1] halkatun
Lam tubḳi [2] li fi 'l-arḍhi shai-an yumlakú [3]
Aslamtu [4] min yóma-izin [5] nafsí ilá
Ya-sin [6] mubídin [7] buttu [8] fíhi uḍhnakú.[9]

---

[1] "caught me up," 4th of درك. [2] "left," aor. apoc. 4th conj. بقى. [3] aor. passive of ملك "to possess." [4] "I resigned," 4th conj. of سلم. [5] "from that day." [6] "despair." [7] "destructive," participle of 4th يبيد باد. [8] 1 sing. pret. from بات يبيت, "to pass the night." [9] "made ill," or "reduced to straits," the last vowel in *yumlaku* and *uḍhnaku* is lengthened by the rhyme. The metre of these lines is *kámil*

⏑ ⏑ —́ ⏑ —   ⏑ ⏑ —́ ⏑ —   ⏑ ⏑ —́ ⏑ —

repeated. The foot ⏑ ⏑ — ⏑ — may become — — ⏑ — provided that at least one foot in the poem is left in its original form.

Wa má ana bi-afínin [10] ḥattá akhálu ’ljurma ‘illatan [11] lil-ḥádithi [12] ka-anna bainahumá ’shtiráka [13] ’ssebebí wa’l musabbabi [14] lakinnaní ashraḥu háhuná kulla má ḳad jará lí ‘ala ’ttatábu‘i [15] wa lá ughádiru [16] min dhálika shai-ammá albattata.[17]

Fa lamma aḍhwání [18] ’nnaháru ṭafaḳtu uṭawwifu [19] ’l-kharáïba [20] fa ra-aitu ’lḥíṭána [21] mutahaddamata [22] illá jidáran [23] lam yabraḥ [24] ḳá-iman waḳad kána ghaira ghalídhin [25] wa mauḳi‘uhu [26] wusṭa ’ddári wa kána mustanidan [27] ilaihi sarírí jihata [28] ra’si maḍhja‘í [29] wa ’ljíru [30] hunálika ḳad kána yadfa‘u [31] ta’thíra [32] ’nnára likaunihi ‘alá ma akhálu [33] maṭlíyan [34] jadídan.

---

[10] “foolish,” “idiotic.” [11] “cause.” [12] “to the event.” [13] “community.” [14] “cause and effect.” [15] “successively,” 5th of تبع “to follow.” [16] “leave,” 4th of غدر. [17] “at all.” [18] “lighted me,” 4th of ضوء ضآء. [19] “go round about, 2nd of يطوف طاف. [20] pl. of خربة “a ruin.” [21] “walls.” pl. of حائط. [22] “thrown down,” 5th of هدم. [23] “a partition wall.” [24] “did not cease.” [25] “thick.” [26] “its situation,” noun of place, from وقع. [27] “leant against,” 8th of سند. [28] “in the direction of.” [29] “my couch.” [30] “and the plaster.” [31] “repel.” [32] “the effect.” [33] “according to what I fancy.” [34] passive participle of طلى “to plaster,” “daub.”

p. 176.

Wa 'jtama'a [1] ḥaula [2] hádha 'lḥáïṭ jamá'atun kathírúna yata-ammalúna [3] juz'an [4] minhu bi kamáli [5] 'lfaḥṣi [6] wat-tadḳíḳi [7] fa ḥaththaní [8] 'stighrábuhum [9] wa ṣarákhuhum [10] "ya lal'ajab!" [11] wa má ashbaha dhálika [12] ila 'l-iṭṭilá' [13] 'alá amrihim fa lamma danautu minhum izá bi-ṣúratin ka-annahá ṣúratu ḳuṭṭin ḍhakhmin [14] maṭbú'atin [15] fí ṣafḥati [16] 'lḥáïti 'lbaiḍháï [17] wa kánat ṣúratan mudhishatan bistikmáli [18] 'lhai-ati [19] wa fí 'unḳi 'lḳuṭṭi ḥablun mubínun [20] fa lammá ra-aitu hádha 'lmandhara 'lháïla [21] wa 'staiḳantu [22] annahu manḳúshun [23] biyadi 'ifrítin [24] fa má kidtu amliku nafsí lifarṭi [25] ma "taráni [26] mina 'l'ajabi wa má nazala [27] bí min arrahbi.[28]

---

1 "assembled," 8th of جمع. 2 "around." 3 "contemplating," 5th of امل. 4 "a portion." 5 "perfection." 6 "investigation." 7 "minute inspection," 2nd conj. of دقّ. 8 "urged me." 9 "their astonishment," 10th of غرب (غريب "strange"). 10 "their shouting." 11 "O what a wonder!" 12 "and the like thereof." 13 "to get information," 8th of طلع, the ت becoming ط by assimilation, see p. 12. 14 "bulky." 15 "imprinted," from طبع. 16 "the surface." 17 "white," fem. of ابيض. 18 "with the perfection of," 10th of كمل. 19 "aspect." 20 "obvious," 4th of بان يبين. 21 "horrible," agent of هال (هول). 22 "I felt certain," 10th of يقن. 23 passive participle of نقش "to engrave." 24 "of a demon." 25 "because of the excess." 26 "attacked me." 27 "alighted on me." 28 "dread."

Thumma akbalat[29] 'alaiya hawájisu[30] 'l-afkári[31] fí ta'wíli[32] hádha 'ssirri[33] 'lkhafíyi fa-khatara libáli anna 'lkutta mashnúkun[34] fi junainatin[35] muttasilatin[36] bid-dári wa lammá tasáyaha[37]

---

[29] "approached," 4th of قبل. [30] "occurring thoughts," "suggestions," pl. of هاجس. [31] "thoughts," pl. of فكر. [32] "interpretation," 2nd conj. [33] "secret." [34] "hanged." [35] "garden," dimin. of جنة. [36] "adjoining," 8th of وصل the و being changed to ت by assimilation. [37] 6th of صاح "to shout."

---

p. 177.

annásu binnári 'mtaliat[1] iljunainatu bilkhalki 'zdihaman[2] falá budda[3] an yakúna ahadu 'nnási kata'a 'lhabla wa anzala 'lhaiwána min faukí[4] 'shshejrati faramá bihi fí shebbáki[5] 'lhujrati[6] 'lmaftúhi[7] wa dhálika liyúkidhaní[8] min al kerá[9] wa lammá waka'ati 'lhítán laffat[10] katílí[11] fa nukishat[12] súratuha fi 'ljibsi 'ttaríyi.[13]

---

[1] "it became full," 8th of ملأ. [2] "in crowds," 8th from زحم the ت becoming د by assimilation; see p. 12. [3] "necessarily," *lit.* "and there (was) no escape." [4] "from off." [5] "window." [6] "apartment." [7] "opened," pass. part. of فتح. [8] "awaken," 4th of يقظ. [9] "sleep." [10] "they involved," fem. sing. used with a broken plural. [11] "my victim," قتيل=مقتول from قتل "to kill." [12] "was engraved," or "depicted," نقش. [13] "fresh," "moist."

LETTERS AND OTHER DOCUMENTS.[1]

صورة تهنئة بزفاف او اكليل

جناب الاخ الاجل الامجد حرسه اللّٰه تعالى

بعد تفقّد الخاطر ومزيد الاحترام نبدى ان الباعث لتحريره اولاً استعطاف الخاطر والاستفسار عن رفاهية المزاج اللطيف وثانيًا تقديم مراسيم التهانى بما منّ اللّٰه تعالى عليكم من الاكليل او الزفاف جعله تعالى مباركاً ورزقكم الذرية الصالحة نرجوه سبحانه وتعالى ان تكون عاقبة هذه النعمة مصحوبة بدوام السرور والاقبال كما اننا نرجو منكم غمض النظر عن التقصير بالقيام بما يليق بالمقام ودام بقاكم

Form of Letter of Congratulation on a Marriage.

His excellency the illustrious, the most laudable brother, may God most High preserve him.

After inquiring after *your* mind (disposition) and increased respect, we state that the reason for writing it (this letter) is first to incline *your* mind towards *us*, and to ask after the comfort of your kind temperament, and secondly to present the usual congratulations for

---

[1] The translation is literal. It must be premised that the hyperbolical and metaphorical expressions employed do not appear strange or exaggerated in Arabic, but are those in every day use in epistolatory correspondence.

what God has favoured you with in the matter of the marriage ceremony; may God make it blessed and bestow upon you righteous (or "sound") posterity! We hope from Him—be He glorified and exalted—that the result of this favour may be accompanied with lasting joy and prosperity; as we hope that you will shut your eyes to *our* shortcomings in performing what is suitable to the occasion, and may your existence remain.

صورة جواب التهنئة

جناب الاخ الاجل الامجد دام بقاه

بعد تقديم الشكر واهداء التحية لجنابكم نبدى انه ورد علينا تحرير مودّتكم فقرأناه مسرورين و كلما تفضّلتم بهِ علينا بمكاتبتكم احاط الذّهن بهِ علماً وصرنا بذلك غريقين ابحُرِ الممنونية متقلّدين عقود الافضال نسأله تعالى ان يديم لنا صداقتكم و يقدرنا على مكافاتكم بالافراح السعيدة والآن اشعاراً بوصول مشرفتكم واظهاراً لممنونيتنا صار تقديم شقة الخلوص بهذا الخصوص وادام بقاكم

Answer to the above.

His excellency the illustrious, the praiseworthy brother, may he endure.

After presenting thanks and offering salutations to your excellency, we state that your affectionate writing has reached us, and we read it with joy; and all that you were good enough to write to us our mind grasped knowledge of; and we became through it drowned in the seas of obligation, collared with the necklaces of *your* favours; we ask Him, most High, to continue to us your friendship and to make us able to repay you for the happy joy *you have given us*, and now, referring to the arrival of your honourable letter and expressing our obligation, the presentation of *this* scrap of sincerity has taken place on this subject.

May (God) preserve you.

صورة تهنئة بمولود

جناب الاخ الاجل المحترم دام بقاه

غبّ مزيد كثرة الاشواق الوافرة لمشاهدتكم نعرض انه فبينما نحن مترقّبون اخباركم السارّة اذ شنفتْ الاذان ببشارة الشرور بظهور نجلكم السعيد فحمدناه تعالى على هذه النعمة الواجبة الشكر اقرّ اللّه بهِ اعيُنكم وجعله من السعداء الملحوظين بنظر العناية والتوفيق والآن تاديةً لفريضة التهنئة بادرنا بترقيم هذه النميقة الى جنابكم ملتمسين عدم المواخذة عن قصور القلم بتحرير ما يليق بالمقام الكريم راجيين تشريفنا بما يلزم ودُمتم

Form of Congratulation on the birth of a Child.

His excellency the illustrious and esteemed brother, may he endure.

After exceedingly many ample longings to behold you, we represent that while we were expecting pleasant news from you, behold! our ears were adorned with glad-tidings of joy of the appearance of your happy offspring and we praised Him, most High, for this favour, which deserves thanks, may God cool (cheer) your eyes therewith and make him one of the happy ones, regarded with the eye of favour and grace, and now, in accordance with the duty of congratulation, we hasten to indite this note to youn excellency, begging for absence of punishment for the shortcoming of the pen in writing what is suitable for the noble occasion, hoping that you will honour us with what *orders* are necessary. May you remain . . . .

صورة دعوة الى عرس

جناب الاخ الحبيب المحترم حرسه اللّٰه تعالى

غِبّ الاحترام لذاتكم الانيسة نبدى انه حيث تفضّل المولى تعالى علينا بهذه المُدّة باكليل احدنا فلان وصارت المباشرة بدعوات الاصدقاء والاحباب الى اكليله صار تقديم هذه الشقة الى ذات محبتكم لأجل تشريفكم الى محآكم لتحوز جمعيتنا بحضوركم المؤانسة وتكون المسرّة مشتركة بيننا زيادة على ممنونيّتنا من جنابكم ولا زلتم مصدراً لملاقاة الافراح والمسرّات نساله تعالى ان يقدرنا على مكافاتكم بامثال ذلك ويزين دياركم بمطالع الهناء والسرور ودام بقاكم

Form of Invitation to a Wedding.

His excellency the brother, the esteemed friend, may God most High watch over him.

After esteeming your sociable self we state that since the Lord most High has favoured us in this period with the marriage of one of us (our family) So-and-so, and it has been arranged to invite our friends and acquaintances to the ceremony, this note (scrap) is presented to your- (*lit.* "to your lovingness") -self that you may honour (us) by being in your place to embrace our party in your sociable presence, and that the joy may be participated among us in addition to the obligation laid upon us by your excellency—may you never cease to be foremost in meeting pleasures and joys, and we ask Him, most High, that he will enable us to repay you with the like thereof, and *we ask Him* to adorn your house with the aspects of congratulation and joy, and may your existence continue.

A Letter of Condolence.

سيدى المحترم

تُبلى الجديدينَ نوائب الدهر ولله كُلّ يوم فى خليقته امر وان كانت اعمار الخليقة كما قيل محدودة الايام فالحىّ مذ يوم يولَد يشرع يسعى الى الحمام والعبرة لنا فيمى غبر فانهم السابقون ونحن على الاثر واننى لفى اشدّ كربةٍ لِماَ آلمَّ بكم ومَنْ يسرُّه سروركم فلا ريب انه يكون فى الحزن شريككم والله المسئول ان يتولّى تعزية قلبكم الحزين انه المستعان على الخطوب كل حين

Esteemed Sir,

The reverses of fortune try (us by) night and day! and God has every day a *fresh* bidding amongst His creatures! Since the lives of the creatures are, as is said, but a limited number of days, and the living being from the day of his birth begins to hasten on towards death! there is a lesson for us in those who have passed away—verily, they have gone before, and we are on their track! Verily, I am in the severest trouble at what has happened to you; he who is joyful at your joy there is no doubt that he will share in your grief! and God is asked that He will rule the consolation of your grieving heart—for He is asked for aid in accidents in every season.

صورة تحرير بعلم وصول رجل الى محله
وتشكّر فضل من كان عنده

جناب سيدى الاجل الاكرم دام بقاه

غِبّ افتقاد الخاطر الشريف والاستفحاص عن رفاهية المزاج اللطيف نبدى انه بحمده تعالى تد تسيّر وصولنا الى محلنا بكل صحة وسلامة ونشرنا الوية الثناء على معروفكم الذى فعلتموه معنا وقد حصلت لنا المسرة التامّة برؤية الاهل والاحباب وما شق علينا سوى فراقكم الذى ما زالت وحشته داخل الخاطر وبما اننا قاصرون عن اداء واجبات التشكّرات المقتضية للجناب اقتصرنا عن الاطناب لعلمنا ان فضلكم السابق غنى بشهرته عن ذكره فلا برحتم اهلاً للمعروف ومصدراً للمحامد من كل شارد و وارد وبناءً على ممنونيتنا اقتضى تقديم هذا التحرير معرباً عن وصولنا والغاية الوحيدة عندنا تشريفنا بما يقتضى ويلزم انه رهين الامر والاعلام وجميع من عندنا يسالون الخاطر الكريم

دمتم

Form of a Letter containing news of one's arrival Home, and thanking the Person with whom one has been staying.

His excellency, my illustrious honoured Sir—may his existence continue.

After inquiring after your noble mind, and investigating the comfort of your kind disposition, we state that with praise to Him, most High, our arrival at our place was brought about with all health and safety, and we spread the banners of thanks for your kindness which you did to (with) us, and there has accrued to us perfect joy at seeing our family and friends, and nothing seemed wretched to us but being separated from you, the feeling of loneliness at which ceases not within the mind; and since we fall short of paying the necessary thanks requisite for your excellency, we moderate flattery because we know (*lit.* for our knowledge) that your former favour is independent through its renown of being mentioned (*i.e.* is already so well known that I need not mention it). May you not cease to be a worthy (dispenser of) kindness and a source of praise for every one who breaks loose or arrives; and owing to (*lit.* founded upon) our obligation it became necessary to present this writing to inform you of our arrival; and the one single object we had (in view) is that you may honour us with the requisite and necessary *orders,* and verily this is pledged to your bidding and your indications; and all who are with us, ask after your honourable mind; and may you remain.

صورة تحرير توصية بصاحب

جناب الاجل الاكرم دام بقاه

بعد اهداه التحيات ووفور التسليمات نبدى انه بهذا الحين متوجّه الى طرفكم فلان بشغل تعرفونه منه وبما ان من الواجب علينا اجرآه المساعدة التآمّة له نظراً لشرف ذاته ووحدة الحال بادرنا بتحرير الوكة ودادنا هذه مؤملين بها من جنابكم معاملته بما يليق به وتدريبه بما يلزمه كما هو معهود من غيرتكم وبذلك نصيرمن جملة المتشكرين لمعروفكم هذا ما لزم ابديناه وعرفّونا عمّا يلزم ودام بقاكم

Form of a Letter of Introduction to a Friend.

His most illustrious and honourable excellency, may his existence continue.

After presenting exceeding salutations and ample greetings, we state that this time there is setting out for your direction So-and-So, on a business which you will learn from himself; and since it is incumbent upon us to extend to him complete assistance, having regard to his own nobility and his being alone, we hasten to write this our communication of affection, hoping from your excellency that you will transact with him what is fitting and set him on the way to what he requires, as is customary from your honour, and that we may thus become of the number of those who particitate in your kindness. This which we require we have stated, and do you let us know what you require; and may your existence continue.

صورة اجارة

الداعى لتحريره

انه بتاريخه ادناه قد اجر زيد ما هو له الى بكر وهو استاجر لنفسه وذلك الماجور هو جميع المحل الفلانى الكاين فى محلة كذا المحدود بكذا على مدة كذا ابتداوها من تاريخ كذا اجارةً واستيجاراً صحيحين بالايجاب والقبول والتسلُّم والتسليم لمثله بالتخلية فارغًا بأجرة قدرها عن مدة الاجارة المذكورة مبلغ كذا حال مقبوض تمامًا من مال المستاجر بيد موجره حسب الاعتراف وبناءً عليه تحرر هذا السند للبيان تحرِّيرا فى

Form of a Lease.

The reason for writing this is—

That on the date of this document (*lit.* of it below it) Zaid has let his property to Bekr, and he has hired for himself and that the thing let is the whole of Such-and-Such a place, situate in Such-and-Such a quarter, bounded by So-and-So, for Such-and-Such a term commencing from Such-and-Such a date, letting and hiring being both in order, with consent and acceptance, and taking over and giving over of the same, without reservation, for a rental amounting from the time of the above-mentioned hiring to the sum of so-and-so, the same being actually and completely paid into the hand of the lessor from the money of the lessee, according to acknowledgement; and thereupon this document is written to explain the same. Written on the ——

صورة كمبيالة

بارة غروش
... .

فقط

المبلغ المرقوم اعلاه وقدره كذا غروش ندفعه لامر فلان بعد مدة كذا من تاريخه القيمة وصلت لنا نقداً او ثمن بضاعة استلمنا منه تحريراً فى
وعنا لامر فلان الفلانى كاتبه

Form of a Bill of Exchange.

—— piastres —— paras, only.

The sum above mentioned, the amount of which is so many piastres, we will pay to the order of So-and-So after such-and-such a period from date ; the value has reached in cash or price of goods, which we have received from him. Written on the ——

And from us (*i.e.* we pay it over to) the order of So-and-So of So-and-So.

(*Signature of the Writer.*)

صورة تحويل

بارة غروش
... .

فقط

نرجو من جناب فلان دفع المبلغ المرقوم اعلاه وقدره كذا غروش لامر فلان والقيمة قيدوها علينا تحريراً فى

Form of a Money Order.

—— piastres —— paras, only.

We hope that His Excellency So-and-So will pay the above-mentioned sum, the amount of which is so many piastres, to the order of So-and-So, and debit us with the value. Written on the ——

ايام الاسبوع . *The Days of the Week.*

الاحد	Sunday.	الخميس	Thursday.
الاثنين	Monday.	الجمعة	Friday.
الثلاثاء	Tuesday.	السبت	Saturday.
الاربعاء	Wednesday.		

الشهور *The Months.*

كانون الثانى	January.	تموز	July.
شباط	February.	آب	August.
اذار	March.	ايلول	September
نيسان	April.	تشرين الاول	October.
ايار	May.	تشرين الثانى	November.
حزيران	June.	كانون الاول	December.

The Mohammedan months are—

محرم	Moharram.	رجب	Rejeb.
صفر	Ṣafar.	شعبان	Sha‘bán.
ربيع الاول	Rabía I.	رمضان	Ramadhán.
ربيع الآخر	Rabía II.	شوال	Shawwál.
جمادى الاولى	Jumáda I.	ذو القعدة	Dhu'lka‘dah.
جمادى الاخرى	Jumáda II.	ذو الحجة	Dhu'lHejjeh

but as they are lunar months reference must be made to the almanacks for the current year in order to find when the first of Moharram occurs.

Money.

The Turkish coinage is current throughout most of the countries where Arabic is spoken, with certain local differences of value and name. In addition, however, to the regular currency, moneys of nearly all the nationalities of Europe pass freely, especially in Egypt and Syria.

Money is reckoned in piastres (قُروش or غُروش sing. قِرْش or غِرْش) and paras, بارا or فضّة, one piastre being equivalent to forty paras in Syria and in Egypt.

The following Table gives the names and value in piastres of the various coins :—

—	Turkish Government Currency.		Syria. Jerusalem.		Syria. Beirút and Jaffa.		Egypt. Government Tariff.		Egypt. Current.		French Equivalents.	
	Piastres.	Paras.	Piastres.	Paras.	Piastres.	Paras.	Piastres.	Paras.	Piastres.	Paras.	Francs.	Centimes.
Piastre	...			40		40		40		20	...	
Fánas	...			20		20	...		...		...	
Zálata	...			30		30	...		...		...	
Baraghút	...		1	5	1	5	...		...		...	
Saghtút	...			5		5	...		...		...	
¼ Mejídí	5		5	15	5	25	...		...		1	25
½ Mejídí	10		10	30	11	15	...		...		2	50
Beshlik	5		5	30 (to 6)	5	20	...		...		...	
Altlik	6		6	10	6	20	...		...		...	
Mejídí	20		21	20-30	22	30	...		...		5	
Shilling	...		5	10	6	10	4	35	9	30	1	25
Franc	...		4	30 (to 5)	...		3	30	7	28	1	
Dollar	...		17	35	18	10	...		...		...	
Rouble	17	20	18	20	19	35	...		...		...	
Spanish dollar (with columns).	...		25		26 (to 26½)		...		...		...	
Napoleon, *lírah Fransáwíyeh* (in Egypt, *Binto*).	86	10	95		100	0	77	6	154	12	20	
Russian imperial . . .	90		97		102		78	20	157		20	
Turkish pound, *lírah Othmáníyeh*.	100		109		115		87	30	175	20	22	75
English sovereign, *lírah Inglízíyeh*.	110		120		126	10	97	20	195		25	25
Egyptian pound . . .	...		...		...		100		200		26	
Egyptian dollar, *riyal masri*.	...		...		...		19	20	39		5	

In Egypt there are really three rates of currency: the Government fixed tariff, the current (which is arrived at by taking a piastre of half the value of the Government as the unit), and the "copper" rate, current in the markets for small coins. All these fluctuate daily to a slight extent.

Weights.

Egypt.

8 Mithkáls	=1	Oḳḳíyah or Arab ounce.
12 Oḳḳíyeh	=1	Ruṭl or pound (about 1 lb. 2 oz. 8 dwt. troy).
$2\frac{3}{4}$ Roṭl	=1	Oḳḳa.
100–150 Roṭl	=1	Ḳanṭár (the number of roṭl in a ḳanṭár varies according to the goods, the average being about 100 lbs. avoirdupois.

For gold and gums, the following weights are employed :—

4 Ḳumḥ (grains)	=1	Ḳíráṭ.
16 Ḳíráṭs	=1	Dirhem.
$1\frac{1}{2}$ Dirhems	=1	Mithḳál (1 drachm to 72 gr. English).
12 Dirhems	=1	Oḳḳíyeh or oz. ($571\frac{1}{2}$—576 gr. English).
12 Oḳḳíyeh	=1	Roṭl.
150 Roṭl	=1	Ḳanṭár.

Syria.

75 Dirhems	=	1 Oḳḳíyeh.
$5\frac{1}{3}$ Oḳḳíyeh	=	1 Oḳḳa.
$2\frac{1}{4}$ Oḳḳa	=	1 Roṭl.
44 Oḳḳa	=	1 Ḳanṭár.

Measures.

EGYPT.

Fitr=span with forefinger and thumb.

Shibr=longest span with little finger and thumb.

Ḳubdeh=the fist with the thumb erect.

1 D'rá'=cubit.

D'rá' Beledí=22–22¾ inches English.

D'rá' Stambúlí=26–26½ inches English.

D'rá' Hindází (for cloth, &c.)=about 25 inches English.

2 Báhs=1 Ḳaṣṣabeh or rod=about 11½ feet English.

333 Ḳaṣṣabeh=1 Feddán or acre.

In Syria the cubit ذراع d'rá'=67¾ centimetres (in Aleppo 79 centimetres).

ARABIC MANUAL.

PART III.—VOCABULARY.

A.

abandon, دمّر , ترك
abide, استقرّ, دام
able, قادر
to be able, قدر على
abound, تكثّر , اكثر
about, حَوْل
about to be, or do, مُزْمِع
above, فَوْق , أَعْلى , على
abridge, اخْتَصَر , اوجز
abridgement, اخْتِصار , ايجاز
abscess, دُمّلة
absence, غَيْبة غياب
absent, غائب
absolute, مُطلَق
absorption, تَنشيش
abstain, زهد عن , عفّ عن
to abuse, شتم
abuse, شتيمة
academy, مَدْرَسَة
to accept, قَبِل
access, دُخول الى
accident, صُدْفة , إتّفاق , عَرَض
accidental, صُدْفِي
to accommodate, وفّق , .حبح

accommodation, حجة

to accompany, رافق , صحب

to accomplish, انهى , اتمّ , انجز

accord, اتّفاق , اجماع

to accost, سلّم , خاطب

account, علم , اشعار , حساب

keep account, أحْسب

to call to account, in money matters, حَاسَب

to accuse, رافع , شكا

accustom, عَوَّد على

to be accustomed to, تَعَوَّد على

to accustom oneself to, أدْمن

to ache, وجع

my head aches, يُوجعنى رأسى

to acquaint, اطلع على , اخبر

acquaintance, اخبار , اطلاع , تعارُف , معرفة

to acquire, كسَب , حصّل

acquirement, كسْب , تحصيل

acquit, برَّأ

acre, فدّان

to act, فعَل , عمل

to act for, ينوب , ناب عن

act, فعْل

action, عَمل

active, عمول , شُغّال

activity, نشاط

to adapt, جعله صالحا ل , أهّل

to add, زاد , اضاف الى

add up, اجمع

additional, مزيد , مضاف

to address, كالم , خاطب

address, خطاب

adjacent, مجاور , متاخِم

adjective, نعْت

to administer, باشر , خدَم

administration, سياسة , ادارة

admirable, بديع , رائع , يُعجب منه

admiral, قبطان باشا , امير البحر

to admire, رِيع , تعجّب من

to admit, قَبل , سلّم ب , اذن ب

to admit of, احْتمل

adieu, خاطرك , وداعاً
to adopt, استحسن , استصْوَب
adore, سجد لِ
to advance, ترقّى , تقدّم
to advance money, سلّف فى , سلف فى
advantage, إفادة , مَنْفَعة
advantageous, مُفيد , نافع
adversary, منازع , مخاصم
advertisement, إعْلان
advice, نصيحة , مشْوَرة
to advise, نصح , اشار بِ
affair, حاجة , امر
affection, حبّ , وداد
affections, اشْواق
afflict, احزن , غمّ
affliction, حُزن , غمّ
afford (expense), اطاق على
afraid, مُشْفِق , خائف
after, ثمّ , عَقِب , بعْد
afternoon, العصر , بعد الظهر
again, كمان , ايضًا
against, على , ضدّ
age, عُمر
aged, طاعِن فى السِنّ , مُسِنّ
agency, وَكَالة
agent, وكيل
agility, خِفّة
ago, سلَف , مضَى
to agree, اتّفق , اتّحد , اجمع على
agreeable, ملائم , موافق
agreement, عهد , شرط
agriculture, حراثة , فلاحة
ague, نفاض , رجيف
to aid, اسعف , اعان , ساعد
aid, إسعاف , إعانة
to ail, مرض , اعتلّ
air, هواء
to alarm, افزع , رَعَب ; (rouse) نَبّه ; frighten, رعب , ارعب
alarm, فزع
to alight, حوّل عن , نزل عن , ترجّل
alike, متماثل , متساوٍ
alive, حَيّ
all, جُملة , قاطبةً , جميع , كلّ

to allow, رخّص فى , قبل , اذن ب , جوّز , اجاز
alluded to, المُشار اليه
almond, لَوْز
almost, الّا قليل
to be almost, كاد يكاد
alone, منفرداً , وحده
along, من جانب
aloud, جَهْرةً
already, آلان , قبل , قد
also, كذلك , ايضًا
to alter, غَيَّر
although, ولَو , وانْ
altogether, معاً , جميعاً
alum, شَبّ
always, على التوالى , دائماً
ambassador, وافد , سفير , ايلچى
amber, كَهْرمان
ambuscade, مَكْمن
amiable, محبوب
ammonia, نوشادر
to amount, علا , يعلو , بلغ
amount, مَبْلغ , قيمة
amply, فسيحًا , وسيعاً
amuse, فرّج , لهّى
amuse oneself, تفرّج , تنزّه
anarchy, عدم الحكم , بلا حكومة
anchor, انجر , مِرسىَ
to anchor, رسا
ancient, متقادم , عتيق , قديم
angel, مَلَك
anger, غيْظ , غضب
angry, مغتاظ , غضبان
animal, حَيْوان
annoy, آذّى
annual, عاميًا , سنويًّا
another, غَيْر , آخر
to answer, لَبىّ , اجاب
answer, تلْبية , جواب
ant, نَمْلة
anteroom, دَهْليز
anticipate, سلفّ , سبّق
antique, متقادِم , قديم
antiquity, تقادُم , قِدْم
an antiquity, أَنْتيِقَه

anxious, متلّهف الى , رَغوب , متشوّق
anxiety, همّ , تلهّف , رُغبة
any, كائناً , ايّا ما كان
apartment, حُجْر , اوضة
ape, قِرْد
apology, عُذْر , اعتذار
apothecary, العطارة , بيع الادوية
apparatus, عُدّة
apparent, ظاهر
an appeal, رفع دعوى الى
to appear, لاح , بدا , ظهر
appearance, مَنْظر , بدو , ظهور
appellation, تسمية , إسم
appetite, اشْتِهآء , شَهْوة
apple, تُفاحة
application, اجتهاد , ملازمة , اقبال على
to apply to, اطلق على , قيّد , شكا الى
appoint, ضرب ميعاداً , عَيّن
appointment, ميعاد
to apprehend, خشى , حذر , ادرك
apprentice, تلْميذ
approach (to), دنا , قَرب مِن , مِنْ
approach, *subs.* قُدُوم
apricot, مِشْمِش
aqueduct, سقاية , قناية
arch (of a bridge), قَنْطرة
arch (of doorway), طاق
architect, مُهَنْدِس
architecture, بِنآء , تعمير
to argue, تحاجَج
argument, بُرهان , قياس , دليل
the arm, ذراع , يد ; the fore-arm, ساعِد
arms, سلاح
army, عسكر , جَيْش
arrange, نظم , نَظّم
arranged, مَنْظوم
arrangement, ترتيب , تنظيم
arrest, قبض على
arrival, قدوم , بلوغ , وصول
to arrive, قدم , بلغ , وصل
art, صنعة

article, صنف , مادّة ; pl. موادّ
artisan, صنائعى
as, كأنّ , كما
aside, على ناحية
to ask, سأل , استفهم
aspect, مَنْظر
ass, حِمار
to assemble, اجتمع , انتدى
assembly, جماعة , مَعْشر
to assert, جزم , اكدّ , حقّق
assertion, تَوكيد , تحقيق
assess, سعّر
assign, حَوَّل , سلّم
to assist, ساعد , اغاث , عاون
assistance, مُساعدَة
associate, شرك , رافق
assortment, نُخبة , صُفوة , جُملة
astern, دابر , عن دُبر
to astonish, حيّر , اذهل
astonishment, تحيُّر , ذهول
astronomy, علم النجوم , التنجيم

at, عند , فى , لدَى , لدُن
atmosphere, الهوآء , الجوّ
atom, ذرة , هبآء
attach, لزق
attack, حمل على
attain, حصّل
to attempt (try), جرّب , امتحن , (strive) سعى فى , قصد الى
to attend, لازَم , شهد , حضر
attendance, حضور , تَبَع
attract, جذب , استجلب
attraction, انجذاب , جذب
auctioneer, دلاّل
aunt (maternal), خَالة
aunt (paternal), عمّة
author, مؤلّف , مصنّف , منشئ
authority, سيادة , رياسة , زعامة
auxiliary, مساعِد
avoid, جانب , اجتنب
awake, نبّه , أيْقظ
away, بُعداً

B.

baby, طُفْل
bachelor, عزب
back, ظهر
bad, ردِى
bag, جُرَاب , زكيبة
baggage, عفْش , أثقال
to bake, طها , خبز , شوى
baker, طاهى , خبَّاز , شوَّا
balance, مِيزان
bale (out water), نزح
ball, كُرَّة
ballast, صبوره
banana, مُوز
bandage, ضماد , رباط
banker, صَرّاف
banner, لِوآء ; pl. أَلْوِية
baptism, مَعْمُودية
bar (to bar the door), دربز
barber, حلّاق , مزيّن , حجام
bare, عُريان , مجَّرد
barefoot, حافى (حاف)

bargain, شرط , عهد
bark (ship), سفينة
bark (of a dog), نِباح
barley, شعير
baron, بارون , بيك
barren (land), اجدب
basin, طشت , ماحور
basket, قُفَّة , ذَنْبِيل
bath (warm) حمّام
battle, قِتال , وقعة
bay, خليج , جون
be (to), كان يكون
bear (animal), دُبّ
bear (to), حمل , احتمل
beard, لحية , دُقن
to beat, ضَرب
beautiful, جميل , مليح
beautifully, بحُسن , بملاحة
beauty, حُسن , ملاحة
because, لِأن , سبب
to become, صار

bed, فرشة , فِراش

bedstead, سرير , تخت

bee, نَحلة

beehive, كُوّارة

beef, لحم , بقر

beer, فقاع , بيرة

beetle, خُنفُسة ; pl. خنافِس

before, اول , قُدام , قبل

beforehand, نقداً , ناجزاً , مقدّماً

to begin, شرع فى , ابتدا

beginning, بدآءة , ابتدآء , بدء

beggar, متسوّل , شحّاذ

to behave, عمل مع , سلك

behaviour, عمل , سلوك

behind, وراء , خلف

to behold, راى , شهد

to believe, اعتقد , امن , صدّق

bell, ناقوس , جرس

belly, بطن

to belong, نسب الى , خصّ ؛

below, اسفل , تحت

bench (stone), مَصْطبة

bend (*v.a.*), لوى ; (*v.n.*) اِلْتَوَى احْتنى

benefactor, مُحسن , مُفضّل

berth, خزنة , مقعد

besides, ما عدا

best, أحْسن , اخْير

to bestow, اعطى , انعم ؛

bet, رهْن

betimes, بداراً , باكراً

betray, خوّن , غدر

better, أحْسن

between, بَيْن

beyond, عِبْر , ورآء

bid, أمَر

bill (of bird), مِنْقار

bill (account), حِساب

to bind, جلّد , ربط

binding, تجليد , ربط

bird, طير , عصفور

birth, ولادة

birthday, مَوْلِد

biscuit, بُقْسُمات

bishop, أسْقُف

bit (a piece), قُطْعه
bite, عَضّ
black, أَسْود
blacksmith, حدّاد
blanket, لحاف , حِرام
to blaze, أجّ . اصطرم , اشتعل
blaze, اصطرام , اشتعال
bleed, نزف
to bless, دعا لـ, بارَك
blessing, دُعا , بركة
blind, أَعْمى
block, خَشَبَة
blood, دم
bloody, دَمَاوى
blotting-paper, ورق تنشيف
blow (to puff), نفخ
blow (the wind), هَبّ
blue, أزرق , كُحلى
boat, قارِب
board, دَفّه , تختة
body, جَسَد , جِسْم , (a corpse) جُثّه
to boil, غلا , سَلَق
bone, عَظْم
book, كتاب
book-case, صندوق الكُتُب , قِمَطْر , غلاف
bookseller, بائع كُتُب , كتبى
boot, جزْمة
borrow, استعار
bottle, شيشة , قنينة
bottom, قعر
box, علْبة , صندوق
boy, ولد , صبى
brain, دِماغ
branch, غُصن , فرع
brass, نحاس اصفر
brave, مقدام , شجاع
bray (as an ass), نهق
bread, عيش , خُبز
breadth, عرض
break, كسر , (v.n.) إنْكَسَر
breakfast, كسر صفرا , فطور , ترويقة
breast, صَدر
breeze, نسيم

to bribe, رشا , بَرطَل
brick, طوب
bridal, عِرس
bride, عَروس
bridegroom, عريس
bridge, جِسْر
bridle, عنان , لجام
bright, زاهى , نوّر , زاهر
brimstone, كِبْرِيت
to bring, حمل , جآء بِ , جلب ;
vulg. جاب يجيب
brink, حافية
broad, عريض , واسع
broker, دلاّل , سِمْسار
brook, ساقية
brother, أخ (اخو)
brown, اسمر
to bruise, رَضّ
to brush, نفض , مَسَح
brush, فُرْشة
brute, بهيمة
bug, بَقّ
to build, بَنَى
building, عمارة , بِناء
bull, ثَوْر
bullet, رصاصة
bundle, رُبْطَة
burden, حَمْل
bureau, مَكْتَب
burial ground, مَدْفَنَة مَقْبَرة
to burn, أحرق
bury, دفن
business, وظيفة , شغل
busy, مشغول
butcher, جزّار , قَصّاب
butter, fresh, زُبدة
butter, salt, سمن
button, زِرّ ; pl. اَزِرّة
to buy, اشترى

C.

cabin, حُرنة , قمرة
cage, قفس
calamity, داهِية , مُصيبة
calico, شِيت

to call, نادى , دعا
to call on (visit), مَرّ بـ , زار
call, دَعْوة , زورة
calm, ساكن , هادى
calomel, زئبق
calumny, بُهتان
camel, بعير , جمل
camp, مَحَطّة
camp (of an army), مَعَسْكر
can (a), تَنَكة
canal, خليج , قناية
candid, سليم , نصوح
candle, شمع
candlestick, شمعدان
cannon, مَدْفَع
capable, اهل لـ , قادر
capacity, ادراك , فهم , اطاقة
capital (stock in trade), رأس مال
capital (of a pillar), راس , قاعدة العمود
captain, رئيس , قبطان
captive, اسير

caravan, قافلة
caravanserai, خَان
carcase, جيفة
to care, تحذّر من , اعتنى بـ
care, حُذر
careful, مُعْتنٍ , متحذّر
carefully, باعتناء , بتحذّرٍ
cargo, شحنة , وسْقة
carpenter, نجّار
carpet, سجادة , طُنْفُسة
carriage, كروسة , عرابة , مركبة
to carry, حمل , رفع
to carve (meat, &c.), قطع , شرّح
to carve (wood, &c.), نقش
cask, بَرْميل
cast, رَمى
castle, قَلعة , قصر
cat, قُطّ
catch, لقف , لحق
cattle, بهائم
cause, عِلّة , سبب , دعوى
caution, تحذر , حزم , احتياط

cautious, متحذّر , حازم

cavalry, خيالة

cave, مَغَارَة , كهف

cease, يزال زال

cedar, ارز

cellar, قابو , دهليز , سِرداب

century, ماية سنة , قرن

ceremony, رسوم , طقوس , تكليف

certain, اكْيد , محقّق , عين اليقين

certainly, يقينا , بالتحقيق , بالتوكيد

chace, قنص , صيد

chain, سِلسِلة , زنجير

chair, كُرسِى

chalk, تباشير

chamber, اوضة , حُجَرة

to change, غير , بدل , صرف

change, تغيير , صرف

small change (money), خُردة

chapter, سورة باب , فصل

character, خُلق , طبع , خصلة

to charge, طلب , تقاضى

charge, طلبٌ , تقاضى

charitable, خيّر , مُحْسِن , ذو فضل

charity, مَحبّة , حُسْن

charm (a), طِلسْم , حمايل

cheap, رخيص

cheat, مكّار , غشّاش

cheek, خدّ

cheese, جبْن

chest, صندوق

chicken, فروخ

chief, مقدّم , اوّل

chiefly, غالبا , بِالأَخصّ , فى الأكْثر

child, طفل , ولد

childbirth, نفاس , توليد , ولادة

childhood, صُغر

chill, بارِد

chin, دُقن

china, صينى

chisel, ازميل , سميل

choice, اصطفاء , انتخاب

to choke, خنق , v.n. اختنق
to choose, انتخب , اصطفى
chopper, ساطور
Christian, نصرانى
church, كنيسة , بيعة
circle, دائرة
to circulate, دار فى , جال فى
circulation, دوران , جولان
circumspect, حريص , متحذّر
circumspection, حرص , تحذّر
circumstance, اعراض , حوادث , أحوال
citadel, قلْعة
city, مدينة , بلد
civil, متمدّن , لطيف , كيّس , ادوب
civility, لُطف , تظرّف
to claim, ادعى بِ , انتحل
claim (a), دعْوى
clap, تصفيق , صفق , تحاك , تصادُم
class, رُطبة , طبقة , باب
claw, مِخْلب

clay, طين
to clean, نظّف
clean, نظيف
clear, واضح , ظاهر , صافى , رائق
clever, ماهر , تقن , شاطر
climate, هوا , مناخ , قطر
climb, ارتقى , ترقّى
cloak, بُرنُس
clock, ساعة , دقاقة كبيرة
close, ملازق , مسدود , مُغلق
closet, مِخدع
cloth, جوخ
clothes, لِباس
cloud, سحاب , غَيم
cloudy, مغيّم
clove, قُرنْفُل
coal, فحم حجرى
coarse, ثخين , خشن , غليظ
coast, شطّ , ساحِل
coat, جُبّة , عباة
cock, دِيك
coffee, قهوة , (in the bean) بُنّ

coffin, تبوت
coin, سِكّة
cold, بارد, (feeling cold), بَرْدان
collect, جمع
college, مدرسة , جامعة
colour, لَوْن , صِبغ
comb, مُشْط
to come, جاء , اتى
come! تَعَال
to command, امر , حكم , اوصى
commandment, وصيّة
to commence, شرع فى
commencement, شروع
commerce, متّجر , بيع وشرا
commercial, متجرىّ
companion, رفيق , مصاحب
company, رِفقة , صُحْبة ; (in trade, &c.) جمعية
to compare, طابق بين , قايس , شبّه
comparison, مطابقة , تشبيهٌ
compass (circuit), دور , دَوْرة
compass, mariner's, قبْله نما
compassionate, رحوم , رؤوف , حنون
compatriot, ابن بلاد
compel, الزم , اضطرّ
competent, قابل , كافى
compilation, مجموع , جمع , تأليف
to complain, تشكّى من , تظلّم
complaint (malady), عِلّة
complement, إتْمام , تتِمّة
complete, تامّ , وافٍ , مُكمّل , تمام , كامل
compliment, تكليف , تحيّة , سلام
compose, الّف , صنّف
composition, انشآء
compound, مركّب , مؤلّف
comprehend, اشمل فى , حوى , ضمّن , اشتمل على
comprehension (mental), إدْراك

compulsion, جَبْر , اِلْزام
concave, اجْوف
conceal, اخفا , كتم
to conceive, فهِم , عقَل
conception, فَهْم
concern oneself, اكْتَرَث بِ
concerning, عن , نحو , من , بخصوص
to conciliate, لاءَم , صالح
concise, مُوْجِز
conclude, أتْمَم , قضى , انْهى
concord, مُوَافَقة
concourse, ازدحام , جمع
to condemn, دان , قضى على , عاب
condition (state), حالة , حال ; (requirement) شرط
conditional, شرطى
conduct, ارشاد , تسديد , سيرة , سلوك
to confess, اعْترف , اقرّ
confidence, إعتماد
confine, احبس
to confine oneself to, اقتصر على
confirm, صدّق
conform, طابق مع
confound (mix), خبّص , خربط ; (silence), افحم
congeal, جمّد
to congregate, اجتمع
congregation, جماعة
congress, مُؤتَمَر
conjecture, تَخْمين
to conquer, ظفر بِ , غلب
conscience, طويّة , نِيّة , ضمير
conscientious, صاحب ذمّة
conscious, مطّلع , خبير
to consent, اجاب الى , رضى بِ
consent, اجابة , ارتضاء
consequence, نتيجة , عاقبة , حاصل
to consider, تأمّل فى , اعتبر
considerably, بزيادة , بكثرة
consideration, عبرة , اعتبار
consign, اودع , سلّم

consignee, مستودَع
to consist, تضمن , اشتمل
consistency, ذات ثبوت , استقامة
console, سلّى
conspire, تحالف
constant, مداوم
constitution (of body), مزاج
construct, عمّر , صنع
consul, قُنْصل
to consult, شاوَر , استنصح
to contain, احتوى , شمل
contemporary, معاصر
contemptible, حقير
contentment, اقتناع
contents, مضمون
continent, برّ
continual, مستدِيم , مستمِرّ
continually, باِستدامة , على الدوام
to continue, داوم , واظب على
to contract, شارط , كمّش
contract (a), عقد , شرط
contrary, خِلاف , ضِدّ
convenience, موافقة , مناسبة
convenient, موافق , مناسب
conveniently, بمناسبة , بتيسّر
convent, دَيْر
to converse, حدّث , حكى
conversation, حديث , مقالة
convex, محدَّب , مقبّب
convict, اثبت على , الزم
convince, حقّق لـ
cook, طبّاخ , طاهى
to cook, طبخ
cool, بارِد , رطب , طرى
copper, صفر , نحاس
copy, نُسخة
to copy, نقل
core, قلب , لُبّ
cork, سدادة
corkscrew, برِيمة
corn (grain), حبّة
corner, زاوية
corporal, جسمى
corporeal, جسمانى , جسدى

corpse, مَيّت , جُثّة
correct, مصحّح , مضبوط
to correct, أصْلح
correctly, بالتصحيح بالضبط
to correspond, راسل
correspondent, مراسل
corresponding to, ملائم , مطاوع
corrupt, فاسِد
to corrupt, فسد
corruption, فَساد
to cost, ساوى , غرّم , كلّف
cost, كلفة , قيمة
costly, غالى , مُثْمِن
costume, ملْبوس , هيئة , زِى
cotton, قُطن
couch, مُتّكِى
cough, سُعال
council, مجلس , مجمع
counsel, مؤامرة , مشْوَرة
to counsel, ايتمر , استشار
counsellor, مُشِير
to count, عدّ

to counteract, نافَى , ضادّ
country, بلاد
courage, جسارة , اقدام , نشاط
courier, بريد , ساعى
course, طَوْر , طريقة
court (yard), صحن , ساحة
courtesy, عطف , لَطافة , لُطف
to cover, غطّا
a cover, غِطا
covet, طمع
cousin, ابن عَمّ
cow, بَقَرَة
coward, جَبّان
crack (burst with a noise), فرقع
to crack, هرط , هشم
cradle, مهد
create, خلق
creature, مخلوقة
Creator, خالِق
credit (repute), اعْتبار
creditor, غريم
creed, مَذْهب , ايمان

crew, حزبة , زُمرة ; (of ship), بحرِيّة
crime, جناح , جُرم
criminal, مُجرِم
crooked, اعْوج
crop (produce), غَلّة
the Cross, صليب
to cross, مرّ , عبر
to crowd, ازْدحم
crowd, جوق , زحام
crown, تاج
cruel, جافى , قاسى
cruet-stand, آنية الابازير , مِقْرَحَة
crumb (of bread), لُبّ
crumble, فتّت
crust, قشر
to cry, بكى , صرخ
cry, بُكآء , صراخ
crystal, بِلّور

cucumber, خِيار
culprit, مُذْنِب
to cultivate, نبّت , حرَث , اتقن
cultivation, تنبيت , حرْث , فِلاحة , اتقان
cup, كاس ; coffee cup, فِنْجان
cupboard, مخدع , خزانة
currency, عملة
current, دارِج , ماشى , سالك
to curse, لعن , شتم
curve, حنو
cushion, وِساد
custom, دَسْتور , عادة
custom-house , گُمرُك
customer, زبون
cut, قطع
cypress, سَرْوة

C.

dagger, خِنْجر
daily, كل يوم , يوميّا

damp, (*s.*) رطوبة , ندآء
damsel, جارية

to dance, زفن , رقص
danger, عطَب , خطر
dangerous, مُعْطِب , ذو خطر
to dare, تجرّاء , تجاسر
dark, مُظْلِم , قاتم
darkness, قتمة , ظلام
to date, أرّخ الكتاب
date (fruit), بَلَح ; (era), تاريخ
daughter, بنْت
dawn, سَحَر , فَجر
day, يوم ; (opposed to night) نهار
dead , ميّت
deaf, اطْرَش
to deal, وزّع , قسّم
dealings, مُخالطة , مُعاملة
dear (in price), غالى
death, مَوْت
debauchery, فسْق
debt, دَيْن
deceased, مرحوم , متوفّي
to deceive, خدع , مكر ; , غشّ

decent, ادُوب , لائق , محتشم
decently, بلياقة , بأدب , بحشمة
to decide, قطع , جزم , فصَل
decision, جَزْم , فَصْل
deck (of ship) سقيفة , ظهر المركب
declare, اشهر
decline (refuse), أبا
to decline (sink), هَبط , تنازل
to decree, قضى
a decree, حُكْم
deep, عميق
defect, تقصير , قصور
defective, مقصّر , قاصر
to defend, دافع , حامى عن
defendant (in law), المُدّعَى عليه
deficient, ناقص
defy, حامَخ
degree, درجة
deign, تنزّل , تفضّل
delay, ابطآء , تاخُّر
deliberate together, إتّمر

delicate (subtle), رقيق , دقيق ; (elegant), ظريف
delicious, طيّب , لذيذ
delight, حبور , سرور , ابتهاج
delightful, سارّ , انيق , بهيج
to deliver from, سلّم من , نجّى , انقذ
to deliver to, سلّم لِ
delude, اغرّ
to demand, تقاضَى , طلَبَ
democratical, شعوبىّ , جمهورىّ
demon, عِفْريت
demonstrate, اوْضح , بيّن
demonstration, بيّنة , بُرهان ; (display), تظَاهر
den, وكْر , جُحْر
denomination, مذهب , تسْميّة
deny, انكر
to depart, فصل عن , افترق
departure, فراق
to depend on, توقّف على
to deplore, تأسّف على , رثى لـ
depose (from office), عزل
deposit (money), وديعة ; (sand, &c.) رُسوب
depôt, مَخْزن , مَحَطّة
deprive, احْرم , اعْدم
depth, عمق
deputy, قائِممقام, نائب
descend, هبط , انحدر , نزل
descendant (from an ancestor), سلالة
descent (going down), نزول ; (slope) حُدور ; (race) نسل
desert, صحرآء , قفر , بادية
desert (merit), استْحْقاق
to desert, ترَك , دشّر ; (as a soldier), هرب
deserve, استأهل , استحقّ
design, قصد
to desire, ابتغى , رام , رغب فى
desk, بِشْتَخْتة
despair, إياس , قنوط
despicable, ذليل , مُهين , حقير
to despise, اهان , احتقر
dessert, نُقل

destination, مَقْصَد
destroy, اباد , اهلك
detain, اخّر , اوقف
determination, عزم , تقرير , جزم
to determine, قرّر على , جزم ب , عزم
to devote, أَهْدَى , نذر
devout, متعبّد , ناسك
dew, طَلّ , ندا
dialogue, مكالمة , محاورة
diamond, الماز , الماس
diarrhœa, إسْهال
dictate, امْلى
to die, توفّى , مات
diet, طعام
difference, مغايرة , خِلاف , مباينة
different, مغاير , مختلف , مباين
difficult, عَسِر , مُبْهم , صعب , عويص
difficulty, ابهام , عُسْر , صعوبة , عَوَص

digest, هضم
diligent, ذو همة , مجتهد , مجدّ
diligently, بهِمّة , باجتهاد
dilute, ب بالماء
dim, سف , مكمّد
diminish, صغّر , قلّل
dimness, غِشاوة
to dine, تغدّى
dinner, غدآء
to dip, غمس
diploma, براءة , فرمان
to direct, سدّد , ارشد , هَدَى
direction, صوب , ارشاد , هُدى , جِهة
directly, دون تورّب , قصداً , توّا , حالاً
dirt, نجاسة , وسخ
dirty, قَذِر , نجِس , غيرنظيف , وَسِخ
disagree, تخالف
disappear, بزال , زال , غاب عن
to disappoint, نغّس , خيّب
disapprove, استهجن , استقبح
disaster, مُصيبة , نحس

discharge (a gun, &c.), اطلق ; (a debt) قضى ; (a servant) صرف , طرد , عزل
disciple, تلميذ
discipline, تأديب ; (of soldiers), ضبط
discord, مخالفة
discount, اسْقاط
to discover, استكشف , وقف على , اطلع على , كشف عن
discovery, كشف , اطلاع , استنباط
discreet, صاحب تدبير , رازن , عاقل , حازم , لبيب
discuss, باحث عن , بحث
disease, مرض , دآء
disembowel, وسّط
disgrace, عَيْب , شَيْن , فازلة
disgraceful, مُفْضِح
disguise, نكّر
to disgust, اقرف من , يشع
dish, صحن
dishonest, غاشّ , غير امين
disinherit, احرمه من الارث , or من الميراث
to disinter, نبّش
to dislike, استكره
dismal, مُوحِش
to dismiss, اطلق , دشّر
to dismount, نزل
disobedience, عصيان , معصية , عتوّ
disobedient, عاصى , عاتٍ , عقوق
disorder, لقبط , قرقب , شواش
to disown, تناكر
to dispatch, ارسل
to disperse, نشر , بثّ , اذاع
to disperse the enemy, هزّم
to display, اظهر
to dispose, دبّر , مَيّل
dispute, جِدال
to disregard, هاون , اهمل
to dissemble, نافق
to dissolve, ذوّب
distance, بُعد مسافة

distant, نآء , نازح , بعيد
distinct, بيّن , مُمْتاز
to distinguish, فضّل , ميّز , فرق
distress, كرب , غمّ , ضيم
distressing, مُحْزِن , مُغِمّ , ضائم
to distribute, وزّع
disturb, اقلق
ditch, حُفْرة , حفيرة
dive, غاص يغوص , غطس
to divide, بعّض , جزّا , قسّم
division, تقسيم , قِسْم
divorce, طلاق
dizzy, دايخ
to do, قضى , عمل , فعل
doctor (learned man), معلّم ; (of medicine) حكيم ; (of laws) فقيه
dog, كلب
doll, لُعْبة
dollar, رِيال
dome, قُبّة
domestic, اهلِي
dominate, استولى على
dominion, قدرة , سلطان , تسلُّط , مملكة
donkey, جحش , حِمار
door, باب
door-post, رِجْل الباب
double, مضاعَف
to doubt, توهمّ , شك , ارتاب
doubt, وهم , شك , ارتياب
doubtless, بلا شك , من دُون شُبه
dozen, دُوزينه
draper, جُوخى
to draw, جرّ , جذب , سحب
drawer, دُرج
to dress, كسا , لبَس
dress, كِسْوَة , لُبْس
to drink, شرب
to drive, سَاق يسوق
dromedary, هِجين
to drop (of liquids), قطر , خرّ ; (of solids) طحّ , سلت
to drown, غرق
due, حقّ , لزوم

duplicity, مـوالسة , نفاق , ريآء
durable, مستمرّ , مستديم
duties (religious), رَوَاتب
dwarf, دِحداح
to dwell, سكن

E.

each, كلّ واحد , فرد , كُلّ
eagle, نَسْر
ear, أذن
early, بكير , بُكرة , باكراً
earn, اكتسب
earnest money, عربُون
earth, ارض
earthenware, فخار
ease, رفاهية , راحة
easily, بالسهولة
east, شرق
eastern, شرقى
easy, هيّن , سهل
to eat, أكَلَ
echo, صدا
eclipse, كسوف
economical, موفّر , مُقتصد , مُدبّر
economy, تدبير , اقتصاد
edge, طرف , حدّ
to educate, هذّب , خرّج , ادّب , ربّى
education, تخريج , تهْذيب , تربية , تأديب
eel, انقليس
to efface, امْحَى , اشال , افنى
effect, نتيجة
effeminate, مخنّث
effort, سعى , جهد
egg, بَيْضة
egg-cup, ظرف
egregious, متفاقم , جزيل
either احد (one)
eject, اخرج
elastic, لدن
elasticity, لدانة

elbow, مِرْفق
elder, اكبر العُمر
an elder, شَيْخ (pl. مشائخ)
eldest, بكر اخوته
elect, مُنْتَقَب , مُخْتار (title of Mohammed) مُصْطفى.
electuary, مَعْجون
elegant, مُسْتظرف , ظريف , لطيف , مليح
elegy, مرثية
element, عُنْصُر ; elements (rudiments) مبادِى
elephant, فيل
elevation, ارتفاع
eligible, جدير
elm tree, دردارة
eloquent, بليغ , فصيح
embalm, بَلْسَم , حنّط
embark, نزل بمَرْكَب
to embark, ركب البحر
embassy, سفارة
emblem, رمز , كناية
embrace, عانق
embroider, طرّز
emerald, زُمُرُّد
emerge, طلع من , برز
emetic, مُطْرِش , مُقيّي
emigrate, ارْتَحَل عَنْ
eminence, سنا , سموّ , علوّ
eminent, رفيع , سنى , شهير
emphasis, اسْتِعلاء , نَبْرَة
empire, سَلْطنة
to employ, استخدم , شغّل
employment, شُغل
empty, فارغ , فاضى
emulation, مُنافسة
enable, اقدر على , مكّن من
enamel, مِينا (a Persian word).
encamp, خيّم , حطّ
encampment, مخيّم , محطّة
enclose, ضمن
enclosed (term used in letter writing), ضِمْنَهُ , طيّهُ

to encourage, شجّع , رغّب
encouragement, تشجيع , ترغيب
encouraging, مُنشْط , مرغّب
to encumber, لبّكَ , ثقّل على
encumbrance, لبكة , تثقيل
end, غاية , آخر , منتهى , ختام
to endanger, غامَر , خاطَر ؛
to endeavour, جدّ فى , اجتهد
endeavour, جدّ , اجتهاد
to endow (a religious establishment, &c.), وقف يقف
endure, كابد , اطاق , v.n. استمرّ , اه تدام
enemy, خصيم , عدوّ
enfranchise, اعْتق
to engage, شَغَل , ألْزم , (in battle) ناوش , قاتل
engaged, مقيّد , مشغول
engagement, شُغل , تعيين , قتال
English, انكليزى

engrave, حفر , نقش
to enjoy, حظى ؛ , تمتّع ؛ , تملّى ؛
enjoyment, تملّى , حظوة , تمتّع
enough, حَسْبُ , وافٍ , كافٍ
to enquire, استَفهم , سأل , استخْبر
to enter, دخل , ولج ; vulgar, خشّ
entire, تامّ , تمام , كامل , مستوفٍ
entirely, جملةً , بالكلية , قاطبة
envious, حاسد , حسود
environs, حوالِي
envoy, رسول
envy, حسد
epithet, لقب , نَعْت
epitome, اخْتِصار
equal, مساوٍ , سوِى
equalize, سَاوى , سَوّى
equator, خَطّ الاعتدال
equip, استعدّ , اعدّ
equivalent, عِوَض
ere, اوّل ما , قبْل

erect, واقف , مُنْتَصَب
error, غلط , غلطة
escape, نجا , سلم من , فلت , هرب من , خلص
escort, شيّع , غفّر
essence, جَوْهر , ذات
estate, عِقار ; (condition) حال
to esteem, اعتبر
esteem, هَيْبة , مراعاة , اعتبار
eternal, اَبَدِىّ
eternity, ازل , ابد
ethics, اخْلاق , ادب
eunuch, خصى , طواشى
Europe, اوربا
evaporate, نشف , تصعّد
even, مساوى , سوى
evening, مساء
event, عارضة , حادثة , مَوْقعة
ever, ابداً
every, كلّ واحد
everywhere, فى كلّ مكان
evidence, شهادة , بيّنة , اِثْبات

exact, مدقّق فيه , مضبوط
exaction, ظُلم , سلب , تغريم
to examine, امتحن , فحص
examination, فحص , اِمْتِحان
example, مَثَل , مِثال , انموذج , عِبرة
exceed, زاد على , جاوز
exceedingly, جِدًّا , الى الغاية
excel, فاق على , فاق , فضل على
excellent, نفيس , فاضل
to except, استثنى
except, ما خلا , ما عدا
excess, زيادة , مبالغة , فضل
excessive, وافر , مُفرِط
excessively, بفرط , بوفور , بإِفراط
exchange, بدّل , بدل
to excite, حرّك , استنهض , هيّج
exclude, منع , طرد , حرم من , ابعد
exclusively, خارج عن , دون غيره
excusable, معذور
to make excuse for, اعتذر من

to excuse, برّأ , قبل عذرًا
excuse, عُذر
to exercise, درّب , مرّن , روّض
exercise, إدْمان , ترويض , ممارسة
exhaust, انفد , نحل
an exile, نفى
exit, خروج
exorbitant, متجاوز , فوق الحدّ
expanse, فسحة
to expect, انتظر , ترقّب
expectation, انتظار , ترقّب
expel, طرد من
expense, نَفَقة , مصروف
experience, خِبْرة , تجْرِبَة
experiment, تجْربة , امتحان
expire, سلّم الروح

explain, شرح , بيّن , عوّل , فهّم
to expose, ابرز , نصب , عرّض لِ
to express, نطق بِ , عبّر عن
extempore speech, اقتراح
extend, امتدّ , طوّل , مدّ ; v.n. امتدّ
exterior, خارج , ظاهر
extinct, مُنْعدم
extinguish, اطفى
extract, استخرج
extravagant, مُسْرِف
extreme, متناهى
extremely, للغاية
eye, طَرْف , عَيْن
eye (of a needle), سُمّ خِياط
eyebrow, حاجب
eyelid, جِفْن

F.

fable, مَثَل , خُرافة
face, مُحَيّا , وَجْه
facilitate, يسّر
factory, كرخان (كارخانة)

to fade, نفض , ذبل , فنى ,
اضمحلّ , انتمس
to fail, خاب من , قصّر عن
fair, رقيق , لطيف

faith, ايمان
faithful, امين
to fall, وقع , سقط
fall, وقوع , سقوط ; (waterfall) هَلَّال
false, مُزَوَّر , كاذب
falsehood, زوْر , كِذْب
familiar, خبير ; , اليف , انيس
family, عَيْلة , اهل
fan, مِرْوَحَة
fancy, خيال , وَهْم , بال , خاطر
to fancy, تصوّر , خيّل
far, بعيد , نازح
fare (boat hire, &c.), أجرة , كرا ; (victuals) معاش , معيشة
to bid farewell, ودّع
farewell! خاطرك , وداعاً , الوداع
fashion, كسْم , هيئَة , زىّ
fast, مستعجل , سريع , عاجل
fast (not eating), صَوْم
fat, s. دُهن , سمن , شحم , دسم
fat, *adj.* دسيم , سمين

fate, قضاء , تقدير , اجل
father, والد , اب
father-in-law, حمو
fatigue, تعب
fault, سهو , غلط
favour, عطافة , معروف , نِعْمة , لُطْف
to fear, خاف يخاف
feast, وليمة , ضيافة
feather, ريش
features, اسِرّة pl. سِرار , سِيما
feeble, ضعيف , ضانٍ
feed, *v. act.* قات يقوت , أطْعم , (cattle) علف ; (graze) رعى
feel (handle), لَمَس
to feel, شعر ; , احسّ ;
feign, صنع
fellow, صاحب , نظير , قرين (vulgar اخو "brother")
female, مؤنّث
a female, أنْثَى
fence, سياج , زريبة , زرب
to fence, زرّب

ferry (ford), مَعْبَر
to fetch, احضر , جآء
fertile, خصيب
fever, حُمَّى
feverish, محموم
fibre, ليف ; (of cloth), نسيج
fickle, متقلّب , متلوّن
fiddle, كمَنْجة , ربابة
field, حَقْل ; (open country), فضاء
fiery, نارِى
fight, قاتل
fighting, مُقاتَلة
figure, صُورة , شكل
to figure to oneself, تصوّر
file (tool), مِبْرد , (rank) صفّ
to filter, صفّى
to find, اصاب , وجد
fine, حسن , لطيف
a fine, جريمة , غرامة
finger, اصْبَع
to finish, فرغ من , اتمّ , انهى
to fire (a gun), فرّغ , اطْلق
to fire at, اطلق على
fire, نار
firm, واثق , ثابت
first, أوّل
fish, حُوت , سمك
fissure, شقّ
to fit (a coat), لبق
to fix, مكّن , ركز , عيّن , قرّر , ثبت
flag, سَنْجق , عَلَم , بيْراق
flap, صفق
flash, وميض , لمع , لمح
flat, مُسَطَّح
to flatter, ملّق
flax, كتّان
fleet, دونَنْمة , اسطول
flesh, لَحم
flight, طَيَران ; (running away), هروب
flint, صوّان
to float, عوّم
flock (of sheep), قطيع ; (of birds), حَوْمة

to flog, ادّب , سوّط
flogging, جَلْد , تسويط
flour, دقيق , طحين
flow, انصبّ , جرى
flower, نوّر , زهر
a fly, ذبابة (دبّانه) ; pl. دِبّان
to fly, فرّ , طار يطير
foam, رغْوة
fodder, علف
fog, شابوره , ضباب
to fold, طبّق , ثنى , طوى
fold (for sheep), حظير
to follow, اتبع , تبع ; (the example of another), تابع على
folly, جهالة , حماقة
fond, مُولع ﺑ , مُغرَم ﺑ
food, غذآء , طعام
fool, ابله , احمق
foolish, ابله , جاهل
foot, قدم , رِجْل
forbid, احْرم , حرّم , منَع
force, غصب , جوْر , جبر ; perforce, غَصْباً علَيْه
ford, مَخَاضة
foregoing, سابق , متقدّم
forehead, جبين
foreign, اجْنبِى , غريب
foreigner, اجْنبِى , غريب
foremost, اقْدم
to forget, سَها عن , نَسى
forgetful, ناسٍ , نسَّآء
forgetfulness, نِسْيان
to forgive, سامح , غفر ﻟ , صفح عن
forgiveness, عَفْو , مَغْفِرة
forgiving, عفوّ , غفور , غافر
fork, مِلْقط , شوكة للسُفْرة
to form, كوّن , احدث , انشأ
form, شكل , صورة
formidable, مُهيب
fortnight, اسبوعيْن
fortune, حظّ , سعد , بخْت
fountain, فوّاره , ينَبوع
fowl, دجاجة
frame, برْواز
fraternal, اخَوِى

fraud, كَيْد , خديعة , مكر

free, حُرّ

freedom, حُرِّيّة

to freeze, ثلّج , جمّد

freight, شحن , وَسْقة , وسق

French, فرنساوى

frequent, كثير الوقوع , مُكرّر

fresh, تازة , غضّ , طرىّ

friend, خليل , صديق , حبيب

friendship, صداقة , حُبّ

frightful, مهول , هايل

from, عَنْ , مِنْ

front, مقدّمة

frontier, حُدود

to fry, قَلَى

frying-pan, مِقْلاة , طاجن

to furnish, احف , جهّز , تأثّث

furniture, اثاث البيت

fruit, فاكهة , ثَمَر

full, مُمْتلِى , مَمْلُوّ , مَلْآن

funnel, قمْع

fye! تبًّا لـ , افّ لـ!

G.

to gain, حصل على , ربح , كسب

gain, رِبْح , كَسْب

gallop, ركض , رمح

to gamble, قامرَ

gambler, مُقامِر

gambling, قِمار

a game, لَعْب

game (prey), صَيْد

garden, حديقة , جُنَيْنة , بُسْتان

garden (artificially watered), غَيْط مسقاوى

garden (only watered by rain), غَيْط بعلى

gardener, بُسْتانجى

gate, باب ; pl. ابواب and بِيبان

gather, جمع
gazette, صحيفة , كزّتة
gender, جِنْس
genealogy, نَسَب , نَسْل
general (officer), جنرال , اميرالاى
general, عَمِيم , عمومى , عامّ , مجمل , شامل
generally, فى الغالب , عموماً , غالباً
generosity, سخا , جود , كرم
generous, سخى , جواد , كريم
genteel, كوَيِّس , هلّبى
gentle, لطيف
gentleman, مخدوم , خواجه
gibbet, مَشْنَقَة
gift, عطاء
gipsy, قُرْباط , نُورى ; pl. نَوَر , غَجَر , زُطّ , زِنْج
girl, جارِيَة , صبِية , بِنْت
to give, وهب , اعطى
glad, مَبْسوط , مسرور , فرحان
glance, لَمحة , نظرة , نظر

glass, طاسة , قدح , كاس
globe, دُنْيا , كُرة
to go, راح , مضى , انطلق , ذهب
goat, معز , عنزة
good, صالح , جيّد , طَيِّب
goodness, احْسان , صلاح , طِيْبة , معروف
goods, سلعة , بضاعة , امتعة
goose, وزّة
gospel, الانجيل
to govern, تسلّط على , حكم
government, تملّك , حُكُومة
the government, المِيرى , الدَّوْلة
governor, حاكم
gradually, هيأً فشيْئاً , بالتدريج
grain, قمح , حبوب
grammar, صرف و نحو
grammatical, على قواعد الصرف و النحو
grand, جليل , عظيم
grandchild, حافد
grandfather, جَدّ

to grant, خوّل , منح , انعم ـ
grape, عِنبَة ; pl. عُنَب
to grasp, مسك على , قبض
grass, حشيش , عُشب
grateful, شكُور
gratis, مَجّانًا
gratitude, شُكر
a grave, قبر
gravel, حَصبة , حَصًا
grease, دُهْن , زفر
great, عظيم , جزيل , كبير
green, اخضر
grind, طحن , جرش ; (crush), سحق
grossly, بجسامة , بجزالة
ground, حضيض , ارض
guard, حارس
to guard, حرس , حفظ
guess, خمّن
guest, نزيل , ضَيْف
to guide, هَدَى , ارشد
guide, هادى , مُرْشِد , قائد
guilty, مُجرم , جانٍ
gun, بنْدقية , بارُودة

H.

habit (custom), إدْمان , داب
habitation, مَسْكَن
habitual, مُسْتَعْمَل
habitually to take or use anything, استعان بشَىْء
hail, بَرَد
hair, شَعْر
half, نصف , شطر
hall, قاعة
to halt, وقَف
halter, مِقْود , رَسَن
hammer, مِرْزبة , مُطْرقة
to hand, ناوَل
hand, يد
handful, قبضة
handle, نصاب , مقْبض

handsome, جميل , لطيف
handy, مطاوع , ملائم
hang (up), علّق; (on a gallows) شَنَق
to happen, حدث , عرض , وقع
happiness, سعادة , غبطة
happy, سعيد , مُغْتبط
harbour, مينا , مرْسَى
hard, قاسى , صلب , يابس
harden, قَسّى
hardly (scarcely), أنْحـق (Turkish)
hardware, آلات حديد
hare, أرنْب
harm, أذى , ضرّر; (there is no harm) لابأس
harness, عُدّة , طَقْم الخيل
harvest, حِصاد
haste, عجلة , سُرْعة
hasty, عَجِل , قَلِق
hat, بُرَنَيْطة
to hate, ابغض , مقت
haughty, مُتكبِّر
hay, حشيش , عَلَف
to hazard, قامر , خطر
hazy, مُكْفَهِرّ
head, رأس; pl. رؤوس
to heal, شفى
health, صِحّة , عافية
healthy, شافى , موافق للصحة
a heap, كَوْمه; (of stones), رُجْم
to heap, كوّم
to hear, سمع
heart, قَلْب , فُؤاد
heartily, بالقلب والارادة , طوعا
heat, حَرّ , حرارة; (of water), سخُونة
the heathen, الوثنيّة
heaven, سماء
heavy, ثقيل
heel, عَقب
height, عُلُوّ; (stature) قامة
heir, وارِث
hell, جهنّم

to help, اعان , ساعد

help, اعانة , مساعدة

hemp, قنّب

hen, دَجاجة

hence, من ثمَّ , من هنا

herb, بقل , نبات , عُشبة

herbage (pasture), كلاء

herd (of cattle), سرب

here, هٰهُنا , هُنا

hero, غازى , بطل

hide, اخْفى ; v.n. استَخْفى

high, رفيع , عالى

highly, بارتفاع , بِكثرة

highwayman, قاطِعُ الطريق

hill, ربْوة ; pl. رُبا

to hinder, صدّ , منع

hint, غَمْزة , اشارة , رمْز

hip, ورِك

hippopotamus, فرس البحر , (in Egypt) بِرْنِيق

hog, خِنْزير

hold, مسك ; (to contain) وسع يسع

hole, ثقَب , بخْش

hollow, اجْوَف

holy, مقدَّس , قدوس

home, محلّ , بيْت , وطن

honest, كريم , امين , حرّ

honesty, كرم , امانة , حرورية

honour, شرْف

to honour, اكرم , كرم

hoof, حافر ; (of camel), خُفّ

hook, عَقْفاء , كُلّاب

to hope, ترجّى , امل , رجا , طمع فى

hope, طمع , امل , رجا

hopeless, مأيوس , قاطع الرجاء

horizon, أفْق ; pl. آفاق

horn, قرْن

horse, حِصان

horseback, ظهر الحصان ,

horse-race, مُسابَقة الخيل

hospitable, مُكْرِم الضيف , مُضيف

hospital, مستشفى , مارستان , شفاخانة

host, مُضيف
hot, سُخن , حامى , حارّ
hotel, لوكانده , منزل , خان , فندق
hour, ساعة
house, دار , بيت
household, اهل البيت
how, أنّى , كيّف
however, كيف كان , كَيفَما
hug, عانق
human, اِنْسانىّ , بشرىّ
humble, خاشع
humility, خضوع
humour (fun), فُكاهة , هَزْل ; (of body), خِلْط
hump, حُدْبة ; (of camel) سَنَام
hunt, اصطاد , صاد
to hurt, اذى , ألّم , ضرّ
husband, بعل , زوْج
husbandman, فلّاح
hypocrisy, نفاق , رِيا
hypocrite, صاحب ريا , مُنافِق

I.

ibex, وَعل ; (in Sinai) بَدَن
ice, جليد , ثلْج (snow)
idea, تصوّر , خيال
idiom, اِصْطلاح
idle, بطّال , كَسْلان
idol, صنم , وَثَن
if, لَوْ , اذا , ان كان , ان
ignorance, جهالة , جهل
ignorant, جاهل
ill (sick), مريض , عَيّان
ill-luck, سوء الحظّ
illustrate, شرح , وضح , صرّح
image, خيال ; (an idol or statue) تِمْثال
imagine, توهّم , تصوّر
imbecile, أبْله

to imitate, قلّد

immediately, على الفور , حالا , لوقْتِه

immoral, فاسق , فاسِد

immortal, دايم , ابدى , صمد , باقى

impartiality, بلا مُحاباة , بلا غرضية

impassable, غير سالك

impede, زَاحَم , صَدّ

imperative, امرىّ , حتمىّ , امر

imperfect, ناقِص

imperfection, نُقْصان , عدم كمال

imperial, هُمايون , سلطانى

implore, اْبتَهل

to imply, دلّ على , عنى يعنى , اشار (يُشير) الى

to import, جَلَب من البلاد البرّانية

important, مُهِمّ

to impose, غبن , غشّ , كلّف ؛

to impoverish, ادقع , أفْقَر

imprisonment, حَبْس , سِجْن

to improve, *v.a.* اصلح , *v.n.* استفاد من

imprudence, عدم فطنة , غباوة

incite, اْسْتحثّ , اغْرى , حرّض

to include, انطوى على , تضمّن

incomparable, غير ذى مطابقة , لا يقايس ؛

incorrect, مختلّ , غير مصحّح

incumbent, واجِب على

incursion, غازية; pl. غَزَوات

to increase, زاد , ضاعف

indecent, عَيْب , غير لايق

indefinite, مُبْهَم

independent, مُسْتقِلّ

index, فِهْرِس

India, بلاد الهِنْد

indifferent, على حدّ سوى , بلا فرق (unconcerned) غَيْر مبالى

indigestible, وخيم

indiscriminately, بلا تمْييز

individual, نفر , واحد

industrious, عَمُول , شغّال , مُجْتَهِد

to infer, استدلّ , أسْتَنْتَج من
inferior, أدْنَى , دَنِي , دون ;
(lower), تحْتانى , اسفل
inference, استدلال , أسْتِنْتاج
to infest, عدى على , نهب
infidel, كافر
to inflict punishment, عاقب , اوجب القصاص
to inform, حدّث , اعلم , اخبر
informer, نمّام
information, اعلام , اخبار
ingratitude, كفران النِّعمة
inhabitant, سكنى
inherent, جِبِلّي
to inherit, ورث
injection (medical term), حُقْنَة
ink, مُركّب , مداد , حِبْر
inkstand, دواة
inn, خمّارة , فَنْدق , لوكنده
(caravanserai), خان
innocence, عِصْمة , براءة
innocent, مَعْصُوم , برِئ

to inquire, أسْتفهم , استقصى
insect, هوامّ pl. هامّة , دويبة
inspiration, وحى , إلْهام
instant, لَحْظة
instead, عِوَضًا عن , بدلاً من , فى محلّ
instruct, علّم , وصّى
instrument, آلة
insult, شَتْم
insurance, سكورتة
intellect, عَقْل
intelligence, إعْلام , اخبار
intelligent, فهِم , لبيب , عاقل
to intend, نوى , عمد الى , قصد , ازمع , عنى
intercede, تشفّع
intercession, شِفاعة
intercourse, مخالطة , معاشرة
interest, استفادة , بغية , رِبح
interesting, مرغّب , مفيد , يدْخل اليه
interfere, تداخل فى
interior, جوانى ; داخلى , (s.) داخل , باطن

interpreter, تُرْجمان , مترجِم (dragoman)
to interrupt, قطــع , عــطّــل , تعرّض لـ
interview, مواجهة , لِقاء , ملاقاة
intricate, مُشْكِل
to introduce, أدْخَــل , عــرّف احداً بِآخر
introduction, فــاتحة , أدخــال , دخول على
invasion, غارة
invent, أبدعْ , وجد , اخترع
inventory, قايمة
invite, عَزَم , دعى
iron, حديد
irregular, غير قياسى , غير مطرد
island, جزيرة
to issue, صــدر , خــرج ; *n.* issue (offspring), سُلالة
ivory, سِنّ الفيل , عاج

J.

jewel, جوْهرة
to joke, مَزَح , هزّل
joke, مَزاح , تهزير
joy, فرح , انبساط
journey, سفر , رحلة
judge, مُفْتِى , قاضى
judgment, رأى , دينونة , قضا , نِيّة
judicious, ذو رأى
jug, قُلّة , كوز
juice, عصارة , مرق
just, عَدْل , قِسط
justice, عدالة , إقْساط

K.

keen, زَرِب , حادّ

keenly, بِجِدّة

to keep, حافظ على , حفظ خزن

to kill, قتل

kind, مُفَضِّل , مُحْسِن

kind, صِنْف , نَوْع

kindness, فضل , احْسان , مَعْروف

king, مَلِك

kingdom, مَمْلكة

kitchen, مَطْبَخ

knife, سِكّين

to know, عَرَف , دری

knowledge, عِلْم , دراية , مَعْرِفة

L.

laborious, كثير الشغل , كادح

labour, شُغل , تعب , كدح

to labour, تعب , اشتغل , كدح

labourer, شغّال , صانع , فاعل

lad, ولد , فتى , غُلام

ladder, مِرْقاة , سُلَّم

lady, خاتون , سِتّ

lame, اعرج

lamp, قنديل , سراج

land, برّ , ارض

landlord, مالك البيت , خاناتى

language, لَهْجة , لُغة

large, واسع , عظيم , كبير

latch, سُقّاطة

late, اخير , موخّر

to lay, بسط , وضع

to lead, هدى , ارشد , دلّ على

lead, رصاص

leaf, ورقة

lean, مهزول , ضَعِيف

to learn, تعلّم

learned, عالم

to leave, تخلّى عن , ترَك

leave (permission), اجازة , اذن

leg, ساق

lemon, لَيمُون

to lend, ادان , قرض , سلف

less, انقص , اقلّ

letter, رسالة , مكتوب , حرف

liable, موجّه الى , معرّض , عرضة

liberty, اطلاق , عتق , حُرّيّة

library, خزانة كُتُب

lie, كِذْب

life, حيوة (pronounced *ḥaiyát*), عيشة

to lift, شال ب , حمل , رفع

light, ضَوْء , نُور

to lighten, اضاء , بَرَق

lightning, برق

likely, مُمْكِن , محتمل

likewise, كذا , كذلك , أيْضًا

lime, جير , كِلْس

to line, حشا , بطن

linen, كتّان

lining, بطانة

lion, اسد

to live, عمّر , عاش

living (livelihood), معيشة

long, طويل

to look, نظر الى, vulg. شاف يشوف

look, سحنة , طلعة , منظر

looking-glass, مِرْآة

to loose, حلّ

loss, خسارة , فَقْد

to lower, حطّ , نقّص , نزّل

lovely, مستحبّ , انيق

M.

mad, مَجْنون

madam, مادامة , سِتّ

madness, جُنُون

magistrate, قاضى , حاكم شرعى

to make, صنع , عمل

to maintain, كَفَلَ , صَانَ , تمسّك ب

man, إنْسان , رجّل

manner, نمط , أُسْلوب , مِنْوال
manuscript, خط اليد
many, وافر , كثير
market, بازار , مبيع , سوق
to marry, تاهّل , تزوّج , زوّج
master, أستاد , خواجه , مُعلّم
mat, حصيرة
matter, قضية , مادّة
mattress, طراحة , الفرشة
meal, مأكول , طعام
to mean, افاد , عَنَى
mean, ذليل , حقير , مهين
means, اسْباب , وسائل
meat, لحم
to meddle with, تداخل , تعرّض
medical, طبّيّ , دوائيّ
medicine, دواء
to meet, صادف , لاقى
meeting, لقاء ; (assembly) مجمع , محفل
to melt, ذاب , اذاب
member, جارحة , عضو

memorandum, تذْكرة
to mention, كنى عن , ذكر
mercantile, بضاعى , متجرى
merchant, بيّاع , شرّا , تاجر
messenger, سفير , بشير , رسول
milk, لبن , حليب
to mind, اعتنى بـ , نظر فى
mind, بال , خاطر , لبّ , عقل
mindful, محترص , ذو عناية
miserable, تَعِس , شقى , نحس
misery, شقاوة , نحس
misfortune, سوء بخت , سوء حظّ
to miss, ما اصاب , اخطاء , طاش عن
miss, سهو , خطأ
mist, ضباب
mistake, سهو , غلط
moderate, متوسّط , معتدل , منصف
modest, محتشم , حييّ , ادوب
modesty, حشمة , حيا , ادب
to molest, نكّد على , عنّى , آذى
molestation, أذى , نكد

moment, لحظة , دقيقة
money, دراهم , فلوس
mood, صيغة , اسلوب , نسق
moon, قمر
moral, ادابىّ , متادّب
morality, آداب , حسُن السلوك
morals, آداب , اخلاق , مكارم
morning, صباح
to mortify, امات , قهر , هضم
mosquito, ناموس , برغش
mother, أمّ , والدة
mule, بغل
muleteer, مكارى
multitude, كثرة , غزارة
to murder, قتّل

N.

name, إسْم
napkin, فوطة
narrow, ضيّق , حَرِج
nation, أُمّة , قبيلة
native, ابن بلد , اهلّى
near, قريب , دانٍ
neat, ظريف , هلبى
neatly, باتِقان , بظرافة
necessary, لازم , واجب , لا غنى عنه
necessity, حاجة , لزوم
need, احتياج , اضطرار
to need, احتاج الى , اضطر الى
needle, اِبرة , مِسلّة
to neglect, اهمل , غفل عن
neglect, إهمال , غفلة
never, ابداً , أصلاً , قطعاً , قطّ
new, جديد , حديث , مستطرف
news, اخبار , احاديث
next, تالى , قادم
night, ليل
no, لا , لَيْس
noble, نبيل , نجيب , جليل
nobly, بنبالة , بنجابة , بجلالة

nobody, ليس احد
noise, لغط , زئطة
nonsense, هذيان , لغو
not, لا , لم , ما
note, حاشية , قايمة , ماحق , علم
nothing, عَدَم , لا شئٌ
notice, نقد , ملاحظة , تنبيد

O.

obedience, اذعان , طاعة
to obey, اذعن , اطاع
to object, خالف فى , عارض
objection, خلاف , اعتراض
to oblige, جعله ممنونًا , الـزم , منّ على
obliging, صاحب معروف , لطيف
obscene, فاحِش
to observe, راعى , لاحظ , راتب
observance, observation, } ملاحظة , مراتبة
obsolete, مُعَتّق , مَنْسوخ , قديم
obstacle, عائق , مانع
obstinacy, عناد , مكابرة
obstinate, معاند , مكابر
obtain, نال , حصّل
occasionally, أحْيانًا
occupation, شغل , تشاغُل
to occupy, استخدم , شغّل
occur, وقع , حَصَل , عرض
to occur to anyone, خطر فى بال
occurrence, عارض , حادث
ocean, الـبـحـر الـمـحـيـط , الاوقيانوس
odd, مُفْرِد , فرد
off, بعيدًا عن
offence, إساءة
to offend, اسآ الى , سآء
offer, اعرض , عرض

to offer, اتحف , اهدى , قدّم

office, خِدمة ; (place of business), مكْتب

offspring, نسل

often, غير مرّة , مرارًا , كثيراً مّا

oil, دهن , زَيْت

oilcloth, مشمّع

old, كبير الْعمر , مُسِنّ

olive, زيتون

omen, فأل

to omit, الغى , ترك , حَذَف

once, دفعة , خطرة , مرّة

one, واحد

one another, بعض بعضاً

only, *adj*. (unique) وحِيد

only, بس , لاغير , فقط

to open, كشف , فتح

open, مكشوف , علانية , مفتوح

an opening, نقب , فتح

operate, عمل

opinion, مذهب , رأى

opium, افْيون

opportunity, فرْصة

to oppose, خالف , ناقض , ضادّ

opposite, قبالة , حذآء , تجاه

opposition, مناقضة , مضادّة

to oppress, جارعلى , ضام , ظلم

oppression, جَوْر , ضيم , ظلم

oppressive, ضائم , ظالم

opulence, جاه , غنى , ثروْة

opulent, ذو غنى , ذو ثَرْوة

or, وَالّا , أمْ , أوْ

orange, بُردقانة , اترنجة

to order, امر ؛

order, امر , تنظيم , ترتيب

ordinary, معتاد

oriental, شَرْقِي

origin, ناهية , اَصْل

ornament, زينة

orphan, يتيم

otherwise, وإن لم , وَالّا

orthography, رسم الخط , رسم الحروف

ounce (weight), أقّة

out, خارج , برّا

outside, الخارج , البرانى

outrage, منقصة , شناعة , فظاعة
over, فَوْق , عَلَى
overbalance, راجح
to overcharge, غالى فى الطلب , بالغ فى
to overcome, ظهر على , غلب
overflow, طفح
overseer, ناظر , مناظر
to oversleep, سبخ , استثقل نوما
overturn, كَبّ
overwhelm, غمّر , غمر
owl, بُومة
own, *adj.* خاصّ
to owe, عليه لـ , اغترم , غَرِمَ
owner, ذو , صاحب , مالك
oyster, اِستِرْدِيا

P.

to pack, ظرّف , اوعى , عَبّا
packet, صُرّة , رَبْطة
padding, حشو
page, صفحة , وجه
pail, عُلْبة
pain, وجع , ألَم
painful, ممضّ , مُوجِع , اليم
pains (care), سَعْى , حِرْص , اعتنا
paint, صبغ , دهن
to paint, لوّن , ادهن ; (delineate), صوّر , نقش
pair, زوْج , اثنيْن
palace, سرايا , قصر
paling, زريبة , زرب
palm (tree), نخلة ; (of hand) راحة
pane of glass, لَوْح قزاز
paper, وَرَق , قِرْطاس
paradise, فِرْدَوْس
paralysis, فالِج
parasol, شمْسِيّة
parcel, رِزْمة

parchment, رقّ
to pardon, صفح , سامح , عفا عن
pardon, عفو , مسامحة
parent, والد
parrot, ببغاء , دُرّة
part, حصّة , قسم , جزء
partake of, تشارك فى
particular, خصوصىّ , مخصوص
partition (wall), حاجب , حايط , حجّاب
partridge, حَجَلة
pass (permission), جواز
a mountain pass, نقب
to pass, مرّ , عبر , جاز
passage, ممرّ , معبر , مخاضة
passion, هوس , هَوَى ; (anger) غيظ , قلق
passport, جواز , تذكرة
passenger, راكب البحر , عابر
past, ماضى
paternal, أبِوى
path, درب , مسلك , سبيل
patience, صبر , تأنّى , اناة

patriot, معزّ وطنه , محبّ مألفه
patron, ولى نعْمة
paunch, كِرْش
pave, بلّط
pavement, بلاط
to pay, ادّى , أوفى
payment, اداء , وفاء
pea (peas), حُمُّص
peace, سلام , سلامة ; (political) صُلْح
to make peace (between two), صلّح
to make peace (with another), صالح
pear, كمثرة , نجاس , أرمود
pearl, لؤلؤ , دُرّة ; pl. لآلِى
peasant, فلّاح
pebble, حصْوة ; pl. حَصًا
peck (at), نقر
peculiar, مخصوص
pedigree, نسب , اصْل
peel, قشر
peg, وتد

pelt, رجم , راشق
pen, قلم
penalty, غرامة , جريمة , جزاء
pencil, قلم رصاص , مِرْسم
to penetrate, نفذ , خَرَق
penitence, ندامة
penitent, نادِم
people, الناس , شعب , قَوْم
pepper, فِلْفِل
perceive, شعر بِ
perfect, وافٍ , كامل , تامّ
perfection, كمال , تمام
perfume, عِطْر , طِيب
perhaps, لَعَلَّ , رُبَّمَا
to perish, فنى , تلاشى , هلك
perjury, حُنْث
permission, اجازة , إذْن , رخصة
to permit, اجاز , اذنَ بِ , رخّص فى
a permit, جواز
to perplex, حيّر , لبك , ربك
perseverance, مداومة , مواظبة
to persevere, داوَم , واظب
persevering, مُداوِم , مواظب
person, ذات , نفر , ظَلم , شخص
personal, شَخْصِى , ذاتى
perspire, عرق
to persuade, أَرضى , أَقنع , امال
perusal, قرآءة , تصفّح , تلاوة
to peruse, قَرَأَ , تصفَّح , تلا
petition, اَلْتماس , عَرض
phantom, طَيْف , خيال
philosopher, فلسفىّ , فَيْلسوف
philosophy, تفلسف , فِلْسفة
phrase, عبارة , اصطلاح , جملة
physician, طبيب
physic, طِبّ
piaster, غِرْش , قِرش
to pick, لَمّ , التقط , لقط
pickaxe, فأس
picture, صُورة
pie, فطير , محشىّ
piece, فلذة , شَرحة , شُقْفة , قُطْعة
piety, صلاح , تقْوى , ورَع

pig, خِنْزِير
pigeon, يمامة , حمام
pile (stake), وَتَد
to pile up, عَرَّم
piles (disease), بَوَاسِير
pilgrim (to any holy place), زائر (pl. زوار); (to Mecca) حاجّ
pilgrimage, حَجّ , زِيارة
pillar, عمود
pillow, مَخَدّة
pilot, مدبّر المركب
pin, دبّوس , اِبرة
pincers, كُلّاب, pl. كلاليب
pinch, قَرص
pine tree, صَنَوْبر
pious, تقيّ , ورع
pipe, شبُك , قصبة
pistol, طَبَنْجة
pit, جُبّ
pitch (tar), زِفْت , قير , قطران
to pitch a tent, ضرب خَيْمة
pith, لُبّ , قَلْب

pitiful, رؤوف , عطوف , شفوق
to pity, ترآف على , تحنّن , توجّع ل
pity, رآفة , تحنّن , توجّع
place, مَوْضِع , مكان , مطرح
to place, وضع , جعل , اقعد
plague, طاعون , وباء
plain (clear), سَهْل , بسيط
plain (level ground), واضح , سهل , بقعة , قاع
plainly, بِوضوح , بصراحة , بيانًا
plaintiff, مُدَّعِي
to plan, قصد , ارتاى , رسم
plan (intention), قَصْد , مَقصد , رای مأرب; (diagram, &c.), رسم
planet, سَيّارة
to plant, غَرَس , زرع
plant, نبات , غرس
plantain (fruit), مُوز
planter, غَرّاس
plaster (for wound), مَرْهَم , لزقة; (cement) جِبْس

plate, لَوْح , صحن
to play, ضرب , عَزَف , لَعِب
play, عزف , لُعب
plaything, لُعْبة
pleasant, مستلطف , بهيج , مستظرف
to please, اعجب , ارضى
pleasure, مسرّة , انشراح , لذّة , انبساط
pledge, رهن
plentiful, كثير , غفير , غزير
plenty, كثرة , غزارة
a plough, محراث
to plough, حرث
pluck (feathers, &c.), قطف ; (fruit) جَنَى ; (hair) نتف
plunge, غاص يغوص , غطس
pocket, جَيْب
poem, شعْر , ارجوزة , قصيدة
poet, شاعر , ناظم
poetry, شعْر , نظم
point, طَرَف , رأس , نُقطة
to point, حرر على , روّس , نقط
to point at, اشار الى
poison, سَمّ
pole (in astronomy), قُطْب ; (stake), عُود
polite, متادّب , كيّس , ادوب
political, حكوميّة , سياسيّة
poll-tax, جِزْية
pool, بِرْكة
poor, حقير , فقير , مِسْكين
popular, محبوب , مشهور , مرغوب
population, الناس , اهال , سُكّان
porch, رواق
porcupine, قُنفُذ
pork, لحم خِنْزير
port, مرسى , مينا
porter (black beer), بوزة , مِذْر ; (carrier) حمّال , شيّال ; (doorkeeper) بوّاب
portion, نصيب , قِسْم
to possess, احرز , ملك , احتوى على
possession, احراز , مِلك

possibility, احتمال , إمكان
possible, محتمل , مُمْكِن
possibly, باحتمال , بإمكان
post, بريد , بوسطة
post-office, محلّ البوسطه
pot, غلاية , طَنْجرة
potato, قلنْقاس , بطاطة
pound weight, رطل
to pound, رض , هرس , دقّ
poverty, مسكنة , فقر
power, عز , قدر , قوّة
powerful, عزيز , قادر , قوِى
practical, استعمالى , عمليّ
practice, تمرّن على , مُمارسة , استعمال
to practise, تمرّن على , مارس , استعمل
praise, اثنى على , مدح , حمد
pray, صَلَّى
prayer, صلوٰة (pron. *ṣalát*)
preach, وعظ , كرز
precaution, تحذّر
precede, سبق
precedence, تقدّم
precious, عزيز
precipice, ورْطة
predecessors, سُلفاء , اَسْلاف
preface, ديباجة , طالعة , مُقدّمة
to prefer, استحبّ , مزّى , فضّل , رجّح
preferable, اولى , مُفَضَّل
preference, ايثار , تفضيل
premier, الوزير الاعظم
preparation, تاهّب , تهيئة , تجهّز
to prepare, تجهّز , تأهّب , تهيّا
prescription (medicine), وصْفة , نسْخة
presence, شهادة , حضرة , حضور
present, هدية , تُحفة
present, شاهد , حاضر
presently, ناجزاً , الآن
preserve, صان يصُون
to press, زحم , عَصّ , كَزّ
pretence, تَعَلّل , عِلّة
pretend, ادّعَى , زعم

pretty, لطيف , ظريف , كويّس , مليح
to prevail, غلب ; (to be general), عم , همّل
to prevent, تعرّض ل , حظر , منع
previous, سابق
price, ثمن , قيمة , سعر
to prick, همز , نقز
pride, تكبّر , كِبر
priest (Christian), قسيس , خوری
principal, اهمّ , اخصّ , اصلىّ
print, طبع
prison, حبس , سِجن
prisoner, محبوس , مسجون
private, ذو انفراد , على حدة
prize, حُلوان , عِوض
it is probable, يحتمل
probably, تخميناً
to proceed, تقدّم , سار , صدر
procession, زفّة , موكب
proclamation, منادية
to procure, حصل على , حصّل , احرز
to produce, ولّد , اثمر , انتج , اغلّ
product, غلّة , حاصل
professor, مدرّس , شيخ , أستاذ
profit, كسب , منفعة , رِبح
to profit, اكتسب , انتفع , ربح
profound, عميق ; (fig.) تبحّر
profuse, مبعزق , مُسرف , مبذّر
progress, ترقّى , تقدّم , نجاح , افلاح
to prohibit, منع , نهى عن , حرّم , حظر
to promise, عهد , وعد
promise, عهد , وعد
to promote, روّج , قدّم
promotion, ترقّى
to pronounce, عبّر عن , لفظ , نطق ب
pronunciation, نطق , لفظ
proof, دليل , حُجّة , برهان , خِبرة , بيّنة
propensity, ميل الى
proper, ملائم , لائق , مناسب , مخصوص

properly, بلياقة , بِمناسبة , بخصوصية

property (wealth), مال , مِلْك ; (peculiarity) خاصّيّة

prophet, نَبِيّ

proportion, تناسب , مطابقة , بقدر

proposal, عَرْض , تَخْيير

to propose, عرض , خيَّر

proprietor, مالك , صاحب

propriety, لياقة , مناسبة , جدارة

prospect, مَنْظَر , مَطْمح

to prosper, افلح , صحّ له , نجح , توفّق

puosperity, توفيق , اقبال

lprosperous, موفّق , بخيت , مُفْلِح

puostrate, مصروح , صريح

to protect, حمى , دافع عن , اجار

rotection, حماية , وقاية , اجارة

roud, متكبّر , مغرور

o prove, برْهَن , دلّ على

proverb, مَثَل

to provide for anyone, رزق

to provide against anything, تدارك

providence, عناية الهيّة , حكمة ربانيّة

province, ايالة , ولاية

provision, ذخيرة , مؤونة , زاد , أُهْبة

prudence, حزم , رشد , فطنة

prudent, حازم , راشد , فطن

psalm, مزمور

public, جمهورى , عامّ , علانىّ

publicly, علانية , عمومًا

to publish, اشهر , اعلن , بثّ , نشر

pudding, بودينة , زردة , نوْع من الحلوآء

to pull, سحب , جرّ , جذب

pulpit, مِنْبر

pump, طُلُنْبة

to punish, عذّب , عاقب , اقتصّ

punishment, عِذاب , عقاب , قصاص

pupil, تلميذ ; (pupil of the eye) حداقة العين
to purchase, اشترى , تبضّع , تسوّق
purchaser, مُشْتَرِى
pure, خالص , صافٍ , نقى
purpose, مأرب , قصد , غايةً
purposely, قَصْداً
purse, كِيس الفلوس
to pursue, طارد , اقتفى , تبع
pursuit, طُراد
to push, ضغط , بهز , دفع
to put, حطّ , وضع
to put on (clothes), لبس
to put off (clothes), خلع
putrid, مُعفَّن , عُفُونى
pyramid, الهَرم ; pl. اهرام

Q.

quail, سُمَّانة , فرَّة
quality, نوع , ماهيّة , كيفيّة
quadrant, رُبْع الدائرة
quadrilateral, مُـرَبَّـع , ذو اربَع ضُلُوع
to quarrel, خاصم , نازع
quarrel, جِدال , خصام , نزاع
quarry, مَحْجَر , مَقْلع ; (prey) صَيْد , قنيصة
quarter, صَوْب , حارّة , رُبْع
quay, رَصِيف
queen, سلطانة , ملكة
quench (fire), أَطْفى ; (thirst) روى
question, بحث , مسئلة
quick, لَقِن , عجول , سريع
quicklime, كِلْس
quickly, على الفور , بِسُرعة
quiet, هادئ , مطمئن
quill, قصب الريشة

quince, سَفَرْجَل
quire (of paper), كُرّاس ; pl. كَرَارِيس, جُز, كَفّ, دِسْتَة
to quit, زايل, خلا
quite, بتمام, بجملة, بالكلية
to quote, ضمّن, اقتبس, استعان ب

R.

rabbit, أَرْنَب
race (stock), نَسَب, أَصْل ; (running) سِباق, مُسابقة
radiance, شعاع
radical, أَصْلِي
raft, طَوْف, رمث
ragged, مخروق, خريق
raid, غَزْوة, غازية
railway, درب الحديد, سِكّة الحديد
rain, مَطَر
rainbow, قوس قزح
rainy, ماطِر
to raise, رفع, انهض, اقام, شال ب
raisin, زبيب
rank, رُتْبة ; (military) صَفّ
ransom, فدية, فِدا ; (blood-money) دِية
rapid, جرى, سريع, فارط
rare, عزيز, تحفة, نادر
rarely, بعزازة, بِنُدْرة
rarity, تُحْفة, نُدْرة
rascal, شرير, خبيث, ابن حرام
rash, مُتهوِّر ; (eruption) طَفْحة
rat, جُرذ
rate (price), سِعْر
raven, غُراب
ray, شُعاع, لمح
razor, موس الحلاقة
to reach, ادرك, بلغ, نال
to read, تلا, قرأ

readily, بخفّة , وشيكا , حالا
ready, عتيد , ناجز , حاضر
real, حقيقى
really, فى الواقع , حقيقية , جَيْرِ , لاجرم
realm, مَمْلكة , مُلْك
ream, رِزْمة , ورَق
reap, حصد
rear (as a horse), تقَنْطر , هبّ ; (of an army), مؤخر
to rear (a child), ربّى
to reason, تعقّل , ناظر فى , حاجّ , تدبّر
reason, عقل ; (cause) سبب , علّة .
reasonable, متعقّل , معقول , متبصّر
to rebel, فتَن , خرج عن , عَصَى , شقّ العصا
rebellion, خروج عن , عُصْيان , فتنة
rebuke, وبّخ
recall, أسْتِعَاد , استرجع ; (recollect) تذكّر
receipt, تمسّك , وصول
to receive, استقبل , قَبِل , تلقّى , ترحّب
reception, تلقّى , قبول
recent, جديد , حديث , طريف , غضّ
recently, ستحدثًا , جديداً
to reckon, عدّ , حسَب
recline, أتّكى , سند
recognize, اكْتشف
to recollect, اذكّر , تفكّر , تذكّر
recollection, اذكار , تذكّر
to recommend, وصف , وصّى فى
recommendation, توصية
to recover, افاق من , شفِي
red, احمر
reed, يراعة , قصبة
reed pen, قلَم
to refer, تعلّق بـ , آلَ الى , نسب الى
to reflect, فكّر , تامّل فى
reform, أصْلح , ادّب
refrain, تورّع

refuge, اَلْتِجاء

refusal, اعراض عن , إباء

to refuse, اعرض عن , أبَى

regard, مراعاة , اعتبار

regiment, كتيبة , الاى

region, كُرة , اِقْليم

regret, تأسّف على ; (to miss) افْتَقد

regular, قياسّى , مطّرد

to reign, تملك

reign (*subst.*), سَلْطَنَة , مِلْك

rein, عنان

to reject, اطرح , طرد , ردّ

to rejoice, سُرّ , انبسط , فرِح

to relate, اخبر , حدّث , قصّ

relation, قرابة , علاقة ; (story) قصّة

release, عتق , سيّب , اطْلق , خلّص

to relieve, اعتق , أنْجى , انقذ

religion, مِلّة , ديانة , دين

religious, تقى , متديّن , ديّن , دينىّ

to rely, وثق ب , اعتمد على

to remain, استمرّ , بقى

remainder, فُضول , بقِية

remains (corpse), اشلو , ميّت ; pl. اَشْلا

to remark, فطن ل , افاد , لاحظ

remark, تنبّه , ملاحظة

remarkable, جدير بالملاحظة , بديع

remedy, تداوى , علاج

remember, تذكّر

remonstrate, عتب على , عاتب , تعتّب على

remote, قاصى

remotest, اَقْصى

to remove, ابعد , نحى , ازاح

rent, اُجرة ; (tear) خِرْق

to repair, عمر , رمّم , عدَّل , صلّح

to repay, اعاد , اوفى

repel, دافع , حامى عن , دفع عن

to repent, اناب , تاب , ندم

repentance, انابة , توْبة , ندَم

to reply, لبّى , احار , اجاب

to reply, جاوب
a reply, جَواب
report, خبر , علم , نبأ
to represent, استحضر , قدّم , مثّل
reproof, تعزير , عَتَاب
reptile, دبيب , هوامّ
repudiate, اطلق
reputation, سمعة , صيت , عِرْض
to request, التمس , طلب
request, التماس , طلب
to require, استلزم , اقتضى ‌ؤ , احْوج الى
requisite, مُقْتضِي
rescue, نقذ , أنْقذ
to resemble, هابه , ماثل
resent, غلّ على , احْرد على
to reserve, ابقى
to reside, اقام , لبث , قطن , استمكن , سكن
residence, مقطن , مقام
resident, قاطِن , مُقِيم

resign, سلّم
resist, قاوم , ضادّ , مانَع
resolution, عزيمة , جزم , ثباث
to resolve, جزم ‌ؤ , حتم
resort to, انتاب الى
to respect, كرّم , فخّم , اعزّ , وقّر
respect, تكريم , تفخيم
respectable, مكرّم , محترم
responsible, مُطالَب , مسئول عن
rest, راحة , استقرار
to rest, استراح , قرّ
restless, قلِق , متشوِّش
restrain, ردع , ضبط
restrict, حرّج , قصّر
result, نتيجة , حاصل , عاقبة
retain, حاش , حَفَظ , وعَى يعَى
retire, تقعّد عن
retirement, تقعُّد , خَلْوة
retreat, رجع , تولّى
to return, رجع , ردّ على , اعاد
return, رجوع , ردّ , اعادة
to revenge, انتقم من , اخذ ثارَةً

revenue, ايراد , دَخْل
reverend, مُحْتَرَم
reverse, عَكْس , نِكْس , تَقْلِيب
review, تصفّح , نقد , عَرْض الجيش
revile, عيّب على , سبّ
revolt (feel disgust), نفّر عن , زهّق
revolution, دَوْران ; (political) اِنْقلاب
to reward, جَزَى , جازَى , كافى
reward, جزآء , مكافاة
rhetoric, البديع , عِلْم البيان
rhinoceros, كَرْكَدان
rhubarb, راوَنْد
rhyme, روىّ , قافية
rhythm, سجع , وزن
rib, ضلع
rice, رُزّ
rich, واسع , غنِى
riches, ثروة , غنا
to ride, امتطى , ركب
ride, ركب

ridge, ظهرة , غارب
right, سديد , صواب
ring, خاتم , حلقة
to ring, دقّ الجرس
ripe, يانع , ناضج , مستوٍ
ripple, غضنة الماآ
to rise, نهض , قام
to risk, خاطر بـ ; (*sub.*) خطر
river, نهر , بحر
road, سِكّة , دَرْب
roam, سرح
to roar, زأر , هدر , قصف
roast, شَوَى
rob, سرق , عصب , سلب
a robber, حرامى
rock, صخرة
rod, عصا
rogue, خدّاع , مكّار
roll, دحرج
roof, سطح , سقف
room, حُجْرة , اوضة , محلّ
root, جذر , اصل
rope, رَسَن , حَبْل

rose, وردة
rot, رمّ
rough, أَخْرَش , خشن
round, مكوّر , مستدير , مدوّر
round, *adv.* حَول , مدار
rub, حَكّ
ruby, يعقُوت أَحْمر , لعل
rude, غَلِيظ
rugged, وَعر
ruin, خَرْبة or خِرْبة , خراب
to rule, تسلّط , حكم على ; (to draw lines) سطّر
ruler, حاكم ; (for drawing lines) مسطرة , مسيطر
to run, عدا , جرى , ركض
to rush, هجم

S.

sad, مغتمّ , كئيب
saddle, برذعة , سرج
safe, سالم , آمِن
safety, سلامة , امن
to sail, اقلع , سافر , سار فى البحر
sailor, نوتى , بحرى
salary, أجرة , مشهرية , جمكيّة
sale, بيع
salt, مِلْح
salutation, سَلَام
salvation, نجاة , خلاص
same, فَرْد , بذاته , عينه ; (vulg. برَضَه).
sand, رمل
sandal (shoe), نَعْل
sanguine, متلهّف الى , ظمآن الى
satiety, شبع
satire, هجو
satisfaction, اكتفا , اقناع , رضى
satisfactory, كافى , مقتنع , مُرْضٍ
to satisfy, كفى , اقنع , ارضى

sauce, مَرَقة , طَرطور
saucer, طاسة
savage, همج , متوحّش
to be savage, جفا , توحّش
a savage, موحّش , وحشى
to save, استبقى , وفّر , خلّص
saw, مِنْشار
to say, حكى , قال
scaffold (for building), صَقالة; (for executions), مَشْنَقة
to scald, سمط
scale, ميزان , فَلْس , قِشْر
scar, داغ , اثر الجرح
scarce, من الشواذّ , شاذّ , نادر
scarcely, انْجق
scatter, نَثَر , بَثّ
scenery, مَنْظر , مرأى , مشهد
scent, هذا , رائحة
scheme, فنّ , قصد , طريقة
scholar, طالب علم , تلميذ , مجاور
school, مكْتب , كُتّاب
science, عِلْم , معرفة

to scold, زجر , وبّخ , عزّر , نَهَر
to scoop up, غرف
scorn, احْتقر
scrap, حَطّة
to scrape, حلّ , بَرَش
scratch, جرّش , خمّش , خرش
scream, صُراخ
screen, حُجاب
screw, لَوْلب , بُرغى , مِلْوى
scythe, منجل
sea, بحر
seal, خاتم , طابع
sealing-wax, لكّ الختم
to search, جاسّ , بحث عن , تطلّب
season, ابّان , زمان , فصل
seasoning, تابِل
seat, كُرْسىّ
second, ثانى ; (moment) دَقيقة
secret, مكنون , مستور , سرّى
secret, سِرّ
secretary, كاتِب

sect, طائفة , مِلّة , فِرقة
secure, سالم , مأمون , آمن
security, طمأنينة , امان , أَمْن
seduce, توّه , اغرّ , اضلّ
to see, عاين , ابصر , راى
seed, بذر , زرع
to seek, فتش , طلب
to seem, علن , ظهر , بدا , بان
to seize, امسك ب , قبض ب
seldom, قلّما , نادرًا
to select, انتخب , انتقى
select, نخبة , منتخب , منتقى
selection, انتخاب , انتقاء
selfish, مستأثر , مُغرض , نفسانى
to sell, باع
to send, انفذ , بعث , ارسل
sensation, حاسّة , حَسّ
sense, حِسّ , عقل
sensible, حسّاس , اديب , عاقل
sensual, نزيز , شهوانىّ
sentence, جُمْلة , كلام ; (in law) فَتْوَى , حُكم
sentiment, اعتقاد , راى

to separate, فصَل , فرَق
separately, بالانفصال , بِالتفريق , فردًا فردًا
separation, تفصيل , تفريق
serious, مُهِمّ , وقور , جِدّ
sermon, خطبة , موعظة
serpent, ثعبان , حيّة
servant, خديم , خادم
to serve, نَصَفَ , خدم
service, طقم , خدمة
serviceable, مفيد , نافع
to set, ركز , حطّ , وضع
to settle, امضى , فصل , انهى
several, بعض , عِدّة , جُملة
severe, شديد , قاسى , عنيف
to sew, لفق , خاط
sex, نوع , جنس
shade, لون ضعيف , فَىْء , ظل
shadow, فىء , ظل
to shake, حرّك , زعزع , هزّ
shame, شنار , عار , عَيْب
shameful, فضيحة , معيب
shape, هَيْئة , صورة , شكل

share, سَهْم , حُصّة
sharp, ذرِب , حادّ
to sharpen, سنّ , حدّ
to shave, حَلَق
shawl, شالة
to shed, سفك , اراق (هراق)
sheep, ضأن , نعجة
sheet, طلحيّة , ملآءة
shelf, تَخْتة
shell, صَدَف
to shelter, احمْى عن , آوى , حَامَى
shepherd, راعى
a shield, تُرْس
to shine, توهّج , تلألأ , لمع
ship, سفينة
shipwreck, اِنْكِسار المركب
shirt, قميص
shoe, صُرْماية , صرمة , خفّ , نَعْل ; (horse-shoe) تاسومة
to shoot, قوّس , رمى , ضرب ب
shop, دُكّان
shore, برّ , شط , ساحل
short, وجيز , مختصر , قصير
shortly, عن كَثَب , عن قريب
shot (for guns, &c.), خُرْدة , خَرْدَق
a shot, طَلْقة
shoulder, منكب , كَتِف
shout, صرخة , صُراخ
shovel, مِسْحاية , مقْلب
to show, ابدى , ابان , ارَى , اظهر
shower, مطر , وبَل , سُبْلة , طشّ , وابِل
shriek, وَلْوَل , زاط
shrink, قصر , تقلّص , كش
shroud, كَفَن
shudder, تَوَهّر
shun, أجتنب , جانب
to shut, طبق , سكّر , اغلق
sick, عيّان , سقيم , مريض
sickle, مِنْجل
sickness, سُقْم , مرض , دآء
siege, مُحاصرة

sieve, مِنْخَال , غِرْبال
side, صَوْب , جهة , ناحية
to sigh, تحسَّر , تأوَّه
a sigh, حَسْرة
sight, مَنْظر , نظر , بصر
a sign, عَمارة , اِشارة , عَلامة
to sign, أَمْضَى
signature, إمْضآء
signet, خاتم
to signify, عرّف بِ , دلّ على
silence, صَمْت , سكوت
silent, صامِت , ساكت
silk, ابرشيم , حرير
silly, بهْلُول , اهبل
silver, فضّة
simple, سادة , ساذج , بسيط
similar, نَظِير
simplicity, ساذجيّة , بساطة
simply, لا غير , ليس الآ , فقط , اِنّما
sin, خطِيَة
since, مِن يَوْم , مُذْ , مُنذ ; (inasmuch as) مِنْ حَيْثُ أنّ
sincere, نصوح , مخلِص , صادق
sincerity, نُصْح , اخلاص , صِدْق
sinew, عَصَب
sing, غَنّى
single, فَذّ , احد , فرد
singly, فرد فرد
singular, غريب , وحيد , مفرد
sink, غَرّق , غَرَق , غار يغور
sip, تَمَصَّص , مصّ
sister, شقيقة , أُخت
to sit, قعد , جلس
sitting, جَلْسة
situate, واقِع فى
situation, وظيفة , منزلة , مقام
size, مِقْدار , حجم , جرم , قدر
skeleton, كرْنِيبة , كركبة
a sketch, مسوَّدة
to sketch, رسم , سوّد
skilful, ماهر , تقن , حاذق
skill, مهارة , اتقان , حذق
skin, بَشَرة , جِلد
skull, جُمْجُمة , قَحْف الرأس
sky, سمِاء , اوج , فضا , جوّ

slack, بطئ عن , مسترخٍ , رخو
slate, نوع حجر , لوح
slaughter, ذبح
slave, رقيق , عبد , اسير
slavery, عبودية , اسر
slay, قتل
to sleep, نام , رقد
sleep, نوم , رقود
sleepy, نعسان
sleeve, رُدْن , كُمّ
slender, ضئيل , مهزول , نحيف
slide, زَلَق ; (for sport) تزلّق
slight, ركيك ; (the slightest thing) اَدْنَى شَيٍّ
slip, زَلَق
slipper, بابوش , بابُوج
slow, متّئد , متأنّ , متمهّل
slowly, رويدًا رويدًا , على مَهْل
sly, داهِي , مُحْتَال
small, صغير
small-pox, جُدارِي
smart, مضّ ; (neat) كُوَيِّس ; (quick) نشيط
to smell, استنشق , شمّ
to smile, تبسّم , بسم
smith, حدّاد , قَيْن
smoke, دُخان
to smoke, تدَخّن , دَخن
smooth, ليّن , املس , ناعِم
smother, غمر , فطّس , خنق
snail, حَلَزُون
snake, افعى , حَيّة , حَنَش
snarl (grin), هدر , اكشر
snarl at, هارس
snatch, خطف
snore, خَنْفَر , شخّر
snow, ثِلْج
snuff, عطوس , نشوغ , نشوق
soak, شرّب , نقع
soap, صابون
society, مُعاشَرة
a society, جَمْعِيّة
sock, جَوْراب
sofa, اريكة , نمرق , مُتّكا , ديوان
soft, ناعم , وثير , ليّن
soften, نَعّم , لَيّن

to soil, طبّع , لوّث
soil, ثرى , ارض
sold, مُبَاع
soldier, جندى , عسكرى
sole, نعل
solely, فَقَطْ
solid, صُلب , صُلد , متين
solidity, متانة , صلابة
solitude, خَلْوة , اِنْفِراد , وَحْدة
some, شى , قدر , بعض
somebody, بعض الناس , اَحَدٌ , شَخْصٌ مّا
somersault, طَفْرَة
sometimes, تارةً وطورا , احياناً
son, ابن , ولد
song, اغنيّة , غناء
soon, عن قريب , عاجلا
sooner than, قَبْلَ
sore, مُوجِع , وجيع
sorrow, غمّ , حُزن
sorry, مغتمّ , حزين
sort, ضرب , صِنْف , نوع
soul, نفس , روح
soup, شوربا
sound, حسّ , صَوْت
to sound, قاس , سَبَر الماء
sour, حامِض
south, قبلى , جنوب
sovereign, حاكم , سُلطان , والى
to sow, بذر , زرع
space, البسيطة , فُسحة
spade, مسحاة , مِحْفَر
spark, شرارة
sparrow, عُصْفور
to speak, نطق , تكلّم
species, صِنْف , نَوْع
spectacles, نظّارة
spectator, ناظر
speech, قَوْل , كلام , مقالة
to spell, تلفّظ , تهجّى
to spend, اضاع , انفق , صرف
sphere, فلك , البسيطة , كُرة
spice, قِرْح , فوحة ; vulg. بهارات
spill, صَبّ , كَبّ
spin, غزل
to spin round, فتل , برم

spirit, نفْس , روح
spit (of iron), سفُّود
to spit, تَفّ , بزق
to split, شقّ , فطر , صدع
to spoil, خسّر , اتلف , افسد
sponge, اِسْفَنْجة
spoon, ملعقة
sport, لَعْب ; (field sports) صَيْد و قنص
spot, لطخة , طبعة , عيب ; (place) موضع
to spread, نشر , انتشر ; (to spread abroad) بثّ , اشاع
to spring, انفجر , انبعث , نبع , طلع
the spring, ربيع ; (a spring) نبع , عيْن
sprinkle, رَشّ
spur, مِهْمَز
to spur, همّز , وكز يكز
to spy, تجسّس
a spy, جاسُوس
square, مربّع
squeeze, عصّ
squeeze out, عَصَر
squinting, اَحْوَل
squirrel, سِنْجاب
stab, نحر
stable, اسْطَبَل
stack (of hay), كُومة
stag, ظَبْى , عفْر , ايّال
to stain, خضّب
stair, مَرْقاة , دَرَجة
stalk, ساق النبات
stallion, فَحْل
stammer, طَمْطم.
a stamp, طبع , مَطْبَع
to stamp, وطئ , داس
to stand, قام , وقف ; (stand up for) حامى عن ; stand against) قاوم
standard (of weight, &c.), عيار ; (banner) بيراق ; (rule) نَسَق
star, نجم , كَوْكب
start (as a horse), جفل.

starve, *v.a.* جوّع

state, حال , نوع ; (condition) حال حالة ; (government) دَوْلة ; (dignity) شأن , جاه

station, محلّ , مَثْوى , مقام , مَنْزِل

stationary, واقف

stationer, ورّاق

stationery, وراقة

statue, تِمْثال , صُورة , صَنَم

stature, قامة

to stay, انتظر , لبث , اقام

steady, ثابت

to steal, اختلس , لصّ , سرق

steel, بولاد , فولاذ ; (for striking fire), زناد ; (flint and steel) قَدْح و زناد ; (for sharpening knives) مُسْتَحَدّ

a steep, عقبه , جُرْف , هُبوط , هاوية

steep, واقف , صَعُود

to steer, دبّر , سيّر

stem (of tree), جِذْع

stench, نَتَن

step, درجة , خَطْوَة

to stew, سَلَق

a stew, يَخْنِى , مَسْلوق

stick, عود , قضيب

stiff, قسيب , صُلْب , يابس

stifle, فطّس

still, ساكت , هادئ

still (yet), ما برح , ما زال , لا يزال

to sting, أَبَرَ , لَسَعَ , عَقَص , نقز

stink, ادفر , أنْتن , نَتَّن

to stir, اجاش , استنهض , هاج

stirrup, غرز , رِكاب

stock, مَبْلغ , جُمْلة , طوق

stocking, قلشين , شُرابات , جَوْرب

stomach, حوصلة , معدة

stone, حصاة , حجر

stoop, تحبّى , حبا

to stop, تأنّى , صبر , وقف

store, انبار , ذخيرة

store (a shop), مخْزن

stork, لقْلق

storm, نَوّ

stormy, نَوْءِىٌّ , ذو نَوْء

story, اسطورة , pl. أَسَاطِير ; حكاية , قِصّة

stout (big), رصين

stove, وُجاق

straight, مستقيم , معتدل

straighten, ثَقَّف

straightforward, دوغـرى ; (fig.) صَادِق

strain, قَنَّب , طَنَّف

a strainer, مُصفّىِ

strange, أجنبىّ , غريب

stranger, غريب , اجنبى

strangle, خنق

strap, سَيْر

to stray, ضاع , تاه

stream, مسيل , سَيْل

street, زُقاق , سِكّة , طريق

strength, شِدَّة , قُوّة

stretch, *v. a.* مدّ ; *v. n.* تمدّد

strict, مدقّق , عنيف , متشدّد

strictly, بتدقيق , بعنف , بتشدّد

stride, فجّ , فشخ

to strike, دقّ , ضرب

string, خَيْط

strip, شلّح , جرّد

strive, تغالب , حاول

strong, شديد , قوىّ

student, تلْميذ , طالب علم

studious, دارِس , مُمارِس

study, مطالعة , درْس

to study, طالع , درَس

to stuff, حشا

stuff (matter), مادّة ; pl. مَوَادّ

stumble, عثر

stun, طوّش

stupid, غشيم , بليد , احمق

style, طَرْز , عبارة , أُسْلوب

to subdue, غلب , دوّخ , اخضع , طوّع

subject, رعيّة , تبع ; (subject matter) مبنَى , موضوع

to submit, عنا , ذلّ , خضع

to subscribe, وقّع , أمْضَى

subsequent, تالى

substance, ذات , جَوْهر , خلاصة
substitute, عِوَض , قائم مقام
subtle, دقيق
subtract, اسْقط , خصم
suburb, ضواحى المدينة
to succeed, اعقب , خلَف
success, فوْز , فلاح , نجاح
successful, فائز , مُفْلح , ناجح
succour, اسعاف , مساعدة , اغاثة
such, كهذا , ونحو ذلك , مِثْل هذا
suck, امْتَصّ , مصّ ; (as an infant) ارتضع , رضع
suckle, ارضع
sudden, فجائىّ , باغت
suddenly, فجاءَةً , بغتةً
to suffer, احْتمل , كابد , قاسى , تألّم
sufficient, مجزٍ , حسب , كافٍ
sugar, سُكّر
suicide, قتل نَفْسَهُ
to suit, وافق , ناسب
suit, طقم , حُلّة ; (at law) دعْوَى
sulphur, كِبْرِيت
sultan, سُلْطان
sum, مبلغ , قيمة
summer, صَيْف
summit, قُمّة , اعلى , ذُرْوة
sun, شمس
sunset, مَغْرِب , غروب
sup, تَعَشَّى
superior, سامٍ , عالٍ , فائق , رفيع
superior of a convent, religious order, &c., رئيس , نقيب
superiority, افضليّة , مزِية , تغلّب
superstition, عقائد فاسدة , اضاليل
superstitious, ذو عقائد فاسدة ذو اضاليل
supper, عَشاء
supple, لَدْن
suppliant, مُتضرِّع
to supply, امدّ , اعان , اغاث , جهّز

to support, مان , انال , اسعف
support, امداد , اغاثة , اسعاف , مدد
to suppose, خمّن , فرض , قدّر
supposition, تَخْمين
to suppress, ابطل , حطّ , خفض
sure, وثيق , يقين , اكْيَد
surely, حقًّا , يقيناً , بتاكيد
surely, يقيناً , على اليقين
surety, ضامِن , ضمين , كفيل
surface, سَطْح , وجْه
surname, اسم , لقب
to surprise, هجم , راع , اعجب
surprise, روْعة , عجب , دهشة
to surround, احدق , احاط ب
to survey, تطلّع الى , استشرف
to suspect, ظنّ , حدس , استشعر ب
suspend, علّق
suspense, حَيْرة , ترادُد
suspicion, ظنّ , تخمين , وهم
to sustain, حمى , اعان , امدّ , حمل
to swallow, استرط , بلع
swallow (bird), خُطّاف , سنونو
swarm, قطيع , سِرْب
to swear, آلى , اقسم , حلف
sweat, رشْح , عرَق
to sweat, رَشَح , عرق
to sweep, قمّ , كنَس
sweet, عذب , حُلو
swell, *v. a.* ورّم ; *v. n.* وَرِم
swift, عجِل , مبادر
to swim, عام , سبَح
swing, جوجح , طوّح , هرهز
a swing, ارجُوحة
swollen, ورْمان
swoon, غشْى
sword, حسام , سَيْف
syllable, حركة , تهجية , وتد خفيف
system, مذهب , هاكلة , طريقة

T.

table, سُفرة , خوان , مائدة , طاولة

table-cloth, غطا السفرة

tailor, خيّاط

to take, اخذ , تناول

tale, قصّة , حديث

talent, مزيّة , مَلَكة , صليقة , قريحه

to talk, حدّث , حكى

talk, تحدُّث , حكى

tall, طويل

tame, جوّى , مُنْقاد , داجن

tap (of a barrel, &c.), لَوْلب

tar, قطران

target, هَدَف

task, مشغلة , مصلحة

to taste, ذاق , طعم

taste, ذَوْق , طعم

tax, خراج , ضريبة , pl. ضرائب

to tax, كلّف بالخراج

tea, شاى

tea-cup, فنْجان الشاى

tea-pot, ابْرِيق الشاى

tea-spoon, ملْعقة الشاى

to teach, علّم , لقّن , درّس

teacher, مُعلّم , ملقّن , مدرّس

to tear, مزّق , شرط

tear, دمعة , عَبْرة

technical, اصطلاحى

tedious, مُعِىّ , مُطوّل

telegram, رِسالة برقيّة

to tell, اخبر , أنبا

temper, مِزاج , خُلق , طبع

temperate, معتدل , مقتصد

tempest, نوء , زعازع

temple, هَيْكل

to tempt, جرّب , ابتلى , امتحن , فتن

tender, ليّن , رخص , ناعم

tent, خيْمة , حباء , خدر , بيْت

term, شرط , لفظ , كلِمة

terms, شُرُوط
termination, رکن الكلمة الاخير , اِنْتِهآء , نِهاية
terrace, طَبَقَة , وجه , سطح
terrible, مخوّف , مُهْوِل
terribly, بِخَوْف , بهول
terror, خَوْف , هَوْل , فَزَع
test, عيار , اِمْتِحان
testament, وصية
testator, مُوَصّي
testimony, بَيّنة , شهادة
text, مَتْن
than, مِنْ
thank, شُكْر
thank you, كَثّر خَيْرك , شَكّر اللّهُ فَضْلَك
to thank, شكر
thankful, شاكر , شَكُور
thanks, اثنية , شكرانات
that, ذلك
that, أَنّهُ , أَنّ
theft, سرقة
then, غبّ , بعد , ثُمّ , حينئذ
thence, من هناك , من ثَمّ
theology, عِلْمُ الكلام , عِلْمُ اللاهوت
there, هُنالك , هُناك
therefore, إِذَنْ , إِذًا , ولهذا , من اجل ذلك
thick, منعقد , غليظ , ثخين
thickness, غلاظة , ثخانة
thief, سرّاق , لصّ
thimble, كِشْتبان
thin, لطيف , دقيق , رقيق
thing, امر , شئ
to think, ظنّ , تفكّر فى
to thirst, ظمأ , عطش
thirsty, ظمآن , عَطْشان
thorn, شَوْكة
though, وَإِن , وَلَو
thought, ظنّ , فكر
thoughtful, مُتَفَكِّر , فكير
thread, سِلْك , خيط
to threaten, توعّد , تهدّد
threat, وعيد , توعّد , تهدّد
thresh, درس

threshing floor, أنْدر
threshing machine, نَوْرج
throne, مِنْبر , كُرسيّ , عرش
through, بينْ , فى
to throw, نبذ , القى , رمى
thumb, ابْهام
thunder, رَعْد
thus, كذا , هٰكذا
a tick, قِرادة
tickle, زغْزغ , دكْدك , دغدْغ , نغْمش
tide (ebb and flow), مَدّ و جَزْر
to tie, هدّ , ربط
tight, مزنّق , محزّق
till, اَوْ , حتّى , الى ان
timber, خَشَب
time, مرّة , زمان , وقت
tin, تنك , صفيح , قصدير
a tin (can), تنكة
tint, لَوْن
tire, اَتْعَب
title, لَقْب ; pl. لِقاب ; (of book) عَنْوان ; (epithet) نَعْت

toast, مقلوّ , محمّص , مجمّر
tobacco, دُخان , تُتُن ; (for a 'narghileh,' or water-pipe) تَنْبَك
toe, أَصْبَع الرِجّل ; (great toe) اِبهام الرِّجل
together, سوية , معاً , جميعاً
tolerable, مقارِب , محتمل , لاباس به
to tolerate, رخّص فى , اباح
toll (payment), مَكْس ; (as a bell) أجرس الجرس , طنّ
tomb, قَبْر
tone, لحن , نغمة , صَوْت
tongs, منقاش , ملْقط
tongue, لهجة , لُغة , لسان
too, أيْضاً , كذلك ; (too much) كثيراً ; (besides) أيضاً
tool, عدّة , آلة
tooth, ثنية , سِنّ
top, قمّة , ذروة , اعلى
topic, مَوْرِد , مَضْمون , موْضوع
torch, مِشْعل

torment, عذّب ; *subst.* عَذَاب

torrent, سَيْل

to touch, لمس , مسّ

tough, كثيف

towards, نحو , الى , صوب , الى طرف

towel, فُوطة

tower, بُرْج

town, بلد , مصر , مدينة

to trace, تتبّع , اقتفى , رَسَم

track, آثر , pl. آثار

tract, كورة , ناحية , بقعة ; (a publication) رسالة , كُتَيِّب

trade, صنعة , حرفة , تجارة

to trade, تسبّب ب , تاجر , باع واشترى

tradesman, صنايعيّ , ذو حرفة , محترف

tradition, رواية , تقْليد

traffic, بيع وشراء , تجارة

train, قطار

traitor, غدّار , خائن

to transact, تعاطى , اجرى

transaction, تعاطِي , اجراء , معاملة

to translate, ترجم , استخرج

translation, ترْجمة , نقل

translator, مترجِم , ترجُمان , ناقل

to transpire, حدث , وقع , حصل

trap, فخّ

to travel, سافر , ساح , طوّف

travel, سفر , سياحة

traveller, مسافر , سائح

tray, طبق , خِوان

tre, treason, } غدْر , خِيانة

to tread, داس , وطئ

treasure, كنز , خَزْنة

to treat, عامَلَ , صنع الى

treatment, معاملة , صنيع

tree, شجْرة

tremble, ارْتعش

to tremble, ارْتعد , ارْتعش

trial, تجْرِبة , فحص

tribe, قبيلة , سبط , طائفة

trick, حيلة
troop, جَوق
to trouble, ازعج , اقلق , سام , شقّ على
trouble, مشقّة , تعب , ازعاج
troublesome, مُزْعِج , شاقّ
true, صحيح , صدق , حقّ
truly, صدقًا , حقيقةً
trumpet, صُور , بُوق
trunk (of a tree, &c.), جذع , ساق ; (box) صندوق ; (elephant's trunk), مُلَمْلَمَة , خُرْطُوم
trust, اعتماد , ثِقة , اتّكال
to trust, اعتمد , وثق , اتّكل
truth, صِدْق , حقّ
to try, اختبر , جرّب
tune, مقام , لحن , نغمة
tunnel, قناية
Turk, تُرْك ; pl. أتراك
Turkey, رُوم
turkey (bird), دِيك هِنْدى
to turn, خرط , برم , دوّر
turn, دَوْر , نَوْبة , برم , تدوير
turnips, شَلْجَم , لِفْت
tutor, مهذّب , مربّى , مؤدّب
twilight, عاتم , شفق , سُدْفة
tyranny, جَوْر , ضَيْم , ظُلْم
tyrant, جائر , ظالم

U.

ugly, مستهجن , شنيع , قبيح
umbrella, شمْسيّة , غاشية , ظُلّة
unanimous, ملتئم , متّحد ,
uncertain, مشكوك , مِتْوهوم , غير يقين , غير محقّق
uncertainty, شك , وهم , دون تحقيق
uncle, عمّ , خال

unclean, وسخ , غير نظيف
uncomfortable, غَيْر متهنّئ , متْعِب
uncommon, نادر , غَيْر شائع
to uncover, اماط , كشف عن
under, دون , تحت
underneath, تحت
to understand, فَهِمَ , عرف , وقف على
understanding, ذهن , فهْم
to undertake, عزم على
undertaking, حتم , عزيمة
to undress, جرّد , نزّع من , عرّى
unequal, غَيّر متساوٍ
unfaithful, غدّار , خائن
unfit, غير لايق ؛
unfruitful, عاقر , عقيم , غير مثْمِر
ungrateful, عديم الشكر , كنود
unhappy, مَنْحُوس , شقِيّ
uniform, على حدّ سوى , موافق
uniform, زِيّ , لبس , طقم
union, اتّفاق , اِتّحاد
to unite, احّد , وفّق , اوْصل ؛
universal, عميم , جامع
unjust, غَيْر منصف , ظالم
unkind, قاسى القلب , عديم الرحمة
unkindly, بقساوة قلب , بلا رحمة
unknown, غير معلوم , مجهول
unlawful, محرّم , حرام , غير محلّل
unlucky, عديم البخت , منحوس , غير مسعود
unreasonable, غير معقول , متجاوز الحدّ
unruly, سائب , مطْلَق , متمرّد , غير مُنْقاد , غير مضبوط
unsheathe, سَلّ
unskilful, جاهل , غشيم , غير ماهر , غير شاطر
unsound, ركيك , ضعيف , غَيْر سالم , مقلق , مكسور
unsteady, متزعزِع , متقلقل , غَيْر رصين , غير ثابت

to untie, حلّ
until, الى , حتّى
untrue, كـذب , مُـزوّر , زُور ,
غير حقيق
unusual, غير معهود , نادر
unwearied, كثير الاجتهاد , لايكلّ ,
غير متعب
unwilling, غير مُريد , آبى
unworthy, غير مستحِقّ
upholsterer, منجّد
uproar, فتنة , سجس , شغب ,
ولولة
upwards, الى فوق , الى العلا
to urge, حثّ , أضطرّ , الحّ على ,
حرّض
urgent, مُستعجل , مضطرّ , ملحّ
urgent necessity, داعٍ ; pl.
ضرورية , دواعى
urinal, مِبولة
urine, بول
use, فائدة , العمل ; , استعمال ,
نفع
to use, عمل ; , استعمل
useful, نافع , مُفيد
usefully, بنفع , بافادة
usefulness, انتفاع , فائدة , افادة
usual, مـألـوف , معـهـود ,
معتاد , على العادة
utensil, آلة , ماعون , متاع ,
اناء , ظرف , وعاء
utmost, انزح , ابعد , اقصى
to utter, تلفّظ
utter, اوفى , اتمّ

V.

vacancy, خلا , خُلو
vague, مُبهم
vain, زهو , ذو كبر , باطل
vale, ابطح , مسيل , وادى
valley, قاع , وادى
value, فضل ثمن , قيمة
to value, قدر , عرف , ثمّن , قوّم
vanity, غرور , عبث , بطل

vapour, بُخار
variation, تغيّر , اختلاف , تنوّع
varied, مُشَكَّل
variety, تغاير , تباين , تخالف ,
  تَلَوُّن
various, شتّى , مباين , متغاير
vast, رحيب , فسيح , واسع
vault, قبُّة , قابُو
vegetable, خضراوات , بقل ,
  نبْت
to veil, برقع , ستر , حجب
veil, برقع , حجاب
vein, حماسة , عرق , شريان
vellum, رِقّ
velvet, قطيفة , مَخْمَل
venomous, سامّ
to venture, غامر , غرَّر , خاطر ,
  جسر
verbally, شفاهاً
verse, سجعة , فقرة , بيْت شعر ,
  نظم
very, كثيراً , جدًّا
vessel, ظرف وعآء ; (ship) سفينة
vestige, اثر ; pl. آثار
to vex, تعدّى على , غاظ , اغضب
vice, رذالة , شرّ , فساد
victuals, مؤّنة , عيْش
vile, رذيل
village, كفر , ضيعة , قرْية
vinegar, خَلّ
virtue, فضل , مزية , فضيلة
vision, رؤية
visit, افتقاد , زيارة
to visit, افتقد , زار
vizier, وزير
voice, لحن , حسّ , صوْت
volcano, جبَل نار
volume, جِلْد , كتاب مجلّد
voluntary, عن ارادة , طوعاً ,
  عن طِيب نفسٍ
vow, عهد , نذر
vowel, حركة
voyage, سفَر
vulgar, عامّ , خسيس , دنيء ,
  دارج
vulture, رَخَمَة , نَسر , عقاب

W.

wafer, بُرشانة

wages, جُعْل , كرا , أُجرة

waggon, عربانة , عرابة

waist, خَصْر

waistcoat, صديرى , صُدْرِيَة

to wait, ترقّب , انتظر

waiter, خادم , السفرة

to wake, به , اهب , استيقظ

to walk, سار , تمشّى , مشَى

walk, مَشْى

wall, سور , جدار , حائط

walnut, جَوْزة

to wander, طاح , تاه , سرب

to want, عَوز , اضطرّ , احتاج , اراد

want, عدم , قلّة , افتقار , اختياج

war, معركة , قتال , حرب

warm, حارّ , حامٍ , سُخن

to warm, احمى , سخّن

to warrant, ضَمِن , تكفّل ب , تقعّد ب

to wash, غسل

watch, ساعة ; (guard or sentinel) عسس , حراسة , خفر

to watch, خفر , حرس , عسّ , سهر .

water, ماء

to water, سقَى

wave, مَوْجَة

wax, شمع

wax candle, شمع

way, سبيل , طريق ; (manner) أسلوب , نوع , وجه

waylay, رصد لِ , تَختّلَ لِ

weak, وانٍ , عاجز , ضعيف

weakness, وِنآء , ضعف

wealth, مال , جاه , غِنىً , ثَرْوَة

wealthy, صاحب ثَرْوَة , وجيه , غنىّ

to wear, توشح , تقلد ب , لبس ; (to wear out) رثّ , ابلى

weary, معيى , مُتْعَب

weather, هواء , زمان , طقْس

to weave, حاك , نسج
weaver, حائك , نسّاج
week, جمعة , اسبوع
to weep, بكى
to weigh, راز , رطّل , وزن
weight, ثِقْل , زِنَة , وزن
welcome, وسهلاً , مرحبا , ترحّب ,
اهلاً
well, حسناً , جيّد , طيّب
a well, بِئْر ; pl. آبار , بِئَار
wet, مشرّب , مبلول
when, حين , لمّا , متى
whence, من , أيْن
whether, سوآء
while, فى خلال , بينا , بينما
whip, كرباج , سَوْط
to whip, جلد , ضرب , سوّط
whisper, سرار , إسرار , وسوسة
white, ابْيَض
wholesome, شافٍ ,
موافق للصحّة
why, لِمَ , علامَ , ما ذا , لماذا
wicked, شرير , خبيث
wickedness, فُجُور , شرّ , خُبْث
wide, واسع
widow, ارملة
widower, ارمل
wife, زوْجة
wild, جافٍ , برّى
will, مشيئة , ارادة
willing, شآء , مُرِيد
to win, قمَرَ , ربح , غلب , عزّ
wind, رِيح
to wind, دوّر ; (twist) فتَل ; (to wind up a watch) ركّب
windmill, طاحون الريح
window, كوّة , طاقة , شبّاك ,
روشن
wine, خمر , نبيذ
wing, جناح
winter, شتاء
to wipe, مَسَح
wisdom, عِلْم , عَقْل , حِكْمة
wise, عاقل , حِكيم
to wish, ودّ , احبّ , اراد

wish, شَوق , ودّ , حُبّ , ارادة
wit, دهآء , ذكآء
within, داخل , جُوّا
without, من غير , من دُون , من ;
(outside) خارج , برّا
witness, استشهاد , شهادة
to witness, شهد , شاهد
woman, امرأة
to wonder, تعجّب من ,
استغرب
wonder, عجب , استغراب
wonderful, عجيب , مستغرَب
wood, حطب , عُود
wooden, من حطب
wool, صُوف
woollen, من صوف
word, كلمة , لفظة

to work, عمل , اشتغل , صنع
work, عَمل , شُغْل
workman, عامل , صانع
world, دُنْيا , عالَم
worm, دودة
worse, أَرْدأ
worship, عِبادة , نسك
worth, استحقاق , قيمة
worthless, لا قيمة له
worthy, مستحقّ , مستاهل
to wrap, لفّ , درج
wretched, صعلوك , دنيء , حقير ,
شقى
to wring, عَصَرَ
wrong, غالط , غير صواب ,
غير صحيح
to wrong, حكر , اساء الى , ظلم

Y.

yard (measure), ذراع ;
(court) حَوْش البيت ; (of
a ship) راجِع

year, سنة , عام , حول
yesterday, البارحة , امْس
yellow, اصْفر

yet, لمّا , بعد , الّا انّ

young, فتَى , مترعرع , شابّ , حديث السِنّ

youth, شباب , فتآء , صغر , حداثة السِنّ

Z.

zeal, غَيْرة , حمِيّة

zero, صِفْر ; pl. اصفار

zephyr, نسيم , صبا

zoology, عِلْم الحيَوانات